A GUIDE TO ASSET PROTECTION
HOW TO KEEP WHAT'S LEGALLY YOURS

Robert F. Klueger

JOHN WILEY & SONS, INC.

New York • Chichester • Brisbane • Toronto • Singapore • Weinheim

For Patricia, David, and Elizabeth

This text is printed on acid-free paper.

Copyright © 1997 by Robert F. Klueger.
Published by John Wiley & Sons, Inc.

This publication is designed to provide accurate and authoritative
information in regard to the subject matter covered. It is sold with
the understanding that the publisher is not engaged in rendering legal,
accounting, or other professional services. If legal advice or other expert
assistance is required, the services of a competent professional person
should be sought.

Library of Congress Cataloging-in-Publication Data:

Klueger, Robert F.
    A guide to asset protection :   how to keep what's legally yours /
by Robert F. Klueger.
        p. cm.
    Includes bibliographical references.
    ISBN 0-471-14886-5 (cloth : alk. paper). — ISBN 0-471-14885-7
(pbk. : alk. paper)
        1. Executions (Law)—United States. 2. Debtor and creditor—
United States. 3. Fraudulent conveyances—United States.
4. Trusts and trustees—United States. 5. Estate planning—United
States. I. Title.
KF9025.K58 1996
346.73'077—dc20
[347.30677]   96-8680
                                                                              CIP

Printed in the United States of America

10 9 8 7 6 5 4 3 2 1

Acknowledgments . . .

A number of people assisted the author, particularly in those areas in which the author required the expertise of others. The author would like to thank Dr. Ataollah Walizadeh of Santa Monica, California, for his assistance in the areas of estate planning, insurance, and life insurance trusts; Steven Fox, Esq., of Tarzana, California, who provided guidance in the area of bankruptcy law; and Michael Tinkler, LlB, who provided continual input and feedback in the area of foreign trusts.

Contents

Introduction   1

    The Case of Dr. John Brown   1

    The Case of Smith v. Brown (Retold)   8

    Bottom Line   10

1   The Need for Asset Protection   11

    A World of Litigation   11

    Juries Won't Help You   17

    Judges Won't Help You   20

    Insurance Won't Help   20

    Avoiding the Litigation Jungle   21

2   In the Belly of the Beast: How Creditors Find and
Get at Your Assets   23

Introduction   23

The Necessity of a Judgment   23

Prejudgment Attachment   28

Debtor Examinations   30

Judgment Liens   32

Execution, Attachment, and Levy   34

State Exemptions   36

3   The 800-Pound Gorilla: The Law of
Fraudulent Conveyances   37

Introduction   37

The Law of Fraudulent Transfers   39

What Is (and What Is Not) a Fraudulent Conveyance   40

Some Cases from Real Life   46

Bottom Line   49

4   *Asset Protection for Married Couples*   *50*

Introduction   *50*

All about Separate Property   *52*

All about Community Property   *58*

Transmutation Agreements   *62*

Shielding the Family Residence from Creditors   *64*

5   *Asset Protection Using Family Limited Partnerships*   *67*

Introduction to Partnerships   *67*

Limited Partnerships   *71*

New Kid on the Block: Limited Liability Companies   *79*

A Word of Caution   *84*

6   *Asset Protection Using Qualified Retirement Plans*   *85*

Introduction to Qualified Plans   *85*

The Anti-Alienation Rule   *86*

Individual Retirement Accounts (IRAs) 88

Nonqualified Retirement Plans 89

Fraudulent Conveyance? 89

7 Using Corporations for Asset Protection 90

Introduction 90

What Is a Corporation? 91

Who's Who in a Corporation 92

All about "Sole Proprietorships" 99

The Limits of Limited Liability 101

A Final Limitation of Limited Liability 106

How Many Corporations Do You Need? 107

8 Using Trusts for Asset Protection 109

Introduction: A Primer on Trusts 109

Can You Avoid Your Creditors with a Living Trust? 115

Revocable and Irrevocable Trusts 117

Irrevocable Trusts and Gift Taxes 121

Irrevocable Trusts and Income Taxes 123

Life Insurance and Life Insurance Trusts 124

9 Foreign Asset Protection Trusts 132

Introduction 132

The Basics of FAPTs 135

Is an FAPT a Foreign Trust? 142

The Anti-Duress Provision 147

The Flight Provision 149

The Spendthrift Clause 151

Who's Who in an FAPT 151

Which Country? 154

Your Access to Your Own Money 158

The Domestic Limited Partnership 158

Who Controls the Limited Partnership? 163

Does the Limited Partnership Distribute Its Earnings? 164

A New Player: The Trust's Protector 166

Conclusion: A Tale from Real Life 167

10   Firing Big Bertha: Filing Bankruptcy to Protect
Your Assets   169

   Introduction   169

   Making the Decision   170

   Chapter 7 and Chapter 13   172

   Are Taxes Dischargeable in Bankruptcy?   178

   Prebankruptcy Planning   179

11   How to Fight the IRS   182

   Introduction   182

   The Big Picture   183

   A Walk through the Maze   191

   Cutting a Deal   197

   The Ombudsman to the Rescue! (Maybe)   207

12   A Final Review   209

   The Prerequisite of a Judgment   209

   The Fraudulent Conveyance Trap   210

   Statutory Exemptions   212

Everyone Is Different   212

Do It Early (One Last Tale from Real Life)   214

Appendices

Appendix A: A Model Transmutation Agreement   217

Appendix B: A Model Family Limited Partnership   225

Appendix C: IRS Form 3520   247

Appendix D: IRS Form 3520-A   250

Appendix E: IRS Form 926   253

Appendix F: IRS Form 90-22.1   255

Appendix G: IRS Forms 433-A, 433-B, 433-D, and 656   257

Index   271

Introduction

THE CASE OF DR. JOHN BROWN

I'd like to tell you the story of Dr. John Brown. Actually, I'd like to tell it twice. First we'll see what happened to Dr. Brown, who was sued but who hadn't done anything to shield his assets from creditors. The second tale—which is considerably shorter—involves the same Dr. Brown, but this time he had the foresight to do something before the lawsuit hit.

Dr. John Brown is a heart surgeon in a large metropolitan hospital. He has been practicing for more than 30 years. He once was extremely successful. He was on the staff of three hospitals and taught at a prestigious medical college. His scholarly papers were published regularly and read with interest.

His success brought him great wealth, with an annual income in the high six figures. He owned a substantial home. He had a portfolio of stocks, commercial real estate, and other investments commensurate with his income. Two children had already graduated from college, and his other two children were about to enter college. He was looking forward to the day when he could cut back on his practice, perhaps even retire and concentrate on teaching, writing, and golf. After all, he thought, he'd earned it.

One day in 1984 he operated on a young woman, Ms. Viola Smith. Although only in her thirties, Ms. Smith had heart disease, caused largely by having smoked three packs of cirgarettes a day since she was 14 years old. The operation was not an emergency, but her condition would only have deteriorated had nothing been done. During the course of her operation, she suffered cardiac arrest and died. Nothing that Dr. Brown and the other attending physicians could do—and they worked feverishly—could revive her. It was not the first time that a patient died during the course of surgery, but that fact did not make it any easier to relay the news to Ms. Smith's brothers and sisters. The worst of it was that Ms. Smith, who herself was a young widow, left two young children who were now orphaned.

After the surgery, Dr. Brown reviewed all of Ms. Smith's medical records searching for any clue to the cause of her death. He found none.

Three weeks after Ms. Smith's death, Dr. Brown was walking into his office when he noticed a rather shabby-looking character seated in his waiting room.

"Are you Dr. John Brown?" he asked.

"Yes," said Dr. Brown, extending his hand.

"Process server. Have a nice day," he said, shoving a sheaf of papers in Dr. Brown's hand as he sped away.

Dr. Brown was stunned. When he recovered his composure, he entered his office, locked the door behind him, sat at his desk, and began reading what had been thrust at him.

It was a legal complaint. Dr. Brown had been sued. Roger Jones, Viola Smith's brother, in his capacity as the executor of the estate of his sister and acting on behalf of her children, was suing Dr. Brown. But not only Dr. Brown. Dr. Bob Abrams, the radiologist, also was sued. So was Dr. Ed Frank, the anesthesiologist. The hospital was also sued, as was Ms. Smith's personal physician. Even one of the nurses was sued, as was Dr. Brown's surgery corporation. (In other words, Dr. Brown's partners, who had nothing whatever to do with the operation, were also sued.) Seven defendants in all.

Then Dr. Brown read the complaint. And as he read he became even more angry. He was sued for negligence, "failure to warn," battery, gross negligence, and wrongful death! As far as he could determine, he was being accused of bungling the operation and failing to tell Ms. Smith that he might bungle it, in which case she wouldn't have consented to the surgery. Then Dr. Brown got to the end of the complaint. He was being sued for $8.5 million in "actual damages" and an additional $20 million for "punitive damages."

Attached to the complaint was a letter from the estate's lawyers, Messrs. Gunn and Nutcracker, Professional Corporation, informing Dr. Brown that he had 20 days to respond to the complaint or suffer a default judgment. It urged him to contact his malpractice insurance carrier immediately.

After a few minutes, Dr. Brown began to calm down. After all, he had reviewed the medical records. There had been no negligence on anyone's part. The whole thing would blow over in a few weeks.

Dr. Brown mailed the complaint to his medical malpractice insurer. He thought that because he paid $75,000 a year in premiums, he might as well let the insurance company worry about it.

A few days later Dr. Brown met with the lawyer for his insurance company, Ray Goode. Goode was an expert in medical malpractice.

The first thing Goode did was ask whether there was any possibility that the operation had been conducted negligently. Dr. Brown assured him there was not. They reviewed the complaint paragraph by paragraph, with Goode explaining the meaning of every allegation.

Finally, Dr. Brown asked Goode what they should do.

"We should settle," said Goode.

"What?" said the astounded Dr. Brown. "Why should I give them any money if I didn't do anything wrong?"

"Because whether you did anything wrong has very little to do with it. At your trial it's going to be a wealthy doctor against two little orphaned children. It's going to be a matter of give the kids a couple of million bucks of our money so they can go to college or let them suffer for the rest of their lives.

"And that's not the worst of it," Goode continued. "A trial like this makes news. The allegation of malpractice could kill your practice. People don't want to go to a doctor thinking they'll never get off the operating table. You'll spend a lot of time away from your practice defending the suit, and after it's over, you may still lose."

"But how could they prove negligence if there wasn't any?" he asked.

"You see that Consent to Surgery form in the file? Did you review it with her before the surgery?" asked Goode.

"Well, no," said Dr. Brown.

"That's their hook," said Goode. "They'll convince the jury that had Ms. Smith known of the risks, she wouldn't have consented to the surgery. She might be a sick woman today, but she'd be alive and her children would have a mother. I'm not saying they'd win, but they could. Don't be a sap. Settle."

"How much do you think it will cost to get this suit to go away?" he asked.

"As your part of the settlement, anywhere from $100,000 to $200,000. The others would have to kick in, but yours will be the lion's share. You were the surgeon."

"Well," said Dr. Brown, "it's your money. That's what I pay malpractice insurance for."

"Not exactly," said Goode. "Your policy has a $50,000 deductible. The first $50,000 comes out of your pocket. But that's still better than risking a trial. Your policy is only for $2 million per occurrence. You're being sued for $8.5 million. The rest is yours. You have $6.5 million to spare?"

"And I suppose that after this is all over my malpractice premiums will increase?" asked Dr. Brown, knowing the answer.

"You can count on it," said Goode. "By at least 50 percent."

"So I spend $50,000 to buy off a ridiculous lawsuit and pay increased insurance coverage for the rest of my life just to keep out of court?" said Dr. Brown.

"You can't afford the alternative," said Goode.

I wish I could report that Dr. Brown took Lawyer Goode's advice. But Dr. Brown was a proud man, whose principles refused to allow him to pay for something he hadn't done. He knew he hadn't been negligent, and he had been taught to believe that, one way or another, justice ultimately would triumph. He refused to settle.

His insurance company handled his defense. Dr. Brown had to pay the first $10,000 in legal costs, which was not covered by insurance. He spent countless hours conferring with lawyers—time he should have spent conferring with doctors. As Goode had predicted, the lawsuit made the newspapers, and his practice suffered. Dr. Brown noticed that certain "friends" he had known for years weren't quite so friendly anymore.

But he hadn't been prepared for the worst. Because he was being sued for "punitive damages," the plaintiff's lawyer, Mal Gunn, had the right to request, and to receive, copies of tax returns and statements showing all of Dr. Brown's assets. These documents revealed to Lawyer Gunn that Dr. Brown was worth $3.4 million.

A full 18 months after the suit was filed (and before a trial date was even set) the time came to take Dr. Brown's deposition. As his lawyer explained, a deposition is an interview under oath. The plaintiff uses it to help prove his case. The deposition lasted four days. It was the worst week of Dr. Brown's life. The plaintiff's lawyers probed everything. They asked what training Dr. Brown had in advising patients about the risks of surgery. As Dr. Brown had graduated from medical school in 1951, he couldn't recall any. They asked what written procedures his medical corporation had established regarding Consent to Surgery forms. There were none. It went on like that for four days. Dr. Brown felt somewhat soiled by the time it was over.

During the course of the litigation, one thing happened that really shocked Dr. Brown: Three of his fellow defendants sued him! They alleged that if they should be found guilty, Dr. Brown should have to reimburse them for what they owed.

After numerous delays (the lawyers said this was common), the case came to trial a full four years after that day when the process server met Dr. Brown. The jury consisted of a postal worker, a bartender, a retired fireman, and three housewives. The trial lasted three weeks. Ms. Smith's children, aged seven and ten, were present throughout the trial. An economics expert testified as to the value of Ms. Smith's lost services to her children.

Lawyer Gunn made a very emotional appeal to the jury. He didn't discuss the facts of the case. He did dwell at considerable length on Ms. Smith's children's future needs.

The jury deliberated for two hours. They awarded the estate $4.3 million.

Little did Dr. Brown know that his problems were only beginning. Dr. Brown had no idea how he was going to pay a judgment that was $2.3 million in excess of his insurance coverage. That's what Ms. Smith's lawyers had a right to find out. Two weeks after the judgment was handed down, he received in the mail a *subpoena duces tecum*. It required him to appear in court to answer questions, under oath, regarding the whereabouts of all his assets. He was required to bring all of his bank records, copies of his stock certificates—everything.

Some years back, Dr. Brown, while vacationing in Geneva, had established a numbered Swiss bank account. He figured it was a little bit of insurance against the unforeseeable. There was $269,000 in the account. During the course of the questioning, Lawyer Gunn asked Dr. Brown the following question:

"Dr. Brown, do you have an interest in a bank account outside of the United States?"

Dr. Brown turned to his lawyer. "Do I have to answer that?" he asked.

"Yes, you do," he was told. "You're under oath. Failure to answer truthfully is a felony."

"What about Swiss bank secrecy laws I keep hearing about?" he asked.

"That prevents the bank from disclosing the existence of the account, not you."

So Dr. Brown told them about the Swiss bank account. He gave them the account number. He told them everything. By the time it was over, Gunn knew where all of Dr. Brown's assets were located, and was preparing to seize them.

The last we heard, Dr. Brown was consulting with a bankruptcy lawyer. His retirement plans were on hold.

THE CASE OF SMITH V. BROWN (RETOLD)

Let's add one fact: A few years before Ms. Smith's surgery, Dr. Brown created a foreign asset protection trust. (We'll discuss in Chapter 9 at great length how this works. But for now, all we need know is that Dr. Brown had one.)

We pick up the story shortly after Dr. Brown received the complaint from the process server. Dr. Brown turned over the complaint to his lawyer, John Swift. Swift read the complaint and called Lawyer Gunn. He asked for a meeting in Gunn's office. Gunn was happy to comply, thinking it was the start of settlement negotiations that would lead to big bucks.

"There's one thing I need to tell you right at the start," said Swift. "Dr. Brown has no malpractice insurance. None whatever. Anything you get you'll have to get directly from Dr. Brown."

Gunn went pale momentarily, but he recovered quickly.

"That's okay," said Gunn. "Dr. Brown is a rich man. We'll go after him if we win."

"I don't think so," said Swift. "You see, Dr. Brown doesn't own any assets, either. All the money that Dr. Brown ever made, and all the assets he ever owned, are now owned by a trust."

Gunn went pale again. This time he didn't recover so quickly. "Well," said Gunn, "we'll go after the trust. We'll sue the trustee."

"I don't think so," said Swift. "The trustee of the trust is the Central Pacific Trust Company."

"So?" asked Gunn.

"The Central Pacific Trust Company is located in Rarotonga, on the island of Avarua, in the Cook Islands," said Swift. "The Cook Islands are located in the South Pacific, 1,000 miles east of Western Samoa. The Cook Islands is a country that doesn't recognize foreign judgments. If you want to go after the trust's assets, you'll have to sue in the Cook Islands. You'll have to bring all your witnesses over to the island of Avarua. And you won't win, because the Cook Islands has no personal jurisdiction over Dr. Brown."

"I'll get a court order requiring Dr. Brown to turn over the trust's assets," said Gunn, with little confidence in his voice.

"It wouldn't do you any good," said Swift. "The Central Pacific Trust Company is under orders to move the assets to some other part of the world if they ever hear of such a court order. We'll move the assets to the Cayman Islands or to the Isle of Man in the Irish Sea. And they will hear of the order. I'll tell them.

"Here's what it boils down to," continued Swift. "You're handling this litigation on a contingency basis. You get paid a percentage of what you can collect. But you'll never be able to collect anything.

You'll spend the rest of your life trying to find the money, and all you'll get is tired. I may give you a few bucks for your efforts, but that's it."

Roger Jones, the executor of the estate who brought the suit, was told of the existence of the foreign asset protection trust. He was told there was little chance his lawyer would ever be able to get his hands on Dr. Brown's trust's money, assuming the lawsuit was won. Ms. Smith's lawyer recommended taking the few dollars offered, because the lawyer didn't want to spend years chasing rainbows. There were other cases in his office that presented a better prospect for payment. They accepted the offer.

It was all concluded in a matter of days. Dr. Brown retired, as planned.

BOTTOM LINE

Same story, different results. With no planning, you walk through a world populated by predators, relying solely on luck and fate. With planning, you get to keep what you may have spent a lifetime earning.

1

The Need for Asset Protection

*Six hundred thousand lawyers in America—
hungry as locusts . . .*

Hon. Warren E. Burger
Chief Justice of the United States (Ret.)

A WORLD OF LITIGATION

There was a time when a person got hauled into court only if actually guilty of something, for instance, committing a crime or causing an injury to someone's person or property. There was a time when a person possessed of common sense knew what it took to get sued. If you drove your car while drunk and hit a pedestrian, you could get sued for negligence—that's what the courts are for.

Those days are long gone. Today, it seems as if everyone in the United States is either suing someone or getting sued. Is this because people have suddenly become more negligent? Of course not. The reason is that litigation has become the United States' Number One indoor sport. People are now willing to sue at the drop of an insult, an imagined slight, or the mere suggestion of an injury. And with 600,000 hungry lawyers out there ready to help, anyone can be a target.

But not everyone gets sued. There's no point in suing someone who can't pay. Only people with real (or perceived) "deep pockets" are potential targets. Any professional with a high enough annual income, or any businessperson with an ongoing business whose assets can be seized is a target.

Here are some recent dispatches from the litigation wars:

- A 92-year-old widow living on a pension loaned some of her money to her nephew to help him buy a car. The nephew bought the car and proceeded to injure a pedestrian. The nephew was sued—and so was she! The legal theory by which she was hauled into court is something called "negligent entrustment." Rather than spend the last of her days in peace, she had to spend her time and energy fighting a lawsuit. *The New York Times* reported that it was only the settlement of the suit (for an unspecified amount) that kept her from losing her home. In order for this unhappy story to be told, not only must a fellow citizen and his lawyer have brought the suit, but also a judge must have allowed it to happen. The judge didn't throw out the suit. They rarely do.

- A depressed woman went to her priest seeking psychological counseling. For whatever reason, the priest's ministrations were unsuccessful; the woman attempted suicide. When she recovered, she sued the priest for "negligent counseling."

- A prisoner in a state penitentiary attempted to escape. (Attempting to escape from prison is itself a crime.) As he fled from the prison, he injured himself. After he was recaptured, he sued the prison authorities and the state for "negligent

care." The proof of the negligent care was the fact that he
had escaped!

- Bill Lear was the developer of the Lear Jet. Before his death,
  his company began work on a new lightweight jet that would
  be able to fly at high speeds using less fuel than any jet then
  on the market. Bill Lear died before he could complete the
  research and development. As a tribute to her late husband's
  work, however, his widow refused to abandon the project. But
  the plane was never brought to market. The result? Bill Lear's
  children sued their mother on the theory that she had negligently dissipated their inheritance.

- A deranged man committed suicide by jumping from a plat-
  form into the path of an oncoming subway train. His estate
  sued the train's engineer and his employer—the City of New
  York—for failure to stop the train in time.

- A couple in Nashville sued a local hospital, claiming they were
  subjected to "callous, distressing remarks" from the hospital
  staff because some nurses nicknamed their newborn baby
  "Smurfette." The baby had been born temporarily blue after
  the mother had been injected with a blue dye 12 hours before
  the baby's birth to combat a urinary tract infection in the
  mother. The couple's lawyer claimed that the mother and the
  baby suffered "extreme, distressing, and permanent emotional
  damage, humiliation, and ridicule." They sued for $4 million.

How is all this possible? In addition to an increased willingness
on the part of many people to sue, and the availability of lawyers
willing to help, the principal reason these and thousands of other
ridiculous suits are brought is the recent expansion of permissible
legal theories.

No area illustrates the expansion of legal liability better than the
booming area of product liability. There was a time when if you
were injured by a defective product, you had to show that the

manufacturer had been negligent in designing or making the product. But that proved too difficult. So the courts adopted the doctrine of "strict liability." Under this theory, you don't have to show that the manufacturer was negligent; you just have to show that the product was unsafe when you used it, and that you were injured by it. Not only that, but also in many states the manufacturer is prevented from showing that you were negligent when you used the product. For example, if you were injured when using an unsafe ladder, it didn't matter that you were drunk when you used it.

But things were only getting started in the product liability arena. If you didn't have to prove that the manufacturer was negligent, at least you had to prove that you bought the product. The theory was that the manufacturer owed a duty to properly design and build products only to those people with whom it intended to deal: the buying public. Those days are gone. Today, anyone who is injured can sue.

There was a time when you could sue only if you used the product for the purpose for which it was intended. A chair should be safe only for sitting—that's what chairs are for. But what about a chair that collapses under the weight of a person who stands on it? That person too can sue, on the theory that a certain percentage of the population will stand on chairs, and that the manufacturer should make them safe for standing as well.

But at least you were limited to suing the manufacturer, the company that built the product and who at least had some control over what was made. Today, anyone who moved the product through the "stream of commerce" can be held liable. If you fell off an unsafe ladder—even if you were drunk at the time—you could sue the manufacturer who built it, the importer who imported it from a foreign country, the wholesaler who distributed it, the retailer who sold it, and even the leasing company that leased it to you. The fact that all these other parties didn't have anything to do with whether the ladder was safe is irrelevant. Remember: You won't have to show that any of them were negligent.

Having come this far, you won't be surprised to learn that, under the "product line" doctrine, a manufacturer can be held liable for a negligent product it didn't manufacture. Here's how it works: Let's say that Acme, Inc., manufactures Acme Ladders, and one of them is defective. Zeno, Inc., would like to make Acme Ladders. Zeno buys Acme's factory, hires Acme's employees, and manufactures Acme Ladders under a license from Acme, paying Acme a royalty for each ladder it makes. It never makes a defective ladder. Can Zeno be liable for the defective ladder it didn't make? In a number of states, including California, it can be, as long as it continues the "product line" of its predecessor. You can be sure that other states will adopt the product line doctrine in due course.

The expansion of liability to defendants who didn't—and couldn't—act negligently is not limited to product liability. One of the most recent—and astonishing—expansions of liability is in the environmental area. The Comprehensive Environmental Response, Compensation, and Liability Act (CERCLA), the federal cleanup law, and a number of state laws, have one thing in common: If you ever had any interest in a parcel of land, these laws require you to clean up an environmental hazard on the land even if you didn't cause it or know about it. If you don't clean it up, the government will clean it up for you and send you the bill.

These laws are very tough. Here's an example of how they work: Assume that 30 years ago a glue manufacturer created a toxic waste dump on a piece of vacant land. A developer, who didn't know about the toxic waste, bought the land and built factories on the site. The developer sold the factories to a number of buyers. Thirty years later, you lease a factory from one of them. Along comes the Environmental Protection Agency, which discovers the toxic waste deep in the ground, and orders it cleaned up. The glue manufacturer is long since gone. But you're not. The EPA can order you to clean up the site. If the cost of cleaning up the site is enough to wipe out your business, it's too bad. (It will wipe out your business, because the EPA will order your factory closed until you complete the cleanup.) Remember, you didn't cause the mess; you didn't even own the land—you're just a tenant. It doesn't matter.

We have already seen how the widow who loaned her nephew money to buy a car got caught on the theory of "negligent entrustment." Here are some other examples of the expansion of legal liability:

- There was a time when a person couldn't sue if that person was himself guilty of negligence; that is, if the plaintiff had contributed to his or her injury. Not anymore. Moreover, in many states the plaintiff can sue—and collect damages from the defendant—even if the plaintiff is more negligent than the defendant! That's why an escaped convict can sue the prison.

- There was a time when only the actual victim of an auto accident could sue. Today, many states allow passersby, who only witnessed the accident, to sue for their "mental distress."

- Until recently, a bank could lend its funds or decline to make a loan as it pleased. No longer. Under the new and growing doctrine of "lender liability," a bank had better be careful if it turns someone down. If the plaintiff can prove that he was somehow led to believe that the bank would grant the loan, and acted on that belief, the bank can be liable for the plaintiff's losses resulting from the refusal to lend the money.

- Employers once knew that they could hire and fire as they pleased, provided their decisions were not the result of race or sex discrimination. Those days are gone. Increasingly, employees have a legally enforceable "expectation" of continued employment and can sue if they are fired. And if you do fire someone, be careful about the negative (but truthful) things you say when the next prospective employer calls. The result could be a lawsuit alleging "invasion of privacy."

- Think again about serving drinks to your friends at your next party. If they leave a bit tipsy and rear-end another car while driving home, you could get sued.

- Certain types of suits that never could have been brought now may be brought. Under the doctrine of "intrafamily immunity," children were not permitted to sue their parents on the sound rationale that to allow otherwise would be an invitation to commit insurance fraud. Now, you can. Here's a recent example: A newborn baby brought suit against her mother for injuries the baby alleged to have suffered in an automobile accident that occurred prior to birth. How could an infant sue its mother? Easy. The child's father, who was still happily married to the mother, sued his wife on behalf of the child. The insurance company argued that this was nothing more than a ploy to get them to pay for the child's medical care. After all, how seriously would the mother defend the suit? An Illinois court permitted the suit to proceed.

Are these extreme, isolated examples? They are extreme, but they aren't isolated. The bizarre has become the norm in the litigation circus.

JURIES WON'T HELP YOU

It's one thing to bring a lawsuit. It's another thing to win. Surely the jurors—your fellow citizens—won't abide by the nonsense that is presented to them, would they?

They do, and the reason that they do is that too often they are confronted with a defendant who appears to be wealthy, or at least comfortable. The plaintiff is likely to be poor, or at least to appear to be. There aren't too many corporate presidents on juries. They are likely to be convinced that whatever they award the plaintiff will be paid by an insurance company anyway. It's simply too tempting: Here is their one chance in life to play Robin Hood and shift around a little wealth. The plaintiff may have some very real medical bills to pay, and may have been thrown out of work. If the defendant didn't actually cause the plaintiff's injury, no matter.

The Wall Street Journal reported that Jury Verdict Research, Inc., reports on results and trends in jury verdicts. It publishes a newsletter, *Lawyer's Alert*, which plaintiffs' lawyers consult in order to be brought up to date on ever-expanding theories of liability and how juries are responding. Here are some results:

- A college student was attacked and beaten at a college fraternity party. He couldn't sue his attackers because he didn't know who had attacked him. He was quite drunk at the time. So he sued the fraternity, claiming, in part, that the fraternity was negligent for having served him alcohol, even though he was under the legal drinking age, thereby making him less able to defend himself. He also sued the college on whose property the party was held, alleging that the college was aware that the fraternity frequently threw wild parties and failed to stop them. *Lawyer's Alert* predicted that a jury would find for the college student 97 percent of the time, and that a jury in Bronx County, New York, would award him $250,000.

- "Willa," a 19-year-old hairdresser, was caught shoplifting in a Mobile, Alabama, department store. At the time she was caught, she had several items of jewelry in her purse, having tried to leave the store without paying for them. Security officers released her, and warned her not to return to the store. Willa claimed that she had been verbally abused and threatened, which resulted in her missing several days of work and seeking psychiatric help. She claimed $200 in lost earnings and $500 in psychiatrist's bills. *Lawyer's Alert* reported that 53 percent of jurors would find in Willa's favor, and that a jury in Mobile, Alabama, would award her $36,000. If there is a moral to the story, it is that for some quick unearned income, suing beats shoplifting.

- "Rhonda," a model, burned her scalp and lost most of her hair when she used a home hair-coloring product. She claimed loss of income, because she couldn't work with her hair in such a condition, as well as emotional distress. The manufacturer contended that the product was not dangerous. Rhonda had suffered an allergic reaction to one of the ingredients in the dye. Because a small number of users will suffer an allergic reaction, the label on the box recommends that each user perform a simple skin-patch test before trying the product. Rhonda didn't follow these directions. *Lawyer's Alert* reported that 89 percent of jurors would find in Rhonda's favor, and that a New York City jury would award her $41,000.

These case histories have something in common: In each case, the plaintiff was an individual suing an institution, be it a university, a department store, or a manufacturer. In each case, the jury could easily assume that what they awarded the plaintiff would be covered by insurance. In the jury's mind, it's a simple matter of taking a little spare cash from a large insurance company so that the individual plaintiff can benefit. The fact that in none of these cases was the defendent negligent or even remotely contributed to the plaintiff's injuries didn't seem to matter.

You can be sure that these cases have one other thing in common: All were brought by lawyers working on a contingency fee basis. Their clients had little to lose. If they won, they kept anywhere from three-fourths to one-half of the money recovered. If they lost, they lost little more than time. For the defendant, however, it was a different story. You can be assured that none of the defendants paid their lawyers on a contingency basis: They had to pay their lawyers, win or lose. Recently, a bill was sponsored to Congress that would adopt the "English" system: If the plaintiff loses, he or she must reimburse the victorious defendant for legal fees. Who do you think is working hardest to defeat this measure? The American Trial Lawyers' Association, the trade group of plaintiffs' personal injury lawyers. To assure that they never run out of plaintiffs, they now advertise for more.

JUDGES WON'T HELP YOU

But won't the judges—who are sworn to do justice—separate the real lawsuits from the frivolous suits designed to badger the wealthy into settlement? No, they won't.

Here is a direct quote from Justice Richard Neely of the Supreme Court of West Virginia:

> As long as I am allowed to redistribute wealth from out-of-state companies to injured in-state plaintiffs, I shall continue to do so. Not only is my sleep enhanced when I give someone else's money away, but so is my job security, because in-state plaintiffs, their families, and their friends will re-elect me.

Justice Neely is by no means alone in his hostility toward wealthy defendants. How much chance is there that you will be subjected to the tender mercies of Justice Neely or his fellow justices?

Pretty good. Most states have very broad "long arm" statutes. If you have an auto accident in another state, or do business in that state, or mail a contract into that state, you'll be sued in that state, not in your home state. You'll have to hire a lawyer there and subject yourself to a jury comprised of the plaintiff's neighbors, not your own. The sympathy you receive from those jurors will be no greater than the sympathy you receive from Justice Neely, particularly if you appear to be wealthy.

INSURANCE WON'T HELP

There are entire communities in the United States whose citizens cannot engage the services of a single obstetrician. This is not because this branch of medicine has gone out of style. It is because few doctors can get affordable—or *any*—malpractice insurance. Every so often the newspapers report the sad story of a doctor who left his practice because he could not get insurance.

Even if you can get insurance, it may not help. Did you ever read your insurance policy? Very few people have. Of course, the insurance company that wrote the policy read it. You can be sure that the policy was written not to broaden their liability, but to limit it. Take the case of the university sued because of the brawl at the fraternity house. Many policies that cover negligence suits don't cover intentional wrongdoing such as assaults and batteries. Many policies exclude coverage if there has been a violation of the law. That might eliminate coverage if the insurer could show that serving alcohol to a minor is something the university knew of.

Even if insurance is available, it covers only the actual jury award or settlement, which may only be covered in part. No amount of coverage will prevent the loss of time, the invasion of privacy, and the agony of a lawsuit.

AVOIDING THE LITIGATION JUNGLE

If you're wealthy—or appear to be—you're a potential target. As we've noted, the fact that you're not negligent is no guarantee that you won't be sued. And if you are sued, you'll find yourself at a huge disadvantage. You'll be subject to attorney's fees and litigation expenses right from the start. The plaintiff, operating on a contingency basis, won't have to pay anything. Even if you win the lawsuit (an increasingly problematical effort) you'll still have to undergo the waste of time, the harassment, and the publicity of a suit.

You really can't win a lawsuit; your best hope is to mitigate the damage. The best you can do is avoid being sued. The best way to avoid a lawsuit is to make it clear to the plaintiff, right from the start, that even if the battle is won, the war is lost. The plaintiff must learn that no matter how protracted the litigation, and no matter how large the judgment won, collection on the judgment will never be possible—the plaintiff will never get any money; he or she will just get tired.

Making certain that your creditors will never be able to touch your assets requires careful planning. That kind of planning is what this book is all about.

2

In the Belly of the Beast: How Creditors Find and Get at Your Assets

INTRODUCTION

There isn't much good news in this chapter. The good news comes later, when we discuss the panoply of weapons at our disposal to defeat the claims of creditors. Here we need to look at the weapons in the creditor's arsenal. The defensive measures we must take are largely a function of the creditor's weapons. Most asset protection planning is undertaken with one eye over our shoulder at the creditor's arsenal, and we cannot plan intelligently unless we know what a creditor can do.

THE NECESSITY OF A JUDGMENT

The one vital datum that remains a mystery to most nonlawyers is exactly *when* a creditor becomes a serious threat; that is, when the creditor legally can go after the debtor's assets. It's one thing for a creditor to possess a legal right; it's quite another thing to have someone else's unfriendly hands in your pockets.

The answer to the mystery is this: Before a creditor can ever go after any of your assets, the creditor must first obtain a *judgment* from a court. That's good news, because very often months or years transpire before the creditor can get that judgment, and in the interim we can undertake any number of defensive measures.

Let's track a typical debt from creation to judgment. Let's assume that Mr. Smith borrows $1,000 from Mr. Jones. The promissory note that Mr. Smith signed says that the principal and interest is due on April 1, 1996. April 1 comes and goes, and Mr. Jones still hasn't been paid. Can Jones go after Smith's bank account, house, or car? Not yet, he can't. Let's assume further that Jones hires a collection agency. They send Smith threatening letters demanding payment lest they take Smith for everything he's worth. Can they do anything? Not yet.

Let's assume further that the collection agency hires a lawyer, who writes a series of increasingly hostile letters to Smith, demanding payment on behalf of Jones and the collection agency. Smith neatly deposits the lawyer's letters in the trash.

What can the lawyer do? If a creditor wants to get paid, the creditor first will have to file a lawsuit. In order to get the lawsuit rolling, Jones' lawyer will have to personally serve a *summons* and a *complaint* against Smith. If neither Jones nor Jones' lawyer can find Smith, they may have a problem ever serving Smith with the summons. Every state has a law providing for some form of *substituted service,* permitting the service of the summons by mail or at Smith's place of employment, to prevent Smith from bolting the door and hiding under the bed every time the process server comes around. But if Jones' lawyer cannot comply with the local substituted service requirement, Jones may never be able to sue successfully on the debt. It happens every day.

Let's assume that Jones' lawyer is successful in serving Smith with the summons and complaint. Can the lawyer now go after Smith's assets? With one exception discussed later in this chapter, the answer is still no. Smith still has the opportunity to prove that he doesn't owe the $1,000. What possible defenses might Smith have? He could prove that Jones also owes him money. Or he might allege that Jones promised he would seek payment from someone else. The list of possible defenses is endless, even with respect to something as seemingly cut and dried as a suit on a promissory note.

In order to determine if Jones really is entitled to the money, there will have to be a trial. In every state, Smith will be entitled to a jury, if he asks for one. Jones will have the burden of proving that Smith owes the money and that there is no defense to payment. Let's assume that the jury returns a verdict in Jones' favor, stating that Smith is indeed indebted to Jones for the $1,000. Can Jones' lawyer now go after Smith's assets?

Not yet. Jones' victory at trial entitles Jones to a judgment against Smith in the amount of $1,000. Armed with the jury's verdict, Jones' lawyer may now apply to the court for the entry of a judgment on the court records. The judgment—and nothing else—is what says Smith owes Jones $1,000. Until Jones obtains the judgment and has it entered on the judgment roll at the courthouse, Jones has nothing.

But even with a jury verdict, Smith has a few possible tricks up his sleeve. Smith's lawyer might ask the judge to defer the entry of a judgment by asking for a new trial. More likely, however, Smith's lawyer will apply for a *stay of execution* of the judgment by appealing the jury's decision to the state court of appeals. Getting a stay pending appeal usually involves posting an *appeals bond* with the judge. Smith will have to pay a certain percentage of the jury award to get an appeals bond. If he has no assets, or no credit, Smith may have a difficult time obtaining an appeals bond. But if Smith does get one, Jones may have to wait additional months or even years—until Smith's appeal is decided—to have the judgment take effect. Until then, Jones gets nothing.

The point in all this is to show that from the time Smith stops paying on the promissory note until the time Jones gets his judgment can be a frightfully long wait for Smith. In the interim, all sorts of asset protection planning is possible.

Default Judgments

Let's back up a few steps. Let's assume that Jones' lawyer serves Smith with a summons and complaint. About one month goes by, during which Smith does nothing. At that point Jones' lawyer may apply for a *default judgment*. If one is granted (which shouldn't be too difficult to obtain, because Smith has already rolled over and played dead), it means that Smith wll never be able to contest the merits of Jones' claim. He won't be able to appeal, and Jones' lawyer will be able to go after Smith's assets immediately.

Most debt collection cases end as default judgments. Even if a debtor owes the money the creditor says he owes, allowing a complaint to proceed to default should be avoided at all costs for a number of reasons. First, every lawyer who represents creditors knows how uneconomical it is to take a claim to trial. That means that almost any claim can be settled for less than what the creditor alleges is owed in the complaint.

Second, if a debtor allows a collection case to go into default, everything the plaintiff alleged in the complaint, no matter how outlandish, is taken as proved. Here's an example of how disastrous that can be: Let's assume that when Jones' lawyer drafts the collection complaint against Smith, not only is it alleged that Smith failed to pay, but it is also alleged that Smith *defrauded* Jones into lending him the money. Jones didn't defraud Smith; the lawyer is just using a little poetic license. So what? Let's assume that next year Smith files for bankruptcy, washing out his $1,000 debt to Jones, along with scores of other debts. But debts incurred as a result of fraud aren't dischargeable in bankruptcy, and the allegation of fraud, which wasn't defended, it taken as proved. The result is that a debt that otherwise would have been washed out in bankruptcy now cannot be.

So here is an iron-clad no exceptions asset protection rule:

> Never let a complaint go to default.

Consent Judgments

Smith might hire a lawyer to defend the collection action, but the case still might not proceed to a jury. Let's assume that the case cannot be settled for less than what is owed. Smith's lawyer sees the handwriting on the wall and convinces Smith that it's just a matter of time before Jones will obtain a judgment. So Smith's lawyer settles the case with Jones' lawyer on this basis: Smith will pay Jones $100 per month for ten months. Smith will agree to the entry of a judgment against him for the full $1,000, but Jones' lawyer will, in effect, keep his judgment against Smith in his back pocket provided that Smith makes the payments on time. If not, Jones is given the right to enter the judgment with the court clerk and go after Smith's assets.

Sister State and Foreign Judgments

Let's assume Jones obtained a judgment against Smith for $1,000. Jones' problem is that the judgment was entered in Bronx County, New York, which is where Smith borrowed the money and the trial took place. Smith now lives in Los Angeles, and that's where his money is. Can Jones use the Bronx County judgment to go after Smith's assets in Los Angeles?

Not yet. Jones must first *domesticate* the judgment of a sister state. (Even though the judgment is one of a sister state, it is referred to as a *foreign* judgment.) That's not difficult to do. If the Bronx County judgment appears valid on its face, the clerk in Los Angeles County will make it a Los Angeles County judgment, permitting Jones to go after Smith's assets in Los Angeles County. Jones won't have to retry his lawsuit anew in Los Angeles. Why? Because the Full Faith and Credit Clause of the Constitution requires Los Angeles County to treat a New York jury verdict the same way it would one of its own. It's one of the things that makes the United States a nation and not just a collection of principalities.

Let's assume that Jones' lawyer arrives at the courthouse in Los Angeles armed not with a judgment awarded by a jury in Bronx County, but with a judgment against Smith awarded by a judge in France. No Full Faith and Credit Clause here, to be sure. Will the clerk in Los Angeles enter the French judgment?

Probably. One reason is that there is a treaty between the United States and France that requires it. But even absent a treaty, a doctrine known as the *comity of nations* may compel the clerk to give effect to a foreign judgment, provided that the foreign country has some semblance of a system of justice with due process protection. (No North Korean judgments, please!)

As we show later, it is important to know which foreign nations will refuse give effect to a judgment entered in the United States, requiring the judgment holder to retry his case in the foreign country. Those nations will be leading candidates for foreign asset protection trusts.

PREJUDGMENT ATTACHMENT

There is one exception to the general rule that a creditor needs to obtain a judgment in order to be able to go after the debtor's assets. In certain narrow situations, the laws of the states permit the *attachment* of a debtor's assets before the creditor has obtained a judgment.

There was a time when creditors had little difficulty seizing a debtor's assets absent a showing that the creditor was entitled to anything. The result was that consumers who owed as little as a few dollars from the installment purchase of a sewing machine had their property seized and their wages garnished without so much as a by-your-leave from the creditor. But the U.S. Supreme Court, in two landmark cases, *Snaidach v. Family Finance Corp.* in 1969 and *Fuentes v. Shavin* in 1971, put a stop to all that. The result is that the prejudgment attachment laws of many states were declared unconstitutional as being a violation of the Due Process Clause of the Fourteenth Amendment, and had to be rewritten.

Today, if a creditor wants to attach the debtor's property before obtaining a judgment, there are a number of things that must be done. First, the creditor must begin the lawsuit seeking a judgment. It must then be proved to the judge that not only will the creditor likely prevail in that suit, but also that obtaining an attachment at the early stage of the proceeding is absolutely necessary. The most common allegation along these lines is that the defendant is dissipating and/or hiding assets, so that there is likely to be nothing left when the creditor wins, making the victory a Pyrrhic one.

But that's not all. Most states require a creditor requesting prejudgment attachment to post a bond. The purpose of the bond is to compensate the debtor for the debtor's losses if the debtor ultimately proves that the creditor isn't entitled to a judgment. Here's an example: Let's assume that Jones sues Smith on a debt. Jones shows the court that the only asset Smith has worth taking is an apartment building. Jones asserts that the rental income from the apartments should not go to Smith during the lawsuit, because they will be lost forever to Jones once Jones gets the judgment. Jones wants those rents now. But if Jones gets the rents now, and then Jones loses the lawsuit, Smith may be the one who's stuck forever. So the judge will likely make Jones put up a bond in the amount of the rent Smith will be deprived of. If Smith wins and can't recover the rent, Smith will be able to go directly after the bonding company to recover the lost rents. As you can imagine, Jones will need both a good case and good credit in order to obtain an attachment bond.

Obtaining prejudgment attachment doesn't mean that the creditor gets the attached property while the lawsuit is pending. If the creditor can get an attachment order, the local attachment officer—usually the sheriff or the marshal—is ordered to seize designated property and hold it during the pendency of the lawsuit.

Prejudgment attachment isn't limited to assets in the hands of the debtor. If some third person holds assets for the debtor or is himself indebted to the debtor, the creditor may obtain prejudgment attachment against the asset that the third person holds for the debtor.

Most often, prejudgment attachment is used as a lever to soften up the debtor. It's a device to get the debtor to settle on favorable terms. But as we shall soon see, there are all kinds of assets that are exempt from attachment. Using those exemptions to our advantage is a principal asset protection tool.

DEBTOR EXAMINATIONS

One thought goes through the mind of many debtors. Although often unspoken, it goes like this:

> My creditors and I are all located here in Los Angeles. But all my cash is located in the Second National Bank of Fargo, North Dakota, in the name of my Uncle Irving. My stock portfolio is owned by the Hocus-Pocus Investment Corporation of Las Vegas, Nevada, of which my Uncle Irving's son, Ethelbert, is the sole shareholder. My home is owned by The Uncle Irving Trust, a trust I established for that purpose. I tend to be very close-mouthed about my financial affairs. *So how will my creditors ever find where my assets are?*

How will they find out? They'll ask!

Once a creditor obtains a judgment, the creditor is permitted to require the debtor (who is now the *judgment debtor*) to appear in court to answer detailed questions about his or her finances, all with the express purpose of aiding the creditor in satisfying the judgment. The procedure goes by a variety of names, variously called a *debtor's examination, supplementary proceedings*, or *proceedings in aid of execution.* The procedure sometimes entails the debtor actually answering questions in the presence of a judge or a referee, but usually consists of the judge swearing in the debtor and having the debtor and the creditor's attorney depart to a nearby conference room or a vacant jury room.

The key to this is the part about *swearing in.* The debtor's exam is conducted under oath. A debtor lying about assets while under oath is committing perjury, a criminal offense. That's why citizens who have judgments against them but who aren't criminals cannot hide their assets. Few law-abiding citizens want to commit a crime and risk a prison term to keep assets from creditors.

Another bit of unpleasantness about creditor exams is that the attorneys who conduct them, being the attorneys for collection agencies, are paid on a contingency basis; they get paid only if they collect. That makes some collection attorneys the "junkyard dogs" of the legal profession. Suffice it to say that they are almost as motivated to get at your assets as you are to keep them. They are not easily deflected or fooled.

What's worse (it gets worse?) is that the creditors' attorneys aren't limited to just asking questions. They have the right to subpoena all of your financial records to the debtor's exam. If you fail to honor a subpoena, it's contempt of court.

In the example noted using Uncle Irving, it won't take a smart collection attorney long to find out where all your assets are. Subpoenas will be issued for all of your bank books, certificates of deposit (CDs), and other banking records. If you don't have any records, you will be asked if you have any interest in any bank account. If you are asked if you own any real estate and you answer no (because technically the trust, not you, owns the house you live in), eventually you will be asked if you ever set up a trust, or have an interest as a beneficiary or trustee of any trust. In short order, it will be discovered that the house is owned by the trust.

Some people believe that they can't lose if they lie on a debtor's exam because there's little the creditor can do to determine whether the debtor was lying. That's a very high-risk approach. There are plenty of ways a creditor can find out if you lied on a debtor's exam. For one, the creditor has the right to subpoena anyone for an exam who might have knowledge of your finances, such as your banker, insurance agent, the Department of Motor Vehicles (DMV), or your Uncle Irving. They might not be willing to lie to protect you, and it's hard to tell what little nuggets of information they might have. For example, if you financed the purchase of a car, the DMV probably has a record of it. That will lead the creditor to your bank, which in turn will lead the creditor to your credit application. Your credit application may have told a far rosier story about your finances, and it too was provided under penalty of perjury. If that's the case, what started out as a manageable creditor problem has become a less manageable criminal problem.

There is no need to lie on a creditor exam. As we shall see throughout this book, there is no need to hide assets. We have better ways. We can arrange your financial affairs so that even if your creditors know where your assets are, they can't get at them.

JUDGMENT LIENS

Once a creditor obtains a judgment, the first thing he or she will do is record an *abstract of judgment* with the county clerk in any county in which the creditor believes the debtor owns real estate. The lien itself doesn't require the judgment debtor to turn any property over to the creditor, but it does assure that if the debtor owns any real estate in the county, the judgment creditor eventually will be paid. That's because if the debtor ever decides to sell the property, a title search will reveal the existence of the lien, and no one will buy the property until the judgment lien has been removed. In this respect, a judgment lien operates the same way that a mortgage does. And what is worse is that the judgment lien is effective against any property the debtor acquires in that county, even property acquired after the judgment lien is filed.

Judgment liens can also operate against personal property. By recording a judgment lien with the personal property clerk in the county clerk's office, a lien will attach to all personal property. The result is that no one will buy the personal property unless the debt is first paid.

Sound hopeless? It isn't. The thing to remember is that the lien attaches only to property in the exact name of the debtor. For example, if the creditor sues John Smith, and a judgment is entered against "John Smith," the judgment lien can be recorded only against "John Smith." If property is owned by "Smith Enterprises, Inc.," the judgment lien will not cover that property, even if John Smith owns all of the stock of Smith Enterprises, Inc. The only way for the creditor to get the judgment to stick to Smith Enterprises, Inc.'s assets is to file an entirely new lawsuit for the purpose of proving that John Smith and Smith Enterprises, Inc. are one and the same. A lot can happen before that proof is obtained. In the interim, there is nothing that prevents Smith Enterprises, Inc. from selling its real estate.

Here is a rule of thumb that should be self-evident: Because judgment liens are effective against property that is acquired even after the recordation of the judgment lien, but only against the person who is the judgment debtor,

> Never acquire property in the same name as the name in which a judgment was or might be entered.

EXECUTION, ATTACHMENT, AND LEVY

If these terms sound like something out of the Spanish Inquisition, you're not far off. These are the terms (they vary somewhat from state to state) describing the weapons at the creditors' disposal for doing what is our worst nightmare: taking the debtor's property. *Execution* generally refers to the steps that a creditor uses to obtain money. *Attachment* refers to what the creditor does to obtain personal property and real estate. *Levy* refers to the act of the appropriate officer, such as the sheriff or the marshal, in seizing the assets.

The procedures vary from state to state and very often from county to county, but one thing is certain: Unless an asset is exempt by statute from levy, execution, or attachment, the sheriff can get the asset *if the judgment debtor owns it.* For example, accounts receivable are subject to attachment, as are intangible assets such as patents and copyrights. Negotiable instruments such as warehouse receipts can be attached, as can a debtor's interest in the estate of a relative who died. Even a judgment debtor's interest as a plaintiff in another lawsuit is subject to attachment.

But only the assets owned by the judgment debtor and the debts that others owe to the judgment debtor are subject to attachment and levy. Let's assume a judgment is entered against "Bob Brown." A local sheriff will not hesitate in going after a house titled in "Bob Brown." He may very much hesitate before going after real estate titled in the "Bob Brown Irrevocable Trust." Before that happens, the creditor might have to prove to a judge that the assets of the Bob Brown Irrevocable Trust really should be subject to levy. How does he do that? By claiming that Bob Brown's transfer of the property to the Bob Brown Irrevocable Trust was a *fraudulent conveyance* that the court should ignore. (More on that in Chapter 3.)

Wage Garnishment

There is probably nothing nastier than a wage garnishment. For a judgment debtor who receives a paycheck, having a portion of one's pay intercepted by the judgment creditor is both damaging and insulting.

A wage garnishment is directed at the employer, not the debtor. It orders the employer to deduct a portion of the debtor's pay and remit it to the creditor. Most employers feel obligated to comply, because the employer can be held liable, either for damages or contempt, if they ignore the garnishment. But if your employer is friendly to you, and if you live in a state whose garnishment law isn't too tough, there may be a way out. Most garnishment laws operate only to intercept what the employer owes the debtor as of the date the garnishment is received. If you have a friendly employer (or if you control the employer) you should be able to time the receipt of income so that the employer doesn't owe you any wages on the day the garnishment hits. Here's an example: Fred is paid on the first and fifteenth of every month for the prior fortnight. The garnishment hits on the sixteenth. The most that Fred's employer owes Fred is one day's wages. The creditor is entitled to no more than a portion of that.

Fortunately, creditors can't take all that much by way of garnishment. There is a federal statute that limits any garnishment to 25 percent of the debtor's disposable income—that is, 25 percent of what's left after required withholding. Some states go further: Florida, Texas, and Pennsylvania prohibit all wage garnishment, the federal statute notwithstanding.

Many people are aware that a creditor's ability to garnish wages is severely limited. What many aren't aware of is that the one creditor who isn't subject to either the federal or any state law limitation on wage garnishments is the Internal Revenue Service (IRS). Sadly, the IRS can take the lion's share of tax debtor's pay.

STATE EXEMPTIONS

Every state exempts certain property from the clutches of creditors. We've just seen that certain states limit all wage garnishments. As we see in Chapter 4, many states have liberal *homestead* exemptions, prohibiting creditors from attaching all or part of the equity in the family home.

State exemptions are not limited to personal residences. To a greater or lesser extent, every state exempts a certain amount of cash, personal effects, and business assets.

It is imperative to check what property your state exempts from the clutches of creditors. Here's an example: California exempts up to $4,000 of the cash value of a life insurance policy, as well as the entire death benefit. In other words, if you own a fully paid life insurance policy that has a $1 million death benefit and a $4,000 cash surrender value, your creditors can't touch it. But if the policy has $100,000 in cash value, the creditors can get at $96,000 of that cash value. California also has a $75,000 homestead exemption. Let's assume you owned a home in California that had no mortgage and was worth $200,000. If you did nothing, your creditors could get all but $4,000 of the life insurance policy. They could also force the sale of your home, subject to your right to receive $75,000 of the sale proceeds. But if you borrowed $100,000 from your life insurance, and also borrowed $125,000 on your home, your creditors could get neither the home nor the life insurance. That's what asset protection planning is all about.

3

The 800-Pound Gorilla: The Law of Fraudulent Conveyances

INTRODUCTION

I wouldn't have to worry about my creditors if I could only go to my Uncle Irving:

ME: Uncle Irving, I've got a problem, and only you can help me. I've got these creditors to whom I owe lots of money. There's no defense. If they sue me, they'll get judgments, and after they get judgments they'll place liens on my real estate. They may even try to attach my bank accounts. I'll lose everything. Here's the favor I'd like to ask of you. Why don't I give you the cash in my bank account for safekeeping. I'll also transfer the titles of my real estate to you. They won't be able to sue you, because you don't owe them any money; they don't even know you. Some day, maybe months or years from now, the creditors will get tired and give up. Then you can give the property back to me.

UNCLE IRVING: You've always been a favorite nephew of mine. I'll be glad to help. Not only will I take custody of the cash and take title to the real estate, but whenever you're short of cash, you just come to me, and I'll "lend" you your own money. Of course, you can live in the real estate, because its really yours.

ME: Sounds like a plan. Thanks, Uncle Irving.

We know what happens next. The creditors sue, and if there really is no defense, they reduce their claims to judgment. When they try to find any of my assets, I merely turn my pockets inside out, reminding them of the difficulty in squeezing blood from a turnip. If they don't have the wit to ask about Uncle Irving or anyone else with whom I may have parked my assets, so much the better.

But what if they do ask about Uncle Irving? Because they've never heard of him, the questions will be a bit more general, such as:

CREDITOR: Have you, or anyone acting for you, under your direction, or with your knowledge or consent, transferred, assigned, or otherwise conveyed any asset worth more than $1,000 to any person within the last two years?

Now I have a little problem. I can't lie about the transfers of my assets to Uncle Irving, because I'm under oath. Lying under oath is perjury, which is a crime everywhere. I have to tell the truth—that Uncle Irving is holding my money and my property.

What may the creditors do when they find out that I transferred my cash and my real estate to Uncle Irving? That's where the law of fraudulent conveyances comes in.

THE LAW OF FRAUDULENT TRANSFERS

Talk about an old law! It all started with something called the *Statute of Elizabeth,* which was enacted in England in 1570. Four-hundred-plus years later, we have the *Uniform Fraudulent Transfers Act,* which (with minor variations) is the law in 33 states and isn't much different than the Statute of Elizabeth. It replaced the *Uniform Fraudulent Conveyances Act,* which is only slightly different and is still the law in ten other states. Fraudulent conveyances are governed by state law; there is no nationwide law governing fraudulent conveyances.

But just what is a fraudulent conveyance? In its simplest form, it is the conveyance of property by one person to another without adequate consideration, made for the purpose of "delaying," hindering or defeating" the claims of creditors. The transfer of my assets to Uncle Irving is the classic fraudulent conveyance. I knew I was about to get into trouble with my creditors. In order to "hinder, delay, or defeat" them, I transferred my assets to Uncle Irving, and didn't require Uncle Irving to give me anything in return.

But what does it matter if a transfer is ruled to be a fraudulent conveyance? It matters a lot. My creditors have no right to sue Uncle Irving, because Uncle Irving doesn't owe my creditors any money. However, if the transfer is ruled to be a fraudulent conveyance, *my creditors can ignore the transfer, and sue the transferee,* who in this case is Uncle Irving. They also can ask the judge to nullify the transfer, ordering Uncle Irving to transfer the property back to me. That's it, in a nutshell.

In all of the asset protection we do, we must, at every step, look over our shoulder at the fraudulent conveyance law. The fraudulent conveyance law is like an 800-pound gorilla who has plopped himself down in our living room. He will make our lives miserable if we try to ignore him; we must deal with him. Every asset protection tool we employ must take one (or both) of the following approaches:

> Approach #1: We may have moved assets out of the hands of the debtor, but the transfer did not constitute a fraudulent conveyance.

If that doesn't work, or isn't feasible, the asset protection tool we employ must take a bolder approach:

> Approach #2: Even though what we did was a fraudulent conveyance, it doesn't matter. We have so wired the transaction that, try as you may, you'll still never get at the money.

Obviously, not every transfer of property is a fraudulent conveyance. If I give my Uncle Irving a tie for Christmas, and he doesn't give me anything in return, the cash I used to pay for the tie is gone forever as far as my creditors are concerned, but no one in their right mind would call the transaction a fraudulent conveyance. However, if I give Uncle Irving 1,000 shares of General Motors stock for Christmas a few days before a lawsuit is filed against me, that Christmas present might well be a fraudulent conveyance.

Between these two extremes, there's a big gray area. We need to structure any transfers of property so that they fall outside of the definition of a fraudulent conveyance.

WHAT IS (AND WHAT IS NOT) A FRAUDULENT CONVEYANCE

Under the fraudulent conveyance law of almost every state, there are two types of fraudulent conveyances. The first involves *actual intent* to defeat or to delay your creditors. If the creditor can prove that you actually intended to cheat your creditors when you transferred property to someone else, the transfer is a fraudulent conveyance. If you had that actual intent (which in many states must be shown by "clear and convincing evidence"), the creditor need not prove anything else. What is worse, if you had an actual intent, the transfer can be set aside by any of your present creditors *and any future creditors*. For example, if you had the prohibited intent in 1985, when you transferred your assets, and a creditor arises in 1987, that creditor can also show that you had the prohibited intent against them, even though that creditor didn't materialize until two years later.

Fortunately, it's very difficult to prove that a transfer was made with the actual intent to defeat a creditor, because most people with any brains at all don't go about advertising their intentions. That's especially true for anyone who is doing some asset protection planning.

The second type of fraudulent conveyance is more subtle, and the one with which we need to concern ourselves. In this, the more common area, the creditor cannot prove that the transfer of property was made with actual intent. Instead, the creditor can show that there existed one or more circumstances that accompanied the transfer that point to the debtor's intent to defeat or hinder his creditors. The more circumstances, known as *Badges of Fraud*, that accompany the transfer, the greater the likelihood that a judge will call the transfer a fraudulent conveyance. It is what the lawyers call a "smell test." The greater the smell, the more likely the judge will hold his nose.

If we're going to plan to avoid having a transfer of assets recharacterized as a fraudulent conveyance, we've got to deal with the badges of fraud. We'll discuss each of them at some length, but in summary form, here they are:

The Badges of Fraud

• The Transferor's Insolvency

- Lack of Consideration for the Transfer

- The Relationship between the Transferor and Transferee

- The Pendency or Threat of Litigation

- Secrecy or Concealment

- Unusual Business Practice

- Reservation of Benefit or Possession of the Asset

It's often said that only one badge of fraud won't result in a fraudulent conveyance; there must be more. Don't believe it. If the transfer is smelly enough to the judge, the judge will find more than one badge of fraud.

The most important badges of fraud are the first two: insolvency and lack of consideration for the transfer.

1. *Insolvency.* Under the Uniform Fraudulent Conveyance Act (UFCA), a person is "insolvent" if the present saleable fair value of assets aren't sufficient to pay existing debts as they come due. In the extreme case, if you give away all your property so that you can't pay your rent, you're insolvent. The UFCA goes further, saying that if the transfer of your property is what makes you insolvent, it's a fraudulent conveyance, regardless of your actual intent.

   Generally, a transfer is not a fraudulent conveyance if you're not insolvent as a result of the transfer, even if you become insolvent *later*.

   As we see in later chapters, it's unwise to transfer all your assets to any person or entity. It's best to keep enough assets so that you can show that, after the transfer, you had enough assets to pay your debts as they came due, that you *did* pay your debts as they came due, and would still be able to pay your debts, but for this unfortunate and unexpected judgment creditor who keeps hounding you. We'll state this a hundred times in this book: Avoiding fraudulent conveyances (and thereby avoiding your creditors) entails *planning*.

2. *Lack of Consideration.* This should come as no surprise. If you part with your assets and get nothing in return, it's not hard to conclude that you did so because you had your creditors in mind. After all, why else would you give something away and receive nothing in return?

Let's say you have two creditors: creditor A and creditor B. You pay off creditor A, which leaves you insolvent. It also means you don't have any money left to pay creditor B. Is preferring one creditor over another a fraudulent conveyance? Generally, it isn't. If both debts were legitimately incurred, preferring one creditor over another isn't a fraudulent conveyance. There's an exception: If creditor A *knew* that you had other creditors and *knew* you would be insolvent after being paid, it might be a fraudulent conveyance. In other words, if one creditor knowingly participates in other creditors being defeated, a court might well punch through the transaction and call it a fraudulent transaction.

As we see in Chapter 5, when we discuss transfers of assets to limited partnerships and limited liability companies (LLC), placing your assets to a limited partnership or an LLC might make it a lot harder for a creditor to get at the assets, but the transfer of your assets to a partnership or an LLC generally isn't considered a fraudulent conveyance, because you are getting something in return: You receive a partnership interest when you transfer the assets to a limited partnership, and a membership interest when you transfer your assets to an LLC. The transfer may leave you so illiquid that you can't pay your debts as they come due, but a creditor won't be able to say you received nothing in return.

3. *The Relationship between the Transferor and the Transferee.* Let's not forget that the question of whether a transfer is a fraudulent conveyance isn't cast in stone; it's a smell test. If you transfer your assets to your spouse (or your Uncle Irving),

the transaction produces a greater odor than if you transfer the assets to a finance company. Everyone knows (including the judge) that Uncle Irving is more likely to have agreed to a sham transaction than is your local finance company.

Unfortunately, we don't want to give our assets to finance companies. If we're going to part with our assets, we want to make sure we'll get them back. That means transferring our assets to entities such as partnerships, corporations, and trusts that we may appear not to control, but actually do. It also means, in an extreme case, transferring our assets to entities we control but that the creditors can't get to. (More on that when we discuss Foreign Asset Protection Trusts in Chapter 9.)

4. *The Pendency or Threat of Litigation.* Again, the smell test. Dr. Jones transfers his assets to a limited partnership eight years before being sued by his creditors. Dr. Smith transfers his assets to a limited partnership the day after being sued by a creditor. Which transfer is smellier? If Dr. Jones' creditors argue to the judge that Dr. Jones transferred his assets with the intent of defeating his creditors, Dr. Jones has a pretty good defense:

> DR. JONES: Creditors? What creditors? When I transferred the assets to the partnership, nobody was suing me. I couldn't possibly have anticipated that a full eight years later I would be sued for negligence, and that a full two years after that I would be found culpable. I'm a neurologist, not a psychic.

What argument does Dr. Smith have? Not much.

Once again, it boils down to *planning*. A great asset protection technique can be no technique if it's started too late.

5. *Secrecy or Concealment.* Let's say that Dr. Jones doesn't transfer his assets to a limited partnership. Instead, he sells his home, his three apartment buildings, his portfolio of stocks and

bonds, and his valuable art collection. These sales result in lots of cash. He doesn't buy anything with the cash. He doesn't even put the cash in the bank. Instead, he boards a plane to New Zealand and stuffs the cash in a hollow tree 200 miles from the nearest town. Would you surmise that Dr. Jones is trying to hide his assets? Does your nose detect an odor in Dr. Jones' actions?

If the fraudulent conveyance law is smell test, nothing is more pungent than hiding your assets. There's no reason to hide your assets other than people might want to get at them, and people who want to get at your assets are generally known as creditors.

Money launderers, criminals, and other assorted lowlifes hide their assets; upstanding citizens never do. As we shall see in later chapters, in all the asset production planning we do, we never attempt to *hide* any assets. Indeed, on occasion we may even advertise what we're doing by recording the deeds of transfer with the county clerk, giving notice of what we're doing to everyone in the world.

With the asset protection tools at our disposal, we don't have to hide assets. We have a better way of defeating creditors. We'll make sure that even if our creditors know exactly where our assets are, they can't get at them.

6. *Unusual Business Practice.* How do you explain stuffing $100 bills into a hollow tree in New Zealand? You can't.

   Whatever asset protection device we employ, we'll need to make it look like something that people do when they're not just seeking to avoid their creditors. We'll want to paper the transaction so that it looks like we're planning for the succession of a business to a younger generation, or seeking to reduce estate taxes, or to avoid the probate of an estate, or even to reduce income taxes, which is a legitimate business purpose. What we will not do is anything that points only in the direction of a fraudulent conveyance.

7. *Reservation of Benefit or Possession.* The last badge of fraud looks at what actually happened to the asset after the transfer. If you're allowed to live in the home after the "transfer," maybe the home wasn't transferred at all. Maybe all that happened was that the title was changed. Similarly, if the income from the bank account comes to you after you supposedly transferred the bank account, maybe you didn't really transfer it.

All of these badges of fraud are designed to provide evidence of what motivated the transfer of an asset. Although one badge of fraud can sink a purported transfer, generally more than one must be found in order to have the transfer recharacterized as a fraudulent conveyance.

Here's some good news: In most courts, the burden of proof is on the creditor to prove that a transfer of property was a fraudulent conveyance. That burden isn't easy to meet, because the creditor must overcome a general presumption against fraud. But the creditor will be able to overcome the burden if the transfer flunks the smell test.

Have creditors been able to overcome the burden? Let's take a look.

SOME CASES FROM REAL LIFE

It might come as a surprise, but the courts haven't been jammed with fraudulent conveyance cases. Those few cases that have been decided point to only one conclusion: It's impossible to predict when a transfer will be stamped as a fraudulent conveyance. That's good news. It means that with careful planning done well enough in advance, we can structure a transfer of assets so that it avoids all or most of the Badges of Fraud.

Here is an example of a classic no-planning fraudulent conveyance. In *Reddy v. Gonzalez*, a recent California case, a man held title to real estate with his wife. California is a community property state, meaning that half of the property is deemed owned by the husband and half by the wife. The husband knew that a judgment would soon be entered against him by one of his creditors. His half of the property was valuable enough to pay the creditor's debt. Knowing that, he transferred his half of the property to his ex-wife for safe-keeping, receiving nothing in return. It wasn't hard for the court to find that the transfer was a fraudulent conveyance.

That one is easy—most cases aren't. In another recent California case, *Wyzard v. Grolier*, a debtor knew that a judgment would soon be entered against him, just as in *Reddy*. But instead of transferring any property to an ex-wife, in *Wyzard* the debtor transferred the property to his attorney, who was also a close friend. He gave the attorney a promissory note and a deed of trust (i.e., a mortgage) for the property, which was ostensibly for the purpose of securing the payment of preexisting legal fees. When the legal fees weren't paid, the attorney foreclosed on the property. The attorney had never required the client to sign a promissory note before. Isn't this just a little bit smelly?

Who won, the creditor or the debtor? The creditor lost, the court holding that the transfer to the attorney wasn't a fraudulent conveyance. The reason for the decision is that—as we've noted previously—it isn't a fraudulent conveyance to prefer one creditor over another, provided the debt you pay was a real debt previously incurred.

How do you reconcile *Reddy v. Gonzalez* with *Wyzard v. Grolier*? Easy. In the former, there was no asset protection planning until it was too late. In the latter, they planned to avoid the fraudulent conveyance more carefully.

The fact that you can't predict the results is made evident when you compare *Wyzard* with *Berger v. Hi-Gear Tire & Auto Supply*, a 1970 case from Maryland. In *Berger*, Mr. and Mrs. Berger were franchisees in an auto parts business that went bad. They couldn't meet the required royalty payments, and the franchisor sued them. After the franchisor sued the Bergers, they gave Mrs. Berger's father a promissory note for money that Mrs. Berger's father had ostensibly loaned them during the marriage. The promissory note was secured by a deed of trust on the Bergers' home. Throughout their marriage, the father had never required his daughter or son-in-law to sign a promissory note for the money he had ostensibly loaned. Mrs. Berger's father never showed up at the trial.

The court's decision is interesting, but what the court said is more interesting. The court held that there's nothing wrong with preferring one creditor over another, even if the creditor you prefer is a close relative, even if you become insolvent in the process, provided that the creditor you preferred doesn't participate in the fraud. Nevertheless, the court held that the creation of the promissory note and the deed of trust in favor of Mrs. Berger's father was a fraudulent conveyance. The key factor seems to be that Mrs. Berger's father didn't show up for the trial. After all, if the debt to him was real, you would think that he would show up to protect his interest. The fact that he didn't show seems to indicate the whole thing was a paper concoction that Mrs. Berger's father wasn't even aware of.

With *Berger* in mind, consider *McCrary v. Bobenhausen*, a 1979 case from Florida. In that case, Boucher was indebted to Bobenhausen. After Bobenhausen brought a lawsuit against Boucher to recover the debt, Boucher sold an income-producing property to McCrary, who knew of Boucher's debt to Bobenhausen and of Bobenhausen's lawsuit. It appears that McCrary paid Boucher fair value for the property. Bobenhausen sued to overturn the transfer, claiming it was a fraudulent conveyance. He lost. The court held that not every conveyance of property made during the pendency of a lawsuit is fraudulent. Bobenhausen, the court held, didn't overcome the presumption against fraud. Perhaps the fact that McCrary paid fair value for the property was dispositive. In other words, the "lack of consideration" badge of fraud was absent.

Consider *DeRicciulli v. State,* another case from Florida, and its planning implications. In *DeRicciulli,* a debtor borrowed money and gave the lender a security interest in the property. According to the court, the lender didn't rely on the general creditworthiness of the borrower when he loaned the money; he relied only on the value of the property that secured the repayment of the debt. Consequently, when the borrower gave away *another* piece of property, that transfer couldn't possibly have been a fraudulent conveyance, because the lender had never relied on the existence of that other parcel of property.

BOTTOM LINE

Can't predict the outcome of these cases? No one can. But they teach us a lesson. We have a far greater chance of beating a claim that a transfer is a fraudulent conveyance if we plan carefully and *early* than if we wait until it's too late.

4

Asset Protection for Married Couples

INTRODUCTION

We saw in Chapter 3 that protecting our assets from the clutches of creditors would be relatively easy if we had a willing Uncle Irving. All we would need to worry about is the Fraudulent Conveyance Law and all we would need to do is plan around it.

Not all of us have a willing Uncle Irving. But for the millions of us in stable marriages, we may have someone far closer to us than Uncle Irving who may be an immediate—and ideal—source of asset protection: our spouse. Moreover, with careful planning we won't ever have to transfer our assets to our spouse; our spouse will have owned the assets long before creditors come calling.

Using the marital unit as a source of asset protection assumes one thing: that one of the spouses runs a high risk of being a target for creditors, and that the other spouse is a low risk. Let's take a typical example. Dr. Bob Smith is an anesthesiologist, one of the highest risk medical specialties. Dr. Smith's wife is a homemaker. Dr. and Mrs. Smith reside in a home valued at $1 million. Who should own the residence, the investment portfolio, the art collection, and the equipment and furnishings that make up Dr. Smith's medical prac-tice—Dr. Smith, who as an anesthesiologist has a target painted on his chest, or Mrs. Smith, who is far less likely to be the target of a lawsuit? The answer is obvious. But the system isn't foolproof. Dr. Smith may never be sued, and Mrs. Smith may have a few beers on the way home from a PTA meeting and run down a school bus. But playing the odds dictates putting the assets out of reach of the creditors of the spouse more likely to be sued.

Note the qualifying phrase used above: Using the family unit as an asset protection device should be used only in a *stable* marriage. If you've been married 30 years, odds are it will last. If you've been married 30 weeks, perhaps we should employ different asset protection strategies.

The stability of the marriage isn't the only variable governing our ability to use the marital unit as an asset protection device. A more basic consideration is the state you live in and, if different, the state or states in which your property is located.

Each state uses one of two systems of ownership of property be-tween spouses. Most states have a system of *separate property*, al-though a few states have a system called *community property*.[1] Whereas there are some subtle differences among individual sepa-rate property (also called *common law property*) states and among

---

[1] The community property states are Louisiana, Texas, Arizona, New Mexico, Nevada, California, and Washington. The easy way to remember which states are community property states is that, with the exception of Washington, they are contiguous.

individual community property states, the real difference is between the separate property states and the community property states. From an asset protection standpoint, the big news is that separate property is good news and community property is bad news. Creditors have a far easier time getting at a family's assets in a community property state, especially if no asset protection planning has been done. Living in a community property state puts a premium on careful—and early—planning.

ALL ABOUT SEPARATE PROPERTY

Separate property is exactly what its name implies: If an asset is titled in the name of only one spouse, it's considered owned by that spouse to the exclusion of the other spouse. It follows that if an asset is owned by only one spouse, the creditors of the other spouse cannot get at it.

With that in mind, we encounter a significant asset protection technique:

> In a separate property state, always title as much property as possible in the name of the spouse who has the lower risk of being sued.

There are a few exceptions to the rule that if the property is in the name of only one spouse, the creditors of the other spouse cannot attack the property. The first exception involves debts incurred by a spouse for *necessaries*. For example, if only one spouse runs up a big bill to pay for the family's groceries, you can rest assured that the grocer will be able to attach all of the family's assets, regardless of how the assets are titled. Just what constitutes "necessaries" varies from state to state, but will almost assuredly include clothing, rent, and doctor and dental bills for every family member.

The second exception is trickier and more important. Spouses may own property in their individual names for 50 years, and it will remain their separate property throughout their marriage. But should they get divorced, the nature of the property then changes, and becomes either their separate property or *marital property*. Getting divorced will obviously affect your life. But it can also affect how protected you are from your creditors.

Divorce in a Separate Property State

Divorce laws vary, but as a general rule the property that was acquired during a marriage in a separate property state becomes marital property in the event of a divorce. The property that one spouse owned prior to the marriage, or received by gift or inheritance during the marriage and that was not commingled with the marital property, remains that spouse's separate property in the divorce.

The divorce courts in separate property states generally divide the marital property according to *equitable principles*. What does that mean? It doesn't mean dividing the assets in half. It means taking a look at a range of factors, such as the length of the marriage, the separate assets of each spouse, the ability of each spouse to earn a living after the divorce, and so on. If two people get a divorce after ten months of marriage, all that the judge will likely award each party is half of the wedding presents. But let's assume that a couple was married for 30 years. One spouse went to medical school while the other spouse worked nights so that the first spouse could attend medical school. After the student/spouse graduated, the worker/spouse cared for the children so that the doctor/spouse could build a medical practice. In the divorce, do you think the spouse with little education, who helped the doctor/spouse develop the ability to earn a substantial income, will be left holding the bag? Not likely. An equitable division will result in a substantial percentage of the assets going to the spouse with the lesser ability to earn a living.

How does all this affect your creditors? Remember, marital property arises in a separate property state only in the event of a divorce. During the marriage, which spouse's name is on the title matters very much. Let's assume that two spouses acquire 1,000 shares of General Motors common stock, using their combined earnings. Obviously, the stock should be titled in the name of the spouse with the lower risk of being sued. But doesn't this mean that the spouse whose name is on the stock certificates will get the stock in a divorce? Not at all. The stock, and all of the other property acquired during the marriage, becomes marital property in the divorce and is subject to equitable division.

All of which brings us to another separate property planning tool:

> Make gifts of marital property from the high-risk spouse to the low-risk spouse.

This technique doesn't work as well as placing the assets in the name of the low-risk spouse because gifts, even to spouses, are subject to attack as fraudulent conveyances.

The property that one spouse brings into the marriage, or that is received by one spouse by gift or inheritance, doesn't become marital property unless it is commingled with the marital property. For example, if you inherit $10,000 from your Uncle Irving, and you put the $10,000 into a joint bank account with your spouse, you most assuredly have commingled it, at which point the $10,000 has lost its character as separate property and has become marital property, subject to equitable division in the divorce.

Property that a creditor couldn't touch during the marriage, because it was titled in the nondebtor spouse, might well be subject to the clutches of creditors if the property falls into the hands of the debtor spouse following the equitable division of the marital assets. That means that if one spouse has creditor problems and knows that a divorce is in the offing, proper planning might dictate working out those problems before acquiring a load of marital assets in the divorce.

Co-Ownership of Property: Joint Tenancy

In 1962, history was made when a required notice first appeared on every cigarette package. It read:

> CAUTION: The Surgeon General has determined that cigarette smoking may be hazardous to your health.

A similar notice should be required to appear on every real estate deed and stock certificate in the United States. It should read:

> CAUTION: The Attorney General was determined that joint tenancy may be hazardous to your financial health.

If we took a sampling of the real estate deeds in any county of any state, we would find that most residential real estate owned by married couples is titled to both spouses as joint tenants. Title companies and escrow agents—even lawyers who should know better—routinely prepare deeds placing property in joint tenancy.

Why? There once was a legitimate reason. Joint tenancy was used to avoid probate when one of the spouses died. That's because the essence of joint tenancy is that when one joint tenant dies, the surviving joint tenant automatically ("by operation of law") gets the property. Because the transfer to the surviving joint tenant is automatic, there is nothing for the Probate Court to do. Hence, the property in joint tenancy "avoids probate." For the same reason, you can't leave joint tenancy property to anyone in your will; the property automatically goes to the surviving joint tenant.

Here's an example: Mr. Green and Mr. White are partners in the real estate business. They own three apartment buildings as joint tenants. Each invested $1 million toward the acquisition of the real estate, and both have contributed to make the monthly mortgage payments. Mr. Green has a wife and three children. Mr. White has a wife and four children. Each has a will naming their respective wives and children as beneficiaries. Mr. Green dies. What happens? What happens is that Mr. White gets all three apartment buildings and Mrs. Green and her children get nothing. Do you think that's the result Mr. Green and Mr. White intended? Not likely.

Do you think you've seen the worst about joint tenancy? You haven't. Here it is: *Property in joint tenancy is subject to attachment by the creditors of either joint tenant.* In the foregoing example, if Mr. Green had judgment creditors and Mr. White had none, could Mr. Green's creditors attach and sell the property to pay Mr. Green's debts? Absolutely.

There is one slight asset protection advantage to joint tenancy, but not enough to warrant placing any assets in joint tenancy. If the joint tenant with the judgment creditors dies, the surviving joint tenant gets the property free of the debts of the deceased joint tenant, because the deceased joint tenant's interest in the property is extinguished by his death. That's true even if the creditors of the deceased joint tenant managed to place liens against the property prior to his death; the liens are automatically extinguished, even *tax liens* of the deceased joint tenant.

We said that probate avoidance was (and still is) the motivating factor for joint tenancy, wrongheaded as that might be. In recent years, with living trusts commonly being used to avoid probate, there is no longer any reason to place assets in joint tenancy. Joint tenancy is like smoking cigarettes. By now, people should know better.

Co-Ownership of Property: Tenancy by Entireties

If you're a married person lucky enough to live in or own property in a separate property state that also permits a form of co-ownership known as *tenancy by entireties,* you have at your disposal one of the handiest asset protection devices available anywhere.

The following permit tenancy by entireties:

Arkansas	Massachusetts	Pennsylvania
Delaware	Michigan	Rhode Island
District of Columbia	Mississippi	Tennessee
Florida	Missouri	Vermont
Hawaii	North Carolina	Virginia
Indiana	Ohio	Wyoming
Maryland	Oregon	

Most of these states permit tenancy by entireties only for real estate. Arkansas, Delaware, Florida, Hawaii, Tennessee, and Vermont also permit tenancy by entireties for personal property.

Any two people can own property as joint tenants, but only spouses can own property in tenancy by entireties. The asset protection advantage to tenancy by entireties is simply stated: *Assets held in tenancy by entireties cannot be attached by the creditors of only one spouse.* For example, if Mr. Black has judgment creditors and his wife does not, Mr. Black's creditors cannot touch property held in tenancy by entireties. An obvious asset protection strategy follows:

If you are married or own property in a state that permits tenancy by entireties, that is how your assets should be titled.

What if you own a parcel of real estate in a state that permits tenancies by entireties, but you and your spouse don't live there? That's okay. Whether you can title property in tenancy by entireties depends on the law of the state in which the property is located, not in which state the spouses reside.

How do you title property as tenancy by entireties? Depending on state law, you do it by signing a document, such as a deed, that states that the property is intended to be held as tenancy by entireties. Never rely on an oral understanding that the property is intended to be in tenancy by entireties.

If the property is in tenancy by entireties, it doesn't mean that creditors of the debtor spouse have no rights. It just means that they might have a very long wait. They'll have to wait until a divorce, which severs the tenancy by entireties, or until the death of one of the spouses, which has the same effect. But if the spouses die in the "wrong" order from the standpoint of the creditors, that is, if the debtor spouse dies first, the creditors will get nothing.

ALL ABOUT COMMUNITY PROPERTY

Millions of people have lived in community property states all their lives and don't understand how community property operates. I have had countless people sit in my office (in California) and emphatically tell me, "That property is mine. It's in my name," or ruefully opine: "It's hers. It's in her name."

You can understand most of what community property is all about by understanding this: In a community property state, we don't care whose name, the husband's or the wife's or both, is on the title; titles don't matter. What matters in a community property state is that property that is acquired during the marriage is owned one-half by the husband and one-half by the wife, regardless of whose name is on the title. The same is true of a spouse's earnings. Here's an example: Mrs. Johnson works in a factory. Her husband doesn't work at all. Every two weeks she receives a paycheck for $500. Only her name is on the paycheck, and only she can cash it. Nevertheless, Mrs. Johnson owns only $250 of that paycheck. Her husband owns the rest.[2]

---

[2] If you want to be completely technical, the "marital community" owns the entire $500, and Mr. and Mrs. Johnson each own a one-half share in the marital community by virtue of their being married.

Approximately 99.99 percent of all property owned by husbands and wives in a community property state is community property. But not all of it. During the marriage, property received by one spouse by gift or inheritance or property owned by one spouse prior to marriage that is brought into the marriage *and not commingled with community property*, retains its character as separate property. To this extent, community property resembles the way marital property is treated in a divorce in a separate property state. It's hard to go through a marriage and not commingle your property with your spouse. That's why there's so little separate property. But if more people were more careful relative to their potential creditors, there would be more of it.

A state's community property law exists to answer the following four questions:

1. Who is entitled to the property when one of the spouses dies?

2. Who is entitled to the property when the spouses divorce?

3. Who is entitled to manage the property during the marriage?

4. What property can creditors go after?

It's question number four that we're most concerned with here. However, because we discussed how property is divided in a separate property state in a divorce, let's see how property is divided when spouses in a community property state divorce.

Technically, nothing is "divided" when the spouses divorce. Each spouse gets to keep his or her separate property, if any. Each spouse then gets to walk away with his or her half of the community property. Unlike a separate property state, there is no division along "equitable principles."

Many wealthy people in community property states are afraid that they'll lose their property if they get married and later divorce. If you're afraid that your biggest creditor one day may be your former spouse, all you need to remember is not to commingle the separate property you bring into the marriage with the community property you acquire with your spouse during the marriage. At the very least, that means keeping separate bank accounts and good records. It also means properly titling the assets you intend to keep as your separate property, as follows:

John Jones, a married man, as his sole and separate property.

That's all it takes. But what if you want to take the cash you brought into the marriage out of the separate account and buy a fishing cabin? Does the fishing cabin become community property? Not if you're careful. If you keep careful records so that you can trace the source of the purchase price, and title the fishing cabin in your name as your "sole and separate property," the fishing cabin will stay your separate property.

We began this chapter by stating that, from an asset protection standpoint, community property is bad news. Here's why: As a general rule, a creditor can attach community property to satisfy the debts of one spouse. For example, if all that Mr. and Mrs. Johnson have is community property, and only Mr. Johnson has creditors, Mr. Johnson's creditors can go after all of the community property, even though Mr. Johnson owns only half of it.

And it can get worse. In California, creditors have the right to attach community property to satisfy the debts of one spouse, even if those debts arose prior to the marriage! Here's a sad story, straight from my law practice. A young couple had been married only a year or two. She had taken most of the money she had saved prior to the marriage and applied it to the down payment on their home. Long before they married, her husband had gotten into trouble with creditors. Now the creditors started to come out of the woodwork. She was afraid that she might lose the home due to debts that she had had nothing to do with. Were her fears justified? Absolutely.

There are some exceptions to this draconian rule. In California, the earnings of one spouse cannot be used to satisfy the premarital debts of the other if the earnings are placed in a separate bank account to which the debtor spouse has no access. In Texas, community property that is controlled by one spouse cannot be attached to satisfy the premarital debts of the other. Community property controlled by one spouse might include the shares of stock of a closely held business, where the corporate bylaws, resolutions, or a shareholders' agreement vests control only in the working spouse. Texas also excludes from attachment nontort debts incurred prior to marriage, such as debts incurred in business from a breach of contract or from a business failure.

One reason that 99.99 percent of all property held by spouses in community property states is community property is that these states' property laws have a legal *presumption* in favor of community property. That means that if the deed or the stock certificates say nothing, the property is deemed to be community property. For example, if real estate is titled:

John Smith and Joan Smith

it's community property. If you want the property not to be community property (and, for whatever reason, want it to be held as co-owners) there must be something written to overcome the presumption, as in:

John Smith, a 50 percent interest as his sole and separate property, and Joan Smith, a 50 percent interest as her sole and separate property.

We have already noted that property brought into a marriage retains its character as separate property unless it's commingled with the community property, at which point it becomes community property. Because creditors can attach all the community property to satisfy the debts of only one of the spouses, an obvious asset protection strategy presents itself for couples in community property states:

> If you own separate property in a community property state, never ever commingle it with the community property.

TRANSMUTATION AGREEMENTS

Community property is bad news, but it's not necessarily fatal. It is possible for spouses to sign an agreement that effectively takes them out of the clutches of the community property law. If you live in California, Texas, or any of the other community property states, the effect is as if you had lived in New York or Pennsylvania all along. Your neighbors in San Diego or Houston may be subject to the state community property law, but you and your spouse are not. Agreements that remove you from the purview of state community property laws and effectively place you under separate property are known as *transmutation agreements.*

All this may sound surprising, but it shouldn't. Most people know someone who signed a prenuptial agreement before getting married. Most prenuptial agreements say, in effect, "What's mine is mine, and what's yours is yours." Prenuptial agreements are transmutation agreements.

A transmutation agreement signed by spouses in a community property state says, in effect:

> This is my property. It's my separate property. You have no interest in my property because we choose not to be governed by community property. Ditto for your property. I have no interest in it because it's your separate property. Any property that we hereafter acquire during our marriage is my separate property if it has my name on it, and your separate property if it has your name on it.

A properly written transmutation agreement has the effect of removing the spouses' existing property from community property, and any property that they acquire thereafter. For many couples, a transmutation agreement is all the asset protection that they need.

We must be very careful when we write transmutation agreements, because they are subject to attack by creditors as fraudulent conveyances. That means that when we write one, we need to be careful that it isn't a fraudulent conveyance.

Let's assume that Mr. and Mrs. James, who live in California, have been married for 35 years and own a residence worth $1 million, have $100,000 in cash, yet another $100,000 in investments, and Mr. James is the owner of a business worth $1 million. Let's also assume that the business subjects Mr. James to considerable risks, militating against asset protection. If their transmutation agreement awards all of the assets to Mrs. James as her separate property, leaving nothing to Mr. James, it's not likely the transmutation agreement will survive a challenge as a fraudulent conveyance. But if we divide the assets equally, so that Mr. James gets half of the assets as his separate property, and Mrs. James gets the other half as her separate property, the result is that each has received fair value for the community property interest in the assets each has given to the other. In addition, if Mr. James retains sufficient liquid assets so that he can pay his bills as they come due (i.e., the transmutation agreement doesn't render him *insolvent*), we will be doubly insulated from an attack on the transmutation agreement as a fraudulent conveyance.[3]

The result of the transmutation agreement is that Mr. James' creditors will be able to attach the assets that he retained as his separate property. But that's significantly better than his creditors being able to attach all of the community property owned by Mr. and Mrs. James.

There's one step we'll need to take after we sign the transmutation agreement. You will recall from Chapter 3 that one of the badges

---

[3] See Appendix A for a model transmutation agreement prepared for Mr. and Mrs. Brown.

of fraud used to determine if a transfer is a fraudulent conveyance is whether the transfer is done secretly. We won't do it secretly. To ensure that the courts accept the validity of the transmutation agreement, we'll record it with the county recorder in the county in which the property is located. Recording the agreement means that, technically, everyone in the world has legal notice of the transfer of the assets. No one will ever be able to allege that we did anything on the sly.

Here's the bottom line: Community property is all good news for creditors and all bad news for debtors. The following asset protection strategy is mandated:

> If you are married and live in a community property state, a transmutation agreement is absolutely essential.

SHIELDING THE FAMILY RESIDENCE FROM CREDITORS

For many people, saving the family home from creditors represents the entire asset protection agenda. The reasons are obvious. For many people, the family home represents the bulk of their net worth, representing years of saving and investment. Many people who acquired their residences years—or even decades—ago could not afford to live in a similar residence were they required to buy another.

If you live in a separate property state, titling the family residence in tenancy by entireties, or titling it in the name of the spouse least likely to be the target of lawsuits, is highly recommended. For couples residing in a community property state, signing a transmutation agreement and awarding the family home to the low-risk spouse is the recommended strategy.

But there's one variable that shouldn't be overlooked. We saw in Chapter 2 that certain assets are exempt by law from the clutches of creditors. State laws that exempt the residence, or a part of its value, from the claims of creditors are known as *homestead exemptions*. Homestead exemptions vary widely from state to state, and you cannot know how to plan to protect your home without knowing how much protection your state affords. For example, New Jersey and Pennsylvania provide no state homestead exemption; a creditor can get at the family home as easily as any other asset. New York exempts a measly $10,000 in value. The California homestead exemption is $75,000, but is $100,000 if one of the spouses is elderly or disabled. The Texas and Florida homestead exemptions are practically unlimited. If you live in a city in Texas, the homestead exemption is any one-acre parcel. That means you can sink your entire net worth into a home worth $10 million, and as long as it sits on a lot that's not more than one acre, you're home free. If you live in rural Texas, the homestead exemption is 100 acres! Florida's homestead law is similar, exempting any one-half acre lot in the cities and 150 acres in rural Florida. People with severe creditor problems have been known to move to Florida just to benefit from its very generous homestead exemption.

If you live in one of the many states that, like California, exempt a dollar amount but not the entire home, it means that your creditors can force the sale of your home if the net equity in your home exceeds the homestead exemption, but they cannot if it doesn't. Here's an example. Let's assume that your home is worth $200,000 and has a $50,000 mortgage, resulting in $150,000 in equity. If the state homestead exemption is $100,000, a creditor who is owed $75,000 can force the sale of the home. The creditor gets the first $50,000, and you get the $100,000 exemption. But if the net equity in the home is only $90,000 and the homestead exemption is $100,000, the creditor cannot force the sale of the home.

The resulting asset protection strategy becomes clear: You should keep the home mortgaged to the extent of the state homestead exemption. But what if your home is "free and clear"? Can you place a mortgage on the home up to the state homestead exemption? Probably, but you'll have to be careful. As we've seen, the creation of a debt shouldn't be a fraudulent conveyance unless the new creditor knew that his or her debt was created for the purpose of defeating another creditor. But here's the problem: What will you do with the cash that you receive when you mortgage the property? Ideally, you might use the cash to acquire property that is covered by some other state exemption. If that alternative isn't available, you'll have to place the cash in some entity in which creditors will have difficulty getting at it. More on that in the following chapters.

5

Asset Protection
Using Family
Limited Partnerships

INTRODUCTION TO PARTNERSHIPS

Most nonlawyers have a general idea of what it means to be a "partner" in a "partnership." That idea is usually pretty close to the legal definition of a partnership: "two or more persons in business as co-owners for profit." On numerous occasions, I've had clients who are shareholders in corporations introduce their fellow shareholders to me as their "partners." Even though a corporation has no "partners," we all understand what was meant; they're partners in the business.

When most people think of a "partnership," they think of a *general partnership*, as opposed to its cousin, the *limited partnership*. General partnerships are easily formed; no document needs to be filed with the state or the county. If no particular business license is required, you can form a general partnership and go into business on a handshake; no written partnership agreement is required.

It's so easy to form a general partnership that you can be a partner in a general partnership without knowing it. Here's an example: Bob Smith and Cindy Jones own a duplex. Cindy lives in one half, and they lease the other half to tenants. One day, they agree over lunch that if Bob would pay the remodeling costs, Cindy would handle the trash collection, sweep the sidewalk, and deal with the tenants. They agree to split the rent. Even though they may never have thought off themselves as such, Bob and Cindy are partners in a general partnership, because they're in business together as co-owners for profit. It's as simple as that.

Partners as Agents for the Partnership

It's simple, but it's crazy. And as we shall see, being a general partner in a general partnership can be an asset protection nightmare.

It's crazy because, as a general rule, each partner in a general partnership is the agent of the partnership, with the authority to legally bind the partnership. And that is an open invitation for trouble.

Let's assume that Bob Smith, Cindy Jones, and eight other people form a general partnership named "Real Estate Associates" to own and operate a high-rise apartment building. One day, Bob wakes up and decides he's going to install new carpeting in the entire building. Never mind that the expense will bankrupt the partnership, or that he forgets to inform his nine other partners of the purchase. The purchase order, which is made out to "Real Estate Associates," is signed by "Bob Smith, General Partner." The carpeting is installed, and the bill comes. Is Real Estate Associates obligated to pay it? Absolutely. That's because each partner in a general partnership is an agent of the partnership, with the authority to bind the partnership on contracts, debts, and almost any other legal document.

But let's assume that the ten partners in Real Estate Associates had signed a partnership agreement. The agreement appoints Cindy Jones as the Managing General Partner, giving her the sole authority to make purchases and sign legal documents on behalf of the partnership. Let's further assume that Bob, flying in the face of the restriction in the partnership agreement, goes ahead and orders new carpeting, again signing the purchase order as "General Partner." Is Real Estate Associates still bound by what Bob has done? Yes! That's because as a general partner in a general partnership, Bob has the *apparent authority* to legally bind the partnership, and anyone supplying goods or services to the partnership isn't obligated to inquire into Bob's authority. Of course, Cindy and her eight other partners might well have a claim against Bob for violating the partnership agreement, but that doesn't affect the partnership's liability on the debt.

But that's not nearly the worst of it. Let's assume that Real Estate Associates doesn't have the money to pay the debt. In fact, Real Estate Associates is in bankruptcy, and its building is about to be sold to pay its mortgages. Can the carpet supplier sue Bob on the debt? Absolutely.

Can the carpet supplier (and all of the partnership's other creditors, for that matter) sue the nine other partners? Yes! That's because *in a general partnership, each partner is liable for all of the debts of the partnership.* That means that the partnership's creditors can attach the personal nonbusiness assets of every general partner, even general partners who didn't participate in or have knowledge of the creation of the debt.

Here's an example from an actual case: Two fellows who live in Texas were duped by two con men into investing in a hotel in Idaho. The deal was that the Texans would be passive investors who wouldn't participate in the management of the hotel, which would be entirely in the hands of the con men. They formed a general partnership to operate the hotel. Years went by, and the Texans received no distributions from the partnership. They had been allocated some tax write-offs, so they didn't grieve too badly over the loss of their investment. Years passed, and they heard nothing. But one fine day they were contacted by everyone's least favorite creditor, the Internal Revenue Service (IRS). It seems that the con men not only stole the money the Texans had invested, they also didn't pay the withholding taxes and social security taxes of the hotel's employees, which, with interest and penalties, now amounted to hundreds of thousands of dollars. Because the con men had long disappeared, the IRS decided to collect the money from the Texans. Impossible? Not at all. The IRS reminded the Texans that they had been general partners with the con men in the hotel business, and as general partners they were each liable for all of the partnership's debts, regardless of whether they knew of the debts.

It should be obvious by now that being a general partner in a general partnership can be the very worst form of asset protection. Why, then, do people do it? As we've seen, it's easy and cheap to go into business as general partners. Many people also feel that there are tax advantages, because a general partnership pays no income taxes; the profits of the partnership are passed through to the partners, who pick up their share of partnership profits (and losses) on their individual tax returns.

But as we shall see, all of the advantages of a general partnership are preserved in a *limited liability company,* yet with none of the disadvantages. Today, people who have not been advised or who have been poorly advised of the alternatives form general partnerships. As a general rule:

> Anyone who becomes a general partner in a general partnership is crazy.

Our law firm hasn't written a general partnership agreement since 1990. With the advent of limited liability companies, it is very possible we never will, and if anyone demands that we do, we might refuse. If you ever again become a partner in a general partnership, you've been warned.

LIMITED PARTNERSHIPS

When we consider asset protection in the context of partnerships, we need to distinguish between the need to protect a partner from the debts of the partnership ("inside-out" debt collection) and from the ability of a creditor to reach the assets of the partnership to satisfy a partner's debts ("outside-in" debt collection). As we have seen, the general partnership is a particularly terrible "inside-out" asset protection vehicle. Not only can the creditors of the partnership go after the personal assets of the partner responsible for a partnership's debt, the creditor can go after the personal assets of the other partners as well. However, as we shall see, the limited partnership is a particularly attractive asset protection tool, both from an "inside-out" and an "outside-in" standpoint.

Who's Who in a Limited Partnership

A general partnership can be formed on a handshake, and you can be a general partner without even knowing it. Not so with a limited partnership. Limited partnerships are entirely the creature of state law, and you cannot form one without complying with the requirements of the state's version of the Revised Uniform Limited Partnership Act (RULPA), enacted by every state except Vermont and Louisiana. That usually means filing a limited partnership certificate with the secretary of state of the state in which the partnership will conduct its business, paying the appropriate fees, and naming someone as the agent for service of process in case the limited partnership is sued. The filing requirements and the fees are minimal, but you can't be a partner in a limited partnership until you first comply.

Every limited partnership has at least two partners, one of whom must be a general partner, and the other of whom must be a limited partner. There is no limit on the number of general or limited partners a limited partnership can have, and many limited partnerships have hundreds or thousands of limited partners. Nor is there any limit on who may be a limited partner. A corporation, trust, or even another partnership may be a general or limited partner, as may a noncitizen or nonresident of the state or even of the United States.

The general partner of a limited partnership is no different than the general partner in a general partnership. He or she (or it) is an agent of the partnership, with the apparent authority to bind the partnership legally by his or her (or its) acts. The general partner is also personally liable for all of the partnership's debts, and a creditor can go after a general partner's personal assets to satisfy a partnership's debts ("inside-out" debt collection).

What makes limited partnerships so radically different from general partnerships is how the limited partners are treated. A limited partner has almost no right to manage the affairs of the partnership. Every state gives a limited partner some rights necessary to protect his or her (or its) interest, such as the right to inspect partnership books and the right to vote on the replacement of a general partner, but these rights are very limited. Nowhere may a limited partner sign a contract or incur a debt legally binding the partnership. Any limited partner who tries to assert such authority becomes a general partner, with all the legal liability that that entails.

In return for not having any right to manage the partnership, the limited partners have no personal liability for the partnership's debts, other than the possibility of losing their investment. Thus, for the limited partners, the "inside-out" aspect of debt collection is eliminated. Here's a typical example:

Sue Jackson wants to open a restaurant and catering business. She needs approximately $200,000. Sue forms a limited partnership, "Quick Eats, Ltd." She sells subscriptions to 20 friends at $5,000 per subscription, and invests the remaining $100,000 herself. She will act as the general partner, and her investors will be the limited partners, each with the right to receive two and one-half percent of the annual profits of the business. If there are no profits, each will be allocated two and one-half percent of the annual losses.[1]

Let's assume that things don't go too well for Sue's business. Not only does the business lose money, but also one of Sue's truck drivers injures a pedestrian just before Sue remembers she didn't have insurance. The pedestrian sues for $10 million, as do many vendors. Quick Eats, Ltd. files for bankruptcy.

Can the pedestrian and the other creditors go after Sue's personal assets? Absolutely, because she was the general partner, personally liable for all of the partnership's debts. But the creditors can't sue any of the limited partners. All that they stand to lose is their investment when the partnership goes under, the original $5,000 per

---

[1] Using those losses, however, will not be easy, because each of the limited partners is a "passive" investor. Since 1986, when Congress enacted the "passive loss" limitations into the tax code, a passive investor may not use his or her (or its) passive losses to offset income earned from active sources, such as salaries. The ability to do so was the *raison d'etre* of most tax shelters. Since 1986, a passive investor may offset passive losses from one investment against the passive gains from another passive investment, or may use the passive losses to offset earned income when the investment in the passive loss activity is sold. Until then, a passive investor cannot use his or her (or its) passive losses for tax purposes.

investor. In short, there is no "inside-out" debt collection against limited partners; they are shielded from the partnership's creditors.

The ability to shield one's assets from the partnership's creditors is not an insignificant advantage, but it is far from the principal reason that limited partnerships are effective asset protection devices. A limited partnership can be used as a refuge from one's *personal* creditors, because all that the creditors can do is obtain a charging order, which, as we shall soon see, isn't much.

All about Charging Orders

We saw in Chapter 2 that if your assets are titled in your own name, your creditors will have no difficulty finding them (by asking you, under oath, where they're located) and attaching them. Keeping your valuable assets in your own name makes life too easy for your creditors.

Let's assume that before Sue Jackson started her catering business, she set up a *family limited partnership*, "The Jackson Family, Ltd." She wants to keep all her assets under her control, but she needs to have at least one general partner and at least one limited partner. That's why limited partnerships established for asset protection purposes are family limited partnerships. Sue names her husband, Charlie, as the general partner, with the right to receive one percent of the partnership's profits and losses. Sue is the principal limited partner, retaining the right to receive 97 percent of the partnership's profits and losses. She names her children, Adam and Becky, as one percent limited partners. She accomplishes all this by filing a certificate with the secretary of state and drawing up a partnership agreement (often called "articles of limited partnership") that pays particular attention to asset protection (see Appendix B for a model family limited partnership agreement).

The next and most important thing that Sue does is transfer her assets to the partnership, so that the partnership, not she, owns them. That means that if she owns a few parcels of real estate, she must change all the titles to the real estate. If she owns a stock portfolio, all the stock certificates bearing her name must be torn up and new certificates must be issued showing that the limited partnership owns the stock. Ditto for bank accounts, certificates of deposit, and even other partnership interests. It's work, but it's essential.

Sue won't need to worry about incurring any capital gains taxes by transferring appreciated assets into the partnership. With minor exceptions, the tax code exempts from taxation the transfer of appreciated assets to the partnership. The only notable exception to the rule is if the partnership relieves Sue of debts in excess of her tax "basis" in any of the assets. For example, if Sue transfers a building that she bought for $1 million that she depreciated down to $600,000 and that has a mortgage on it of $800,000 to the partnership, the $200,000 difference between the $800,000 debt and the $600,000 "basis" represents a gain. However, if she's a 97 percent partner, she needs to report only three percent of that $200,000 gain.

Let's assume again that Sue's restaurant business goes under, leaving all sorts of creditors holding the bag. Because she was the general partner in Quick Eats, Ltd., she's personally liable for all of its debts. The creditors obtain judgments against her, and then issue a subpoena to her, demanding that she appear and answer questions, under oath, regarding the whereabouts of her assets.

Sue can't lie under oath, but she doesn't need to. They ask her if she owns any real estate, and the answer is no (the partnership does). Ditto for any cash, stocks, and bonds. Near the end of the inquiry, one of the creditors' attorneys asks her if she owns any partnership interests. Because she's under oath, she must tell the truth. She responds by telling the creditors that, yes, she does indeed own an interest in a partnership: a 97 percent limited partnership interest in "The Jackson Family, Ltd." Sue has been thoughtful enough to bring a copy of the partnership agreement with her.

They ask her about the partnership's assets, and again, she tells them everything.

What can the creditors do to get at the partnership's assets? Not much. That's where the charging order comes in.

At first blush, the charging order sounds like a weapon in the hands of the creditors, and it is. The problem is that it's a popgun where a cannon is needed, but it's the only weapon the creditors have.

Section 703 of RULPA, titled "Rights of Creditors," states:

> On application to a court of competent jurisdiction by any judgment creditor of a partner, the court may charge the partnership interest of the partner with payment of the unsatisfied amount of the judgment with interest. *To the extent so charged, the judgment creditor has only the rights of an assignee of the partnership interest.* This Act does not deprive any partner of the benefit of any exemption laws applicable to his or her partnership interest.

In plain English, the charging order makes a creditor of the debtor–partner the assignee of the debtor–partner's right to receive distributions of partnership income. Let's assume that next year, The Jackson Family, Ltd. decides to distribute $1,000 to its partners. As a 97 percent partner, Sue would be entitled to receive $970.00. Armed with a charging order, the partnership would be required to pay the $970.00 to Sue's creditors, rather than to Sue.

But that's all that the creditors get. They don't get the right to dissolve the partnership, and they certainly don't get the right to any partnership assets. The creditors can't sell the charged interest, because the partnership agreement most assuredly prohibits that. And because Sue was a limited partner, they don't obtain any right to manage the partnership, which remains exclusively in Charlie's hands. And Charlie has a vested interest in seeing that Sue's creditors get nothing. If you have any doubt, reread the italicized language in Section 703. It is explicit in making the charging order the exclusive remedy of the creditor.

Why has the legislature of every state except two enacted a provision that is so restrictive to creditors? The theory is that to permit a creditor to bust up a partnership in order to seize the assets of one of the partners would be unfair to the other partners. And so, to avoid the disruption of a partnership's business, a compromise of sorts is struck. The creditor gets whatever the debtor–partner gets whenever the debtor–partner would get it, but that's it.

The effect of the charging order in the context of a family limited partnership should, by now, be obvious. Nothing requires Charlie to distribute any money to anyone. The creditors will probably have to wait forever to get anything. Rather than wait forever, they might elect to settle the debt for pennies on the dollar.

The charging order concept isn't limited to limited partnerships; it applies to general partnerships as well. But the Uniform Partnership Act (UPA), which covers general partnerships (and limited partnerships unless RULPA has a contrary provision) provides creditors with a far more powerful weapon than does RULPA. Under UPA, a creditor may, in an appropriate circumstance, get a judge to order the sale of partnership assets if the mere assignment of the right to partnership distributions yields the creditor nothing. The inability of the charging order to provide the debtor with any real protection in the "outside-in" debt collection context is another reason limited partnerships are favored over general partnerships.

A Few Words about Phantom Income

But that's not all. There is a particularly delicious quirk with respect to charging orders that may require the creditor to *pay* money to the IRS without getting anything in return. But to understand this little gem, one needs to understand some basics of partnership taxation.

It is a basic principle of tax law that partners are taxed on their proportionate share of partnership income, regardless of whether that income is distributed to them. For example, if I am a 10 percent partner in a real estate partnership, and the partnership has $100,000 in net income during the year, I'm subject to tax on 10 percent of the $100,000, or $10,000. If the general partners decide that they can't distribute the income to partners because they need $100,000 to install a new roof, it's too bad for me. I'm still liable for the taxes on $10,000, even though I didn't receive any cash from the partnership to help pay the tax. This little problem is known as "phantom income."[2]

Now let's assume that I'm no longer a partner, because my creditors obtained a charging order. Are my creditors subject to the phantom income? Must they pay taxes on the *pro rata* share of partnership income that wasn't distributed to them? The law isn't clear on this point. In our previous example, Charlie will certainly send IRS Form K-1 to the creditors around tax time, indicating that they are liable for their share of the partnership's income, even though he distributed nothing to them. It'll make them squirm, and that may be all we need to get the creditors to settle on our terms.

But that's still not all. Depending on how aggressive you want to be, it may be possible to get cash to the debtor–partner, even though the creditor, armed with the charging order, gets nothing. That's because the charging order attaches the partner's right to distributions from the partnership in his or her capacity as a partner. But partners often deal with their partnerships in capacities other than

---

[2] Should the partnership distribute the $10,000 to me next year, I won't be taxed on it when I receive it, because I already paid the tax on the undistributed income.

as partners, and are compensated as such. For example, a partner in a real estate partnership may also act as the partnership's broker or property manager.

Could Sue Jackson get paid as a consultant to the partnership? Perhaps. The creditors will scream to the judge that the whole thing is a sham. But it's something worth considering.

Fraudulent Conveyance?

If you transfer all your assets to a family limited partnership, is it a fraudulent conveyance? It shouldn't be. As we saw in Chapter 3, the *sine qua non* of fraudulent conveyances is the transfer of property without obtaining anything in return; that is, a *gratuitous transfer*. But whenever you transfer assets to a partnership, you do get something in return: a partnership interest. That partnership interest may not be worth much to a creditor due to the charging order concept, but that doesn't make it a fraudulent conveyance.

NEW KID ON THE BLOCK: LIMITED LIABILITY COMPANIES

Consider all of the possible ways to own a business. You can conduct the business in your own name as a sole proprietor, which from an asset protection standpoint, is the worst form of ownership. If there are two or more owners, you have a number of choices. You can form a general partnership. The partnership's income will not be subject to double taxation, because the partnership itself doesn't pay taxes. A general partnership affords its owners a great deal of flexibility, because we can write the partnership agreement to allocate certain accounting items specially to one or more partners to the exclusion of others. For example, if one partner contributes a building to the partnership, it might be fair to allocate all the depreciation deductions attributable to the building to just that partner. We can't do that in a corporation, where every shareholder gets his share of partnership profits and losses, period. But, as we have seen, a general partnership is an asset protection disaster.

A limited partnership affords us the same flexibility as a general partnership. Within limits imposed by the tax code, we can allocate certain tax deductions and credits only to certain partners or classes of partners. If it's properly formed and operated, a limited partnership will also be subject to only one level of taxation. It represents a good asset protection vehicle, but only to the limited partners. The general partners are still personally liable for all of the partnership's debts.

If we want to limit the liability of all of the owners, we might consider forming a corporation (see Chapter 7 for a complete discussion of the asset protection aspects of corporations). We'll get the asset protection we need, but at a price. Corporations don't provide us with the flexibility that partnerships do. We also run the risk of double taxation. If we're not careful (and even if we are and the corporation is very profitable), we'll wind up paying corporate income taxes on the corporation's profits, and a second round of taxes when those profits are distributed to shareholders in the form of dividends.

We can avoid double taxation by filing an election with the IRS to be taxed as an "S Corporation." The result of this election is that our corporation is taxed like a partnership, which means that the corporation isn't taxed at all. The shareholders are taxed on their proportionate share of corporate earnings, regardless of whether those earnings are distributed to them. But not every corporation qualifies to make the election. There may not be more than 35 shareholders, and if just one of those shareholders isn't an individual (no corporate or partnership shareholders please!), and if just one of those individuals is a nonresident alien (no foreigners, please!) it destroys the S corporation election for everyone.

Take a look at Table 5–1. As you can see, there is something wrong with each form of doing business, even though the limited partnership comes closest to satisfying all our needs. Is there a form of ownership that combines all of the advantages of each of these forms of ownership with none of the disadvantages and limitations? There now is.

The limited liability company (LLC) gained rapid acceptance in the late 1980s and early 1990s. As of late 1995, only Hawaii, Massachusetts, and Vermont had not adopted some form of LLC statute (California was one of the last states to permit LLCs, enacting enabling legislation in September 1994). Unfortunately, there is no uniform LLC statute like RULPA for limited partnerships. The result is that state laws regarding LLCs vary to a greater degree than do state laws regulating limited partnerships.

But all state LLC laws strive to do the same thing, which is to keep all of the best features of corporations and partnerships while shedding all the disadvantages. In large part, these laws achieve that goal. If there is any disadvantage to the LLC as a form for holding assets and doing business, it is that LLCs are new. Consequently, many attorneys shy away from recommending them to clients, and many clients fear to form LLCs. But that is a disadvantage that will recede with time.

Since about 1994, many of my clients have asked: "Is an LLC a kind of partnership?" or "Is an LLC a form of corporation?" The answer is that an LLC is neither a partnership nor a corporation, but a new form combining the best of both.

An LLC doesn't have shareholders or partners, but "members," who are like shareholders in a corporation and partners in a partnership in that it is the members who own the LLC. There are no

Table 5–1. *Analysis of Different Forms of Ownership*

	General Partnership	Limited Partnership	Regular Corporation	S Corporation	Limited Liability Company
Formation formalities	No	Yes	Yes	Yes	Yes
Flexibility	Yes	Yes	No	No	Yes
Avoid double taxation	Yes	Yes	No	Yes	Yes
Restrictions re ownership	No	No	No	Yes	No
Asset protection	No	GP: No LP: Yes	Yes	Yes	Yes

GP: general partners; LP: limited partners.

restrictions on who may be a member, which is a big advantage over the S Corporation, which places numerous restrictions on who may be a shareholder, with potentially catastrophic results if those restrictions are violated. Unlike the limited partners in a limited partnership, the members may fully participate in the management of the LLC without losing their limited liability.

An LLC may (but isn't required to) have one or more "managers" who manage the affairs of the business, much like the officers of a corporation or the general partner of a partnership. But unlike the general partner of a limited partnership, no one in an LLC is personally liable for all of the debts of the LLC; there is no "inside-out" debt collection.

An LLC also preserves the tax advantages of a general or limited partnership. If the members so elect, an LLC in most states is not a taxpayer, but instead passes its profits and losses through to its members (an LLC may, for whatever reason, structure itself so that it is subject to taxation). LLCs afford their members the same flexibility to allocate LLC deductions, credits, and items of income among the members as does a partnership. Depending on the state in which the LLC is formed, the "operating agreement," or, as it's termed in Texas, the LLC "regulations," will spell out who gets what income, tax advantages, compensation, and so on.

From an asset protection standpoint, the best part of LLCs is that, in most states, they are governed by the same charging order concept as are limited partnerships. Thus, all that a creditor of a member of an LLC could get is an assignment of the member's interest in LLC distributions; the creditor couldn't force the sale of LLC assets or participate in the management of the LLC.

As a result, the LLC will, in time, replace family limited partnerships as asset protection devices, because an LLC affords the same asset protection without the problem of the general partner's exposure to creditors.

A WORD OF CAUTION

The fact that creditors of the owners of a limited partnership (and an LLC) are limited to the ineffectual weapon of the charging order has bedazzled some people into thinking that limited partnerships and LLCs are a panacea. They aren't.

The reason that they aren't is that, for asset protection, limited partnerships and LLCs rely on a judge to follow the technical requirements of RULPA or a state LLC law. But judges are often sympathetic to the claims of creditors and hostile to debtors, especially those debtors who have engaged in asset protection. The result is that, within the past few years, there have been cases where judges simply have refused to follow the law. They have allowed a creditor to foreclose on the assets of the partnership, permitting the sale of partnership assets to satisfy a partner's debts. These cases result from peculiar sets of facts. But from these cases, we can advise:

> If at all possible, avoid placing personal assets in a family limited partnership.

The reason is as follows: We began by saying that a partnership is an association of two or more persons engaged *in business* as co-owners for profit. You can always make the case that managing your stock portfolio or investment real estate is a business; it's all that some people do. But what's your home doing in a family limited partnership? What does that have to do with any business? That's the argument creditors will—and have—made to the judge to prove that a family limited partnership was nothing but a sham that should be ignored. If at all possible, employ some other asset protection device to protect your home; keep it out of the family limited partnership.

6

Asset Protection Using Qualified Retirement Plans

INTRODUCTION TO QUALIFIED PLANS

We saw in Chapter 2 that every state provides certain exemptions from the assets that a creditor may attach to satisfy a debt. There is one exemption, however, that is not wholly dependent on state law, and that is the exemption provided by the Employee Retirement Income Security Act of 1974 (ERISA) for qualified retirement plans.

The most common qualified retirement plans are

- Profit-sharing plans, often called "defined contribution plans"

- Pension plans, often called "defined benefit plans"

85

- "401(k)" plans, a type of profit-sharing plan in which the employee makes voluntary contributions to the plan

Almost all pension and profit-sharing plans entail contributions by the employer to the plan on behalf of the employee. What makes these plans "qualified" is that they comply with all of the scores of rules promulgated by both the Internal Revenue Service (IRS) and the Department of Labor. For example, there are rules regarding which employees the employer may exclude and/or include in the plan, the amount of benefits that highly compensated employees and employees who are owners can obtain under the plan, and the extent to which an employee may or may not forfeit any of his or her benefits if he or she leaves the employer. But once the plan qualifies, the employer gets a tax deduction merely on making the contribution to the plan, and the employees are taxed on the benefits only when they remove the benefits on retirement, death, disability, or whatever other event the plan permits. If you're already a participant in a qualified plan, you probably already know you are.

THE ANTI-ALIENATION RULE

One of the rules that governs ERISA contains the asset protection that makes qualified plans potentially valuable asset protection tools. The rule states that once a contribution has been made for the benefit of an employee, that benefit cannot be sold or transferred, *and cannot be attached by creditors.* The only exception to the alienation rule is in the domestic relations area. The law does provide for "Qualified Domestic Relations Orders," which permit the attachment of an employee's account to pay for child support and alimony.

Here's an example: Sally has a 401(k) plan with her employer. Every month, $400 is removed from her paycheck and deposited into her account. She gets a tax deduction for the $4,800 she contributes to the plan every year, and the earnings in her account build up tax free. One of Sally's creditors has a $10,000 judgment against her. There is nothing that Sally's creditors can do to get at the money.

The protection that qualified plans afford debtors received a blessing from no less than the Supreme Court. In a 1992 case, *Patterson v. Shumate,* the Court upheld the broad rule that funds in an ERISA plan are exempt from the claims of creditors. In a sweeping and unanimous decision, the Court held that the goal of ERISA was to ensure that amounts contributed to a qualified plan would be available for the employee at retirement, and would not be subject to the vagaries of state law. The case arose in the context of a bankruptcy proceeding, with the court holding that funds deposited in a qualified plan were exempt even from the clutches of a bankrupt employee's bankruptcy creditors. The Court's decision is broad enough to cover retirement plans created by unincorporated employers such as partnerships and sole proprietors. These plans are often called "Keogh Plans."

The Supreme Court's opinion in *Patterson v. Shumate* left open the question of whether a retirement plan that covers only the employee owner would provide the owner with protection from creditors. For example, if Dr. Wilson is the sole employee of "Dr. John W. Wilson, Professional Corporation," and he contributes a certain percentage of his income to a profit-sharing plan, there is some question as to whether that plan is exempt from the claims of his creditors. A number of lower federal courts (not the Supreme Court) have held that a retirement plan benefitting only the owner doesn't provide a shield from creditors.[1] What should Dr. Wilson do? He

---

[1] The fact that ERISA may not provide a shield for an owner-only plan doesn't mean that a state law exemption might not be applicable. In one California bankruptcy case, state law was held to cover a sole owner's $1.8 million plan account covered by a state law exemption.

should make sure that his plan includes at least one other employee not related to him.

Here's a planning tip: Every ERISA-qualified plan places limits on the annual tax deduction that you can claim from a contribution to a qualified plan. But there's nothing that prevents you from contributing more and not taking the tax deduction. The excess amount should, nevertheless, be protected from creditors.

Caution: The Anti-Alienation Rule prevents a creditor from attaching funds in a qualified plan. It does nothing to shield you once the funds have been withdrawn from the plan and reduced to your control.

INDIVIDUAL RETIREMENT ACCOUNTS (IRAs)

IRAs are hugely popular retirement vehicles because they permit the owner to obtain a tax deduction when making a contribution. The earnings build up tax free, and withdrawals are taxed at favorable rates when the owner retires.

Unfortunately, IRAs are not ERISA-qualified plans. As a result, they do not enjoy the asset protection benefits that the anti-alienation provisions of ERISA plans afford participants in ERISA plans.

Some states, notably Texas and Florida, do protect IRAs from the clutches of creditors. California protects an IRA only if the funds in the account are "reasonably necessary" for the owner's retirement. That probably means that someone who is age 55 could shield a large IRA from creditors, but someone age 25 could not!

Participants in qualified ERISA plans often "rollover" their ERISA accounts into an IRA, because a qualified rollover exempts the rolled-over funds from income tax. But the rollover is a mistake from an asset protection standpoint, because the funds are shielded while in the ERISA plan but exposed in the IRA, unless covered by a state law exemption. If at all possible, you should keep the funds in the ERISA plan as long as possible.

NONQUALIFIED RETIREMENT PLANS

A nonqualified retirement plan is a plan that isn't subject to all of the ERISA requirements. The result is that the employer has far more freedom with respect to who may be included and excluded in the plan, and how much of a contribution is made to the account of each employee. The trade-off is that the employer doesn't get a tax deduction when a contribution is made to the plan. Most nonqualified plans are written exclusively for an employer's executives or for a few key employees that management wants to retain.

One of the requirements that nonqualified plans are relieved of by being outside of the scope of ERISA is the anti-alienation provision. But that doesn't mean that all nonqualified plans fail as asset protection devices. A small number of states, including California and Pennsylvania, have statutes that are worded broadly enough to cover assets in both qualified and nonqualified plans.

FRAUDULENT CONVEYANCE?

Is it a fraudulent conveyance to remove an asset from one account, in which it is exposed to creditors, and place it in another account, such as a qualified plan, in which it's shielded from creditors? No, it isn't. It's never a fraudulent conveyance to place your assets in a form in which they qualify for a federal or state exemption. You're not giving your assets away without consideration. In fact, you're not giving assets away at all; you're merely changing the form of ownership.

7

Using Corporations for Asset Protection

INTRODUCTION

The conventional wisdom is that you can protect yourself from your creditors if you form a corporation. To a certain extent, the conventional wisdom is true. Properly formed and operated, doing business in corporate form is one of the best ways to insulate yourself from your creditors. There are hundreds of thousands of corporations in the United States, from the small Ma and Pa grocery to General Motors and Exxon, and hundreds more are formed every day. They all help their owners. Most people in business should incorporate before they ever open the doors and start business.

Most nonlawyers, however, don't know why a corporation insulates them—why it affords them *limited liability*. Because they don't understand how a corporation works, they don't know when limited liability doesn't exist or how it can be forfeited. Before you've completed this chapter, you'll have a good working knowledge of the benefits and limitations of a corporation. The key to understanding the concept of limited liability is in understanding just what this animal known as a "corporation" actually is.

WHAT IS A CORPORATION?

Let's imagine that there are three people, Al, Bob, and Charles, seated around a table in Irvine, California, and they decide to go open a restaurant called "The Eatery." They decide that each of them will contribute $1,000 in seed money to the business, and that each of them will own one-third of the business. Something tells them that they ought to incorporate. Al knows a lawyer who does that sort of work, and so they authorize the lawyer to form "The Eatery, Inc." A few days later, the lawyer informs Al that he has filed *articles of incorporation* with the secretary of the state of California, and that "The Eatery, Inc." is California's newest corporation.

Al, Bob, and Charles are again seated around the same table. But in the eyes of the law, there are no longer three legal persons seated around the table—there are four! The corporation is a separate legal entity, separate from Al, Bob, or Charles.

It is separate in every respect. Just as Al, Bob, and Charles each have a social security number that they will carry through life and that they will use for any number of purposes, the corporation will have its own identification number. If the corporation is wronged, it can sue. If it injures someone, it can be sued. It has most of the constitutional rights of due process, equal protection, jury trial, and so on, as any natural person. As a separate legal person, it is also a separate taxpayer, required to file a tax return and pay taxes on its income. As a corporate taxpayer, it may choose a tax year different from the tax years of individual taxpayers, which always begin on January 1 and end on December 31.

The key to understanding the concept of limited liability is in understanding the separate nature of the corporation. It is, for all purposes, separate from its owners (the shareholders), the directors, and the officers of the corporation. Most people have heard of the doctrine of limited liability, but nowhere will you be able to find it. It's not a law, and no judge ever decreed it. Rather, it's a result of the separate nature of the corporation.

Al, Bob, and Charles will never earn a cent from the sale of restaurant meals and drinks. Once The Eatery, Inc. opens its doors, the Eatery, Inc. will earn the money. That separate person—The Eatery, Inc.—will hire (and fire) the staff, print the menus, cook the food, and pay the rent. If the chef poisons a customer, The Eatery, Inc., not Al, Bob, or Charles, is the guilty party subject to a lawsuit for damages.

WHO'S WHO IN A CORPORATION

A corporation is a legal person, but it's obviously different in many respects from natural persons. It can't sign checks or negotiate contracts; it needs natural persons—people—to do that. As we see later, the roles that people play in a corporation are vitally important in understanding their liability for the corporation's debts. Generally, a person can fill one or more of three roles in relation to a corporation: shareholder, director, or officer.

The Shareholders

The most important position you can have in a corporation is that of a shareholder. That fact comes as a surprise to a lot of people. After all, what would you rather be, a shareholder of General

Motors (GM) or its president? The reason most people would rather be the president of GM than be a shareholder is that being president commands a high salary, whereas being a mere shareholder gives you the right to receive a dividend check every quarter. The right to elect directors at the annual meeting isn't considered much of a benefit to most shareholders.

But GM is the exception, because it's a public corporation with thousands of shareholders. The day-to-day operations of the corporation resides with the board of directors and, more likely, the officers. But most corporations aren't publicly held. Most corporations are privately held (in legalese, they're *close corporations*), in which the real power resides in the shareholders. Most closely held corporations don't pay any dividends on their stock.

If you own more than 50 percent of the voting shares of a private corporation, you effectively control the corporation. Because the shareholders elect the board of directors, if you own a majority of the shares, you have the power to control the board. You don't even have to be a director if you control the shares, because if the directors refuse to abide by your wishes you can fire them. You won't even have to wait until the next meeting of the shareholders; you can call a special meeting of the shareholders and replace them.

The shareholders elect the board of directors and have the right to vote on some extraordinary corporate matters, such as mergers and acquisitions. But that's all they do. They have no right to manage the operations of the business or interfere with or even advise the directors or officers. In many states, shareholders have a limited right to look at some of the corporation's books, but that's it.

You get to be a shareholder by buying the corporation's shares, that is, its stock, either directly from the corporation or from another shareholder. Because the corporation is a person separate from you, the most you can ever lose from the operations of the corporation's business is your investment. If the business loses money, defaults on its loan, poisons a customer, or defrauds the public, you didn't do it, someone else—the corporation—did. Because you're not responsible, you can't be sued. That's the very heart of limited liability.

But just as your ability to lose money as a shareholder of a corporation is limited, so is your ability to make money. The only way you can receive money in your capacity as a shareholder is by being paid a dividend on your stock. But the directors decide when and if to declare a dividend, and there is very little that requires them to do so. They can decide that they would rather save the money to build a new plant than pay you a dividend, and they can build plants all over the world for the next 50 years before they get around to paying you a dividend. Of course, if your stock becomes more valuable while you're holding it you can sell it at a profit, but that's the only way you'll profit from being a shareholder of a close corporation. Close corporations don't pay dividends because the dividends aren't tax deductible. Being a minority shareholder in a close corporation is not the best place to be: You won't receive any dividends, you have no control, and there may not be a market for your stock.

The Directors

The shareholders elect the board of directors. The directors are the persons empowered by law to direct the corporation. They make all the big decisions. If a corporation decides to build a new plant, hire more employees, begin research on a new product, or any one of a thousand things businesses do, it's the board of directors that makes the decision.

Let's return to The Eatery, Inc. Let's assume that Al, Bob, and Charles each own one-third of the corporation's stock, and that each of them is a director. Let's also assume that they have appointed Al as the president. One day Al decides that it would be beneficial if The Eatery, Inc. were to open another store. Could he do it? Probably not. That's not a decision that the president, who is an *officer*, makes. That decision must be made by the directors. Let's also assume that Al and Bob, who represent a majority of the directors, decide to open another store. Can they do it? No! The decision must be made by the board of directors, sitting as a board.

Just as the corporation is a legal person separate from the shareholders, the corporation is also a legal person separate from the directors. Let's assume that one day the chef confuses laundry soap with shortening, poisoning a few customers as a result. Who can the customers sue? They can certainly sue the chef for his own negligent act. They can also sue The Eatery, Inc., because that's the legal "person" who injured them. But they can't sue the directors.

But that doesn't mean that directors cannot be sued for corporate acts. If the directors cause the corporation to do something that's illegal, fraudulent, dishonest, or wasteful, they can be sued—as directors—for their dishonesty or negligence. Very often, directors are sued by the corporation's own shareholders. Here's an example: Let's assume that Bob is a director not only of The Eatery, Inc.; he's secretly also a director of Acme Restaurant Supply, Inc. He convinces Al and Charles that The Eatery, Inc. should buy its tables and chairs from Acme. He doesn't tell them that The Eatery, Inc. could get a better price for tables and chairs if it bought them elsewhere. When Al and Charles find out about Bob's deception, they can sue Bob for *breach of fiduciary duty*—that is, his duty as a director to place the interests of his corporation above his own interests. They can also sue him for fraud. What happened to the concept of limited liability? It doesn't apply. That separate legal person, The Eatery, Inc., didn't commit the fraud—Bob did.

There are a very limited number of circumstances in which the law has abrogated the doctrine of limited liability, enabling a creditor to sue a director. The two most common are employee claims and claims for unpaid taxes.

Employee Claims.   Let's assume that a corporation goes broke and files for bankruptcy. Corporations that go belly up often don't formally file for bankruptcy—they just disappear. Most often, a lot of people who loaned money to the corporation are left holding the bag. But many states have passed laws that enable employees to sue corporate directors, officers, and controlling shareholders if the corporation goes under and they haven't been paid their salaries.

Unpaid Taxes.   Many people assume that if a corporation doesn't pay its federal income taxes, the corporation's shareholders, directors, or officers will have to pay them. To a certain extent this is true, but to a large extent it isn't.

Section 6672 of the Internal Revenue Code governs who is liable for a corporation's unpaid taxes. The interesting thing about §6672 is that it respects the separate nature of the corporation and the concept of limited liability while at the same time creating an exception to it.

Section 6672 imposes a tax equal to the tax the corporation didn't pay on any person in the corporation who had control over the corporation's affairs, and who "willfully" failed to pay it. Generally, that includes any controlling shareholder, the directors, and most corporate officers. But liability under §6672 isn't automatic and doesn't extend to all back taxes. Here's how it works. Let's assume that things are a bit rough in the beginning for The Eatery, Inc., as it is for many businesses just starting out. The Eatery, Inc. has nine employees. Every two weeks or so, when The Eatery, Inc. pays the staff, it is supposed to withhold a prescribed portion of each employee's pay and turn it over to the Internal Revenue Service (IRS). The Eatery, Inc. is also supposed to withhold a portion of each employee's pay to cover social security taxes, and match that amount. But The Eatery, Inc. needs cash to pay for food and to pay the rent and the utilities. It's awfully tempting to withhold the prescribed portion of the employee's pay and not turn it over to the government, in effect making the government an involuntary unsecured lender. Needless to say, this does not please the IRS at all, especially if the corporation goes out of business before they discover what's happened.

Section 6672 allows the IRS to go after the persons "responsible" for withholding and paying the tax, but who "willfully" failed to do so. But if the corporation—that separate legal person—no longer exists, they can't recover it all. They can only recover the employee tax withholding and the employee social security withholding the corporation didn't pay. They can't collect the corporation's social security matching amount and they can't collect any of the corporation's back income tax liability. To that extent, the separate nature of the corporation is respected.

The part that the IRS can collect from a "responsible" person is known as the *Trust Fund Recovery Penalty*. There's a "gotcha" associated with the fact that withheld employment taxes are supposed to be deposited in a trust fund. As we'll see in Chapter 10, it's possible, under certain circumstances, to wash out your federal *income tax* liability in bankruptcy. But you can never wipe out trust fund taxes in bankruptcy.

The IRS can go after you only if you're a person "responsible" for the failure to pay. Needless to say, the IRS takes a very broad view of who is "responsible." If you're a director, the IRS will certainly claim you are responsible, because as a director you are legally responsible for the corporation's acts. If you are the corporation's president or vice president, they'll also claim you were responsible. No matter what your title, if you had any control over who got paid, they'll go after you as well.

The IRS will also have to show that you "willfully" refused to pay. That usually means that you knew about the nonpayment and didn't do anything about it. You might be able to show that you thought the IRS was getting paid but that the bookkeeper was pocketing the checks, but corporate officers and directors rarely beat the IRS on this argument.

People often agree to act as corporate directors as a favor or for an honorarium, pocketing a few bucks for attending directors' meetings. This is crazy. If the corporation doesn't pay its employees or the IRS, both the employees and the IRS can go after all the directors, even those who had very little to do with the operations of the business. All of which brings us to Klueger's First Rule:

> Never agree to serve as a director of a corporation unless you also control it.

Many states permit corporations to have only one director, which is usually the business' president. But many states still require that there be two or three directors. Very often, the directors, needing one or two additional directors, elect their spouses as directors. This means that if creditors can't go after one spouse (because they have carefully planned their affairs and have no assets in their own names) they can go after the other spouse. Which brings us to Klueger's Second Rule:

> Never allow your spouse to act as a director of a corporation merely to fill a vacancy.

The Officers

The officers of a corporation are appointed by the board of directors. Every corporation must have at least one officer, and if there is only one, the officer is the president. Some states require that there be a corporate secretary who is not also the president.

The officers handle the day-to-day operations of the business. They hire and fire the staff, pay the bills, oversee whatever the business does, and carry out whatever the directors order them to do. They serve at the pleasure of the board of directors.

Let's assume again that Bob is the president of The Eatery, Inc., as well as one of its directors. Let's also assume that the chef poisons the customers. We know that the chef and The Eatery, Inc. can be sued, but can Bob, in his capacity as president? Very possibly. Even though The Eatery, Inc. is a separate legal person, Bob could be sued for his own negligence. A customer might show that Bob didn't check the chef's references when he hired him, or permitted the chef to run a sloppy kitchen, or knew about a prior instance of negligence and failed to reprimand the chef. As we've already seen, Bob could be sued for employee back salaries or for certain unpaid taxes.

In most private corporations, the shareholders also act as the directors and at least some of the directors also act as officers. It's certainly true if only one person forms a corporation. But that fact shouldn't deter you from following Klueger's First and Second Rules. Your financial health might depend on it.

ALL ABOUT "SOLE PROPRIETORSHIPS"

Let's assume that Al couldn't convince Bob and Charles to go into the restaurant business with him. Al opened The Eatery by himself. He didn't incorporate. Instead, he operated the restaurant as a "sole proprietorship."

A sole proprietorship is any business that is owned by a single individual and that isn't incorporated. If your Aunt Florie knits sweaters and sells them at a flea market, her business is a sole proprietorship. Being a sole proprietor doesn't mean being in business by yourself. Al can employ 100 people at The Eatery and still be a sole proprietor, as long as he's unincorporated and no one else owns the business but him.

Nothing is easier than going into business as a sole proprietor. Unless you need a special business license (such as a liquor license to open a liquor store), all you need is a business card and you're in business. You don't need to file anything with the secretary of state. That's the one advantage a sole proprietorship has over a corporation.

But that's where the advantages end. Just as the key to understanding limited liability is the separation of the corporation from its shareholders, directors, and officers, the key to understanding the unlimited liability of a sole proprietor and his or her business is the identity of the proprietor and his or her business.

In the eyes of the law, the sole proprietor and his or her business are indistinguishable. If Al operates The Eatery, no one can say where Al leaves off and The Eatery begins. The Eatery's tables and chairs are owned by Al, not by The Eatery, which is nothing more than a name. If The Eatery earns money, Al earns money. There's nothing that prevents Al from taking a few bucks out of The Eatery's cash register whenever he wants; it's his money. The Eatery isn't a separate taxpayer. Al must report The Eatery's profits on Schedule C of his personal tax return. If The Eatery loses money, he can deduct its losses against any other income Al or his wife might have. When Al dies, The Eatery dies with him. And worst of all, *The Eatery's debts are Al's debts.*

Let's assume the worst: Al's chef poisons the customers. They could sue the chef, but there's usually no money in that. They can sue The Eatery, and The Eatery is Al! As we saw in Chapter 1, they will all sue, not only for their medical bills and their real pain and suffering, for their "mental distress," their loss of companionship with their spouses, and anything else their lawyers can dream up. And they'll win. If Al was smart and is lucky, his insurance will cover the judgments that the jurors will surely award. But here we're assuming the worst. Let's assume that part of the judgments aren't covered by insurance.

When the plaintiffs (who are now judgment creditors) come to collect, can they get their hands on The Eatery's bank account, its accounts receivable, its tables and chairs—any business assets—to satisfy their judgments? Of course. Can they also go against Al's house, his personal bank account, and his car? Yes! There's no difference between The Eatery and Al. Can The Eatery go into bankruptcy to avoid the judgments? No! The Eatery doesn't exist—it's just a name. In order to avoid the judgments, Al will have to file for bankruptcy. And, as we saw in Chapter 4, if Al is unlucky enough to live in a community property state, the judgment creditors might be able to go after property that is titled in Al's wife's name but that is really community property. If that's the case, Al's wife will also have to go into bankruptcy.

All of this is a pretty stiff price to pay for not having walked down to the secretary of state with a set of articles of incorporation. All of which brings us to Klueger's Axiom. If you remember nothing else in this book, remember this

KLUEGER'S AXIOM
ANYONE SERIOUS ABOUT MAKING MONEY
IN BUSINESS MUST INCORPORATE.

Klueger's Axiom is limited only to people who are serious about making money—and keeping it. Your Aunt Florie, who every now and then knits a few sweaters and sells them at flea markets, is exempt from the rule. Everyone else must incorporate.

THE LIMITS OF LIMITED LIABILITY

Some people think that the minute they incorporate they've wrapped themselves in an impenetrable bulletproof shield. As we've already seen, certain owners, directors, and even the officers of a corporation may be liable for certain corporate debts, such as employees' wages and certain taxes, as a result of special statutes.

But even without these statutes, there are certain instances when the doctrine of limited liability doesn't apply. Yet all of these exceptions recognize and are consistent with the separation of the corporation and its owners.

Debts Incurred Prior to Incorporation

I once met a woman who was planning to go into business and who understood that she needed to incorporate. Before she incorporated she bought certain supplies and signed an office lease. She asked me if she could avoid personal liability for these business expenses by incorporating. The answer is no. The people who sold her the supplies on credit and the landlord who leased her the office didn't deal with that other legal person—it didn't yet exist. They dealt with her, and nothing can get her off the hook. Of course, that doesn't mean that the corporation, once formed, can't pay the debts and make the lease payments. She can assign the lease to the corporation, and the corporation can assume the debts. But if the corporation can't or won't pay these creditors, they can—and will—go after her.

If you're not careful, you can be personally liable for what you think is a corporate obligation, but which is really your personal debt. Let's assume that the landlord is willing to lease a building to a corporation. Here are two ways in which the lease can be signed by the tenant:

_____

John Smith

XYZ INCORPORATED

BY:_____

John Smith, its president

The signature block on the left is the signature only of John Smith. The signature block on the right represents the signature only of a corporation. However, because a corporation, being a legal—but not a natural—person, cannot sign its name, John Smith is permitted to perform the *ministerial act* of signing for the corporation. But if the rent is unpaid, John Smith won't be liable for the corporation's obligation if he signed the signature block on the right.

Personal Guarantees of Corporate Debts

One of the reasons that the tallest buildings in any city are bank buildings is that bankers aren't stupid. They understand the concept of limited liability and will do anything to avoid it. The easiest way for a lender to avoid limited liability is to require an individual to guarantee the corporation's debt. If the corporation defaults on the loan, the lender ignores the corporation and sues the individual guarantor.

Whether you will have to guarantee a loan, a lease, or other debt is solely a function of your bargaining position. If the landlord is dying to lease the space, you may be able to avoid giving a personal guarantee. A bank usually will try to get a personal guarantee before it lends to a corporation. You should at least try to negotitate a loan without giving a personal guarantee.

Secured Debts

If a bank lends money to your corporation, and that loan is secured by real estate, accounts receivable, equipment, or any other asset, the loan will have to be repaid, at least to the extent of the lender's security. Limited liability won't help. Just as with personal guarantees, the amount of security you'll have to put up is strictly a function of your bargaining power.

"Piercing the Corporate Veil"

This legal doctrine is an exception to the doctrine of limited liability. It allows a creditor to ignore the corporation—and sue the shareholders—if the shareholders themselves ignored the corporation. Here's how it works:

Let's assume that Al, Bob, and Charles file a set of articles of incorporation with the California secretary of state. As far as the State of California is concerned, The Eatery, Inc. is a corporation. The Eatery, Inc.'s lawyer mails the certificate of incorporation to Al, Bob, and Charles. They put the certificate in a drawer—and forget about it. They never hold a shareholders' meeting, they never elect directors, and they never formally appoint officers. The corporation doesn't withhold taxes and social security from Al's, Bob's, and Charles' paychecks, as it should if they truly were employees of a corporation. They don't even file a corporate tax return.

It's easy to forget to hold annual shareholders' and directors' meetings and keep minutes of the meetings, because no one requires that you hold them, and the minutes of the meetings don't have to be filed anywhere.

But failing to do so can be costly. If you don't keep up with the "formalities," you could lose limited liability. A creditor can sue the shareholders of a corporation rather than the corporation itself—"piercing" its "veil"—saying, in effect: "These shareholders ignored their corporation; why shouldn't we?" It's a powerful argument, and often it works.

What a creditor must do to pierce the corporate veil varies from state to state. In some states, proving that the shareholders didn't perform the formalities (directors' and shareholders' meetings, corporate bank accounts, etc.) is all you need to prove. In other states, a creditor must show that the corporation was undercapitalized when it was formed. The rationale is that the shareholders weren't serious about being incorporated if they didn't give the corporation enough money to pay its debts. In order to avoid the undercapitalization rule, shareholders need only to have the corporation be solvent when the corporation is formed, not when it's sued. Of course, as we saw in Chapter 3, if the reason the corporation is insolvent when the lawsuit is brought is due to a fraudulent conveyance to its shareholders, directors, or officers, then the creditors could sue these individuals for this reason.

The piercing of the corporate veil is easy to avoid. You just have to remember to keep timely shareholder and director meetings and document in a corporate minute book all the decisions the shareholders and directors make. Corporate officers should have written employment agreements with the corporation, and should be paid in accordance with the terms of the agreements. The corporation should withhold income and social security taxes from the officers' salaries, just as General Motors would if they worked for GM. Of course, the corporation should be adequately capitalized (i.e., able to pay its debts) when the corporation is formed.

The "Ultra Vires" Doctrine

It sounds like a terrible disease, but hardly anyone flunks this one anymore. This doctrine allows a creditor to ignore the corporation and sue the individuals if the corporation did something its own charter—the articles of incorporation—didn't allow the corporation to do. Let's say that the articles of incorporation of The Eatery, Inc. empowers the corporation to do business only as a restaurant. One day, the shareholders decide that it would be swell if The Eatery, Inc. were also to open a barber shop. If a customer is injured by an inept barber employed by The Eatery, Inc., the customer could ignore the corporation and sue the shareholders.

It's easy to avoid the *ultra vires* doctrine. Most states permit corporations to be formed "for any lawful purpose," in which case all the owners of the corporation need to do is avoid committing illegal acts. If you intend to form a corporation that requires you to spell out in the articles of incorporation all the things the corporation intends to do, just make sure you amend the articles before you do anything not specified in your articles.

Professional Corporations

Most states have special statutes for professional corporations—that is, corporations composed of doctors, lawyers, architects, accountants, psychologists, and so on. In most of these states, you may not be a shareholder or director of one of these corporations unless you're a licensed professional.

Most of these statutes limit or eliminate limited liability with respect to professional malpractice. The theory is that the doctors in a medical corporation should be sued if they're negligent. In some states, all of the shareholders of a professional corporation can be held liable for the negligence of any one of them if the corporation doesn't have malpractice insurance.

Professionals have the most difficult job protecting their assets from creditors, and must use the greatest care. Not only are professionals prime targets for lawsuits, but also their corporations help them the least.

A FINAL LIMITATION OF LIMITED LIABILITY

In Chapter 5 we explored the difference between "inside-out" and "outside-in" debt collection. The same applies here. "Inside-out" debt collection occurs when a creditor of the entity (here, the corporation) tries to go after a shareholder, director, or officer of the entity to collect the entity's debt. Limited liability prevents the creditor from going after the individual for the entity's debt.

But what if the debt was incurred by a shareholder wholly apart from the corporation? For example, let's assume Al, while vacationing in Hawaii, rams a surfer with his jet ski. After the surfer wins a judgment against Al, can the surfer attach The Eatery, Inc.'s assets? In other words, can the creditor collect "outside-in"? Not a chance. If the separate nature of a corporation means anything, it means that the corporation's assets cannot be reached to satisfy the debts of a shareholder.

Is the creditor of a shareholder completely out of luck? Not necessarily. The creditor can't touch the corporation, but there's nothing that prevents the creditor from seizing Al's shares in The Eatery, Inc. His shares are personal assets, just as his jet skis are. There may not be much that a creditor will do with a minority interest in a close corporation, but that's the creditor's problem, not Al's.

HOW MANY CORPORATIONS DO YOU NEED?

You may need more than one. You may need many.

The next time you're at the airport in any large city, take a close look at the long line of taxicabs. They'll all look the same—bright yellow—because they're probably all owned by the same group of individuals. But look carefully at the stenciled letters on the side of each cab. The first cab will have "Acme Cab Company, Inc." stenciled on it. The next will have "Beta Cab Company, Inc.," and somewhere in the line of cabs waiting for a pickup is "Zona Cabs, Inc." Every cab is a separate corporation! What are the assets of each "corporation"? The cab itself, a spare tire, and, depending on local law, the taxicab license.

The reason that the owners make every cab a separate corporation is that when (not if—when!) a cab is involved in an accident and is sued, the plaintiff can recover no more than the assets of the corporation that caused the injury; the judgment isn't made against the assets of the entire fleet. You can be sure that every "corporation" has its own bank account, shareholder, directors, and officers, and that they hold periodic meetings and document their meetings with written minutes.

You may not need a whole series of corporations, but you may need more than one. If you're in more than one business, one that makes "safe" products and the other that makes "dangerous" ones, it's crazy to combine them both in the same corporation. There is no point in exposing the assets of the "safe" business to the lawsuits likely to result from the "dangerous" one.

8

Using Trusts for Asset Protection

INTRODUCTION: A PRIMER ON TRUSTS

Thousands of people have created trusts, and thousands more have benefitted from trusts created by others. Yet most people view a trust as being a plaything reserved for the wealthy, like polo ponies. That may have been true once, but it hasn't been for decades. A trust can achieve a number of personal estate and tax planning goals; asset protection is only one of the potential benefits.

Who's Who in a Trust

Every trust has at least three "players," who are the *settlor*, the *trustee*, and the *beneficiary*. The settlor is usually the person who creates the trust. In some states, the settlor is referred to as the *trustor*, the *grantor*, or the *creator* of the trust. By whatever name it's called, this is the person who deposits assets into the trust. The assets of the trust are variously called the trust *principal*, or, for those of us who love the Latin, the trust *corpus*.

The settlor deposits the corpus with the trustee. The trustee is the most important—and active—player in a trust. The trustee holds and distributes the assets in accordance with the wishes of the settlor. The trustee is a *fiduciary* for the benefit of the beneficiaries. The trustee cannot use the trust corpus for personal benefit unless specifically authorized by the settlor. The trustee is legally obligated to use the trust corpus in a manner requiring at least as much (and often more) care as he or she would their own property. If the trustee messes up, he or she can be sued by the settlor, the beneficiaries, or both. If he or she *really* messes up, it's a crime.

The beneficiaries are the people for whom the trust is created by the settlor, and for whom the trustee manages the assets. They have the most passive roles in a trust, with nothing to do but wait for the trustee to do whatever the trustee is required to do under the trust. It comes as a sad surprise to many people who are the beneficiaries of trusts that they have no say in the operation of a trust.

In most states there is no requirement that a trust be in writing, but most trusts are because it's extremely foolish to create an oral trust. Anyone who wants to assure that the trustee does what he or she is supposed to do, and that the beneficiaries receive what is intended for them, will create a *written* trust. The document embodying the settlor's desires (and the trustee's instructions) is often referred to as the *declaration of trust*, the *trust agreement*, or simply as the *trust*.

Once the trust document is written and signed, the settlor will transfer assets to the trustee, and those assets become the trust corpus.

What tends to confuse many people about trusts is that the settlor, the trustee, and the beneficiaries often are the same people. There is nothing that prevents the settlor from naming him- or herself as the trustee, although, as we shall shortly see, to be both the settlor and the trustee may have negative asset protection and/or tax consequences. The trustee may also be a beneficiary of a trust. Indeed, a person may be the settlor, trustee, and a beneficiary of a trust at once.

Here's a common example. Let's assume Mr. and Mrs. Brown create a trust for their children. They both are the settlors and the trustees. When they transfer their residence to the trust, the deed will include a provision stating:

> John Brown and June Brown, grantors, hereby transfer to John Brown and June Brown, as trustees of The Brown Family Trust, under instrument dated January 2, 1995.

If the trust also provides that Mr. and Mrs. Brown will receive the income from the trust during their lives, then the Browns are the settlors, the trustees, and the beneficiaries of the trust.

Living Trusts and Testamentary Trusts

A trust that comes into being during the settlor's lifetime is often called a *living trust,* or, for the Latin lovers, an *inter vivos trust.* In the previous example, in which Mr. and Mrs. Brown created the trust and signed over the ownership to themselves as trustees during their lifetime, an *inter vivos* trust was created.

Very often, however, a trust is created only when the settlor dies. The trust, created by the settlor's will, is called a *testamentary trust.* Let us assume that Mr. and Mrs. Brown have two young children. During their joint lifetimes, and during the lifetime of the survivor of them, they will care for their children. But if they both should die while their children are minors, they're not likely going to want their children to receive their estate outright; they'll want someone to retain the estate for the children, distributing the assets to them only when the children are adults or otherwise competent to handle them. That's where the testamentary trust comes in. A trustee is named in the decedent's will who takes control of the assets on the decedent's death, and administers the trust in accordance with the settlor's wishes.

Clients often ask me what they can say in a trust. The answer is almost anything. If you want to leave $10,000 to your cousin Sally provided she becomes an Eagle Scout, that's your prerogative. It's your money, and you're limited only by your imagination. The only things you cannot do with your money are a small class of bequests prohibited by public policy. For example, if you write a trust that leaves "Ten thousand dollars to my cousin Sally, provided she divorces her husband Joe," you can rest assured Sally will get the money if she stays married to Joe or not. Similarly, "Ten thousand dollars to cousin Sally, provided she is not married to a black man," will go to Sally, regardless of whom she marries.

Are living trusts better than testamentary trusts? In a few key areas, they are. First, because a testamentary trust only comes into being at the settlor's death, it can provide no asset protection for the settlor. Depending on how the trust is worded, it might well provide a great deal of asset protection for the beneficiaries after the settlor dies.

A second advantage of the living trust over the testamentary trust— and the reason most living trusts are created—is that a living trust enables the settlor's estate to avoid *probate* when the settlor dies; a testamentary trust does not.

Little creates more confusion in the minds of nonlawyers than the whole probate process. Many people are aware that probate is something that needs to be avoided, but they aren't sure why. And if they know why they need to avoid it (because they went through it with a relative), they usually don't know how a living trust helps them avoid it.

Here's how. Let's assume that Mr. and Mrs. Brown own a home titled in joint tenancy. Mr. Brown owns a stock investment account and a certificate of deposit. Mrs. Brown owns a certificate of deposit. Mr. Brown owns a life insurance policy that pays $100,000 on his death to his designated beneficiary, Mrs. Brown. Mr. Brown has a one page will that leaves everything to Mrs. Brown on his death, but no trust.

What happens when Mr. Brown dies? Mrs. Brown will have no problem getting the $100,000 death benefit from the insurance company. Because the life insurance policy is a contract Mr. Brown signed with the insurance carrier, all Mrs. Brown needs to do is present the insurance carrier with a certified copy of a death certificate, and a few days later she'll receive the money. The same is true of the home in joint tenancy. Because the essence of joint tenancy is that the survivor, who has the *right of survivorship,* gets to keep the property when the first joint tenant dies, all Mrs. Brown will need to do is present an affidavit and a certified copy of the death certificate to the county recorder to have the property titled in her name alone. The life insurance and the joint tenancy property pass to the survivor automatically; they're not part of the *probate estate.*

But what of the stock portfolio? Let's assume that Mrs. Brown visits the stockbroker, armed with a copy of Mr. Brown's will (which clearly and unambiguously leaves everything to her) and a copy of the death certificate. Will the stockbroker transfer the stock fund into Mrs. Brown's name? Not likely. The stockbroker will most likely inform Mrs. Brown that he can transfer title to the assets only if Mrs. Brown first obtains *letters testamentary* or *letters of administration.* From whom do you get these? The Probate Court.

Probate is the process of physically transferring the title to assets from a deceased person to living persons. Note that the fact that Mr. Brown had a will that clearly left everything to Mrs. Brown doesn't avoid probate. Mr. Brown's will is a directive; it informs the Probate Court where the assets are supposed to go. But because

Mr. Brown can't reach up out of the grave to sign over the title to the stock certificates from himself to Mrs. Brown, Mrs. Brown needs the Probate Court to get the titles transferred to her.

Why is all of this so awful? If you've had a relative whose estate needed to be probated, you know. Depending on the state in which the estate is probated, the process will range from the merely inconvenient, if you're lucky, to the downright Dickensian, if you're not. You will spend anywhere from six months to two years in the clutches of lawyers. You will need to have the assets appraised, even if you have no intention of selling them. If you want to sell an asset, you'll need the probate judge's consent. You will get writer's cramp signing motions, petitions, and waivers. And the entire process will be completely open to public inspection.[1] So you needn't be surprised if you're inundated by calls and letters from real estate appraisers, liquidators, and financial planners soliciting their services.[2]

It's not only time-consuming and annoying, it's also expensive. Some states, like California, fix the amount the administrator and the lawyer may charge to probate the estate. In other states, it's whatever you can bargain for. But don't be surprised if the probate fees consume five to eight percent of the estate.

For what? For the little piece of paper, the letters testamentary, that you need to transfer the assets in accordance with the decedent's expressed will.

That's the bad news. The good news is that it's all completely avoidable with a living trust to which you have transferred your

---

[1] When actress Natalie Wood died, she owned 29 fur coats. How do we know this? Her will had to be probated.

[2] Florida recently enacted a law making it illegal for a lawyer to contact a decedent's survivor within a prescribed number of days following the decedent's death.

assets. Review the transfer of the residence from Mr. and Mrs. Brown to Mr. and Mrs. Brown as trustees of The Brown Family Trust. When Mr. Brown dies, the property is already in the trust, and Mrs. Brown, as cotrustee, already owns it. When Mrs. Brown dies, a *successor trustee* steps in and takes control of the trust. What is there for the probate court to do? Absolutely nothing. If Mr. and Mrs. Brown make sure that The Brown Family Trust, and not they, have title to the stock certificates, the bank accounts, the certificates of deposit, and the real estate, there will be nothing for the Probate Court to do when either of them dies, and probate is avoided.

Some of my clients often express a concern that the Probate Court judges might frown on this obvious avoidance of the judicial system. Do they? No, they don't, for the same reason the criminal court judges aren't put out by people not committing crimes.

CAN YOU AVOID YOUR CREDITORS WITH A LIVING TRUST?

Dying is, for most people, too extreme a method to avoid one's creditors. We don't recommend death as a planning tool to most of our clients. But while we're on the subject, can you avoid your creditors by dying? If you set up a living trust, the answer is maybe. Here's why.

Let's assume that Debbie Debtor died owing $30,000 on six credit cards. She also signed a $10,000 promissory note, and owed $1,200 to Dr. Smiles, her dentist. She also owed $50,000 on a student loan. Let's further assume that Debbie didn't have a living trust, so that her estate had to be probated. One of the many things that her executor is required to do is publish a notice in a local newspaper stating that Debbie has died, and anyone who was owed money by Debbie should submit a claim to the executor. In most states, a creditor has a very limited time (anywhere from 30 days to six months) to file a claim. If you don't file a claim in that period of time, the executor may distribute the estate's assets to the beneficiaries, and you're out of luck.

Not only that, but 39 states also have a *self-executing statute of limitation.* If a creditor doesn't sue the estate for payment within a certain period of time, the creditor is out of luck. Moreover, these statutes of limitations start to run when the decedent dies, and they're not dependent on the executor ever starting a probate proceeding. The statute of limitations in California, Massachusetts, and Ohio is one year. It's two years in Florida and Illinois, and three years in Michigan. (New York, New Jersey and Pennsylvania, among others, have no such statute.) For example, if Debbie had died a resident of California, her creditors would have one year to sue to recover their debts. If they don't, they can kiss off their claims.

Note that the executor needs only to *publish* a notice that Debbie died and that her probate has been opened. There's usually little chance that her creditors will see the notice. If they don't see the notice, they won't know that Debbie died, and the self-executing statute of limitations will run out before they ever find out that she died! Is this too good to be true?

Yes, it is. In 1988, in the case of *Tulsa Professional Collection Services v. Pope,* the Supreme Court ruled that if you start a probate, and you know a creditor has a claim, telling him about the probate through a published notice isn't enough; it's a denial of the creditor's rights under the Due Process Clause of the Fourteenth Amendment of the U.S. Constitution. If you know of a creditor's claim, you have to give him actual notice, by sending him a letter or by picking up the phone.

But here's where things get technical. The Due Process Clause is violated only where there is some *state action*—that is, where the government somehow is involved in due process being denied. And there's nothing that involves the government more intimately than a probate proceeding.

But what if there is no probate, as is the case where the decedent had a living trust? Let's assume Debbie died on January 15, 1995. If all her assets had been in a living trust, there's no need to inform her creditors, because there's no need ever to start a probate. If Debbie had been a California resident, the clock starts to tick on January 15, 1995, and time runs out on January 15, 1996. If the creditors don't learn of Debbie's death until more than a year has gone by, they're out of luck.

Isn't this a denial of due process? No, it isn't, because there was no "state action." The Supreme Court specifically ruled in *Tulsa v. Pope* that:

> Nor is the State's involvement in the mere running of a general statute of limitations generally sufficient to implicate due process.

Does that mean that Debbie's creditors are completely out of luck? Not necessarily. How did the executor keep the credit card companies from finding out that Debbie had died? Did he make the monthly interest payments on the credit cards, counting the days until the statute of limitations ran? Perhaps the executor himself committed fraud. Even if he didn't, there may be a state law that makes a trust liable for the debts of the settlor.

What about that student loan that Debbie owed? Can her estate use the state self-executing statute of limitations to beat the U.S. Department of Education out of their debt? Probably not. The reason stems from yet another provision of the Constitution, the *Supremacy Clause,* which makes federal laws superior to state laws where they conflict. It isn't likely that a federal debt will ever be barred by a state statute of limitation.

REVOCABLE AND IRREVOCABLE TRUSTS

The most important thing you need to know about any trust is whether the trust is *revocable* or *irrevocable* by the settlor. The asset protection consequences are substantial.

If a trust is revocable, it will provide absolutely no asset protection to the settlor. That makes sense. If the settlor has the power to tear up the trust and retrieve all the assets given to the trustee, there's nothing that should prevent a court from ordering the settlor to exercise that power in favor of a creditor.

In order for a trust to afford any asset protection for the settlor, it must, therefore, be totally irrevocable. That means that, at least technically, once you give the assets to the trustee, you cannot get them back. We say technically because, even though the language of the trust cannot require a trustee to return assets to the settlor, there is nothing to prevent a friendly trustee from voluntarily returning assets to the settlor should the settlor so request.

Creating an irrevocable trust also means that the settlor cannot act as the sole trustee. Regardless of a trust's language, no one is fooled if you create an "irrevocable" trust and then say that you prevent yourself from tearing it up. You're running a risk if you create a purportedly irrevocable trust with yourself and someone else as cotrustees, especially if that someone else is related to you.

It isn't always easy to determine whether a trust is irrevocable. Often the trust will specify that the settlor reserves the right to amend or alter it at any time, or that the settlor may not ever alter or amend it. But often the trust is silent. In that case, it's necessary to check the powers the trust reserves to the settlor, and state law to determine if it creates a presumption in favor of revocability or irrevocability if the document is silent.

Fraudulent Conveyance?

The creation of a revocable trust isn't a fraudulent conveyance, because it isn't a conveyance. In the eyes of the law, the settlor—armed with the power to retrieve the assets—hasn't really transferred them. Because the settlor started out owning the assets and ends up owning them, he or she cannot be said to have made a transfer. That doesn't mean that revocable trusts don't serve useful purposes. As we have already seen, they avoid probate on the settlor's death. They can also serve to care for the settlor during the settlor's disability or the settlor's children or other loved ones.

If a trust is irrevocable, however, it is very definitely subject to the law of fraudulent conveyances. It is so for the simple reason that whenever the settlor transfers assets to a trustee, the settlor receives nothing in return. And as we saw in Chapter 3, one of those badges of fraud is if the transferor received anything in return.

That is not to say, however, that the creation of every irrevocable trust is a fraudulent conveyance. It just means that when we create an irrevocable trust, we need to "jump through the hoops." We need to assure that the settlor isn't rendered insolvent by the transfer, and that the transfer is done openly. And most important (you've heard this before), we need to create the trust and transfer assets to it before creditors come calling. Once again, an irrevocable trust works a lot better to defeat the claims of creditors if it's established before you develop creditors rather than after.

If, however, the transfer of the assets to the trustee is not a fraudulent conveyance, an irrevocable trust serves very well to shield the assets from the settlor's creditors, because an irrevocable trust is, in the eyes of the law, a legal "person," separate and distinct from the settlor. Creating an irrevocable trust is like creating an Uncle Irving if you don't already have one.

Discretionary Trusts

Transferring assets to the trustee of an irrevocable trust doesn't mean, however, that the benefit of the assets are lost to you. Far from it. For example, if you transfer $1 million to an irrevocable trust, and name yourself as an *income beneficiary* of the trust, there is nothing that prevents the trustee from distributing all or a portion of the annual income from the trust to you.

In order to keep your creditors' grasping hands off the annual income, you will need to create a *discretionary trust*, which is a type of irrevocable trust that gives the trustee the complete discretion to decide which of two or more beneficiaries gets paid, and when. Here's an example of a clause that makes a trust a discretionary trust:

> The trustees, in their sole and absolute discretion, may apply the whole, any portion, or none of the net income of the trust to one, some, or all of the beneficiaries of the trust, to the complete exclusion of one or some of the beneficiaries.

If the trust contains this or similar language, and there are in fact two or more beneficiaries, there's little chance a creditor could ever get at the income. Here's why: First, under the technical terms of the trust, no one beneficiary—including the settlor in his or her capacity as beneficiary—has the right to demand any income from the trustee; the trustee could cut the settlor out entirely. Second, there is an ancient principle that a creditor doesn't get an interest in a trust greater than the interest of the debtor. If a particular beneficiary cannot force the trustee to distribute any income to him, the beneficiary's creditors also cannot force a distribution. Of course, should the trustee actually distribute trust income to a beneficiary, the beneficiary's creditors can go after that income. But if the beneficiary has creditor problems, and the trustee is friendly to the beneficiary, a distribution isn't likely to occur.

Spendthrift Trusts

An irrevocable trust can provide asset protection not only for the settlor, it can serve to shield trust assets from the creditors of a beneficiary, provided that the trust contains a special clause making it a *spendthrift trust*. Here's an example:

> No interest in the principal or income of any trust created under this instrument shall be anticipated, assigned, encumbered, or subjected to a creditor's claim or legal process before actual receipt by the beneficiary.

Now let's see how this provision works in real life. Let's assume that your nephew is a beneficiary of a trust you set up that contains the spendthrift language as in the previous quote. Your nephew becomes a stock market addict, throwing all his cash at his brokers. One day, after he's run out of money, he cajoles his broker into lending him more money to buy stocks, based on the fact that in a few years the trustee will be required to make a distribution of trust assets to him. So the nephew signs an irrevocable assignment, assigning his interest in the trust to the broker. When the entire brokerage account is frittered away, the broker knocks on the trustee's door, demanding payment.

Is the assignment enforceable? No, it isn't, due to the language of the spendthrift clause. Read it again. It says that a beneficiary's interest in a trust may not be *anticipated*, which is what the nephew did, or *assigned or encumbered* (i.e., subject to a security interest or lien), which is also what the nephew did.

It sounds too easy to exempt a trust from a beneficiary's creditors merely by adding one paragraph, but that's pretty much how it works. The reason it's so easy is that no one forces anyone to put money into a trust, and if you do transfer your money into a trust you should be able to on your own terms. After all, if you had never established a trust for your nephew (which is your right), your nephew's creditors could never have attached your assets.

IRREVOCABLE TRUSTS AND GIFT TAXES

Most Americans have a pretty good sense of the income tax, because most Americans have a good percentage of their paychecks withheld to pay income taxes, and those who aren't subject to withholding must still file an annual income tax return. Most people have an even closer appreciation of sales taxes, because they pay sales taxes almost every day.

It's the *gift tax* that remains a stranger to most people. A gift tax is due on the value of any gift. Not only that, it is the *donor*, the person who makes the gift, not the recipient (the *donee*), who is principally liable for the gift tax. So why don't I have to pay gift taxes every time I buy a bicycle for my son or a Barbie doll for my daughter? Because every person is allowed a $10,000 per calendar year exemption from gift taxes, per donee. For example, if I give $10,000 in cash to my son on December 31, and stocks and bonds worth $10,000 to my son on the next day, January 1, I pay no gift taxes. But if I give my son $4,000 on May 1, and $7,000 on June 1, $1,000 of the June 1 gift, being the amount in excess of $10,000 for that calendar year, is subject to gift taxes. And I get to pay it, not my son.

Most of my clients are incredulous when they learn about the gift tax. They cannot understand why the government gets involved in this transaction. After all, if I want to give my assets to my children, my nephews, or the Los Angeles Dodgers, that should be no one's business, least of all the U.S. Treasury. And if anyone should be liable for the gift tax, it should be the person receiving the windfall, not the person giving it. What's going on here?

Here's what. The gift tax is a necessary backstop to the estate tax. It prevents people from eliminating their exposure to estate taxes by giving everything away before they die. For example, if Uncle Irving, knowing he is about to depart this mortal veil, calls his relatives to his deathbed and parcels out all the assets, the relatives get everything and the tax collector is left holding the bag. If there's no gift tax, there's no estate tax. That's why there's a gift tax.

If an irrevocable trust really is a separate legal person, we run the risk that a transfer to the trustee of the irrevocable trust will result in an immediate gift tax. Protecting ourselves from the claims of future creditors is one thing. Doing it at the price of an immediate gift tax is something else again.

Fortunately, there is a way out. For gift tax purposes, only *completed gifts* are subject to gift tax. If we purposefully structure the trust so that the gift is incomplete, there is no gift to tax. We can make a gift incomplete by giving the settlor the power to shift distributions among certain classes of beneficiaries. Making a gift incomplete for gift tax purposes should not mean that the trust is revocable, resulting in the continued shielding of the trust's assets from the claims of creditors.

IRREVOCABLE TRUSTS AND INCOME TAXES

Even though we want the trust to be the owner of the assets for asset protection purposes, there are a number of reasons we'll want the settlor of the trust to be the one who is taxed on the annual income from the trust. First, the settlor may need the annual income to maintain his or her lifestyle. Second, the settlor may need the income tax deductions that the assets yield (such as depreciation deductions) to be included in his or her own tax return, rather than on that of the trust's.

There is a simple way to accomplish this end. The trust has to be designed for income tax purposes as a *grantor trust.* We can accomplish this in a number of ways, the simplest being merely to state that the trust's income and deductions go to the settlor. If the settlor doesn't want the income, knowing there is a good chance creditors will get the income if it is distributed to him or her, but wants the trust's deductions, there are other ways we can wire the trust so that it qualifies as a grantor trust. For example, we can give the settlor the power to distribute trust income among a class of beneficiaries other than the settlor him- or herself. That should be sufficient.

LIFE INSURANCE AND
LIFE INSURANCE TRUSTS

Millions of people own life insurance. Considering that fact, it's astounding how little people know about their own life insurance. The reason isn't a mystery. Most people find the charts and projections that insurance agents foist on us to be absolutely incomprehensible and mind-numbing.

Let's review the basics. Every life insurance policy has three "players," being the policy *owner*, the *insured*, and the *beneficiary*. Most people understand that the insured is the person whose life is covered by the insurance. If the insured dies, the insurance company pays the beneficiary. The role that throws many people is that of the owner. As you might suspect, the owner is the person who owns the policy. The owner is usually the insured, but not always. I can own a life insurance policy on the life of someone else, provided I have an *insurable interest* in his or her life. The concept of the insurable interest is what prevents me from taking out a $1 million policy on the life of a Bowery bum and then lacing his next martini with poison. I have an insurable interest in my family members and my key employees, but not in strangers.

If I'm the owner of a life insurance policy, I'm responsible for the premiums. But I also get to make all the decisions. If I wake up one morning and decide I no longer love the named beneficiaries, I'm free to change them. If I decide the policy has become too expensive, I can cancel it.

In spite of the insane complexity of many insurance products, there are basically only two types of life insurance. The oldest type, usually called *term insurance*, has nothing but a *death benefit*. If the death benefit is $1 million and the insured dies, the beneficiaries get $1 million. The second and more modern type of insurance has not only a death benefit, it also carries with it an investment feature.

The premiums are often far higher than the premiums for term insurance, because the premiums go to buy an investment portfolio for the owner. As with any investment portfolio, the invested capital can do well or do poorly. Depending on the type of coverage you buy, however, the success of the investment portfolio may affect the death benefit—or it may not. It may affect your premiums—or it may not. Life insurance that has an investment element as well as a death benefit is often called *whole life* insurance.

From an asset protection standpoint, who the owner is and the type of insurance she or he owns is vitally important. If you're not the owner, then neither the policy itself nor the investment portfolio can be attached by your creditors. If you are the owner, how much, if anything, that is available to your creditors depends on the type of policy it is. If you own a whole life policy, it's likely that your creditors will be able to get at the investment portfolio, commonly known as the *cash value* or the *cash surrender value* of the policy, just as they could with respect to any investment portfolio you might own. But if the policy you own is a pure term policy, being nothing but a death benefit when the insured dies, there's nothing for the creditor to attach until the insured dies.

Even if you own a whole life policy, you may be protected by a state exemption. A number of states, including Florida, Colorado, Illinois, Iowa, Kansas, Michigan, Texas, Ohio, Minnesota, and Wisconsin, exempt either the death benefit or the cash value from the clutches of creditors. But it is vital to check the state exemption. Most states shield the recipient of the death benefit (i.e., the policy beneficiary) from the owner's creditors, but only if the beneficiary is the spouse or dependent of the deceased insured. Other states, including California, Florida, Arizona, and Iowa, also exempt a portion of the cash surrender value. Anyone with creditor difficulties needs to know what the applicable state exemption is, because that's the amount you can safely keep in the policy without worrying about your creditors.

Irrevocable Life Insurance Trusts

There is little in the world of estate planning and asset protection that is more insanely complex than life insurance trusts. If you can't handle too much complexity, all you need to know is that life insurance wrapped inside an irrevocable trust is a very good way to both lower your estate taxes (and the estate taxes of the beneficiary of the insurance) and keep the death benefit and the cash value out of the grasp of your creditors as well as the beneficiaries' creditors. Armed with that, you can skip to the next chapter. If you want to know how irrevocable life insurance trusts (ILITs) work, stick around.

Most people know that the proceeds of life insurance aren't subject to income taxes. What many people don't know (because insurance agents don't tell them) is that if you own a life insurance policy, or are the beneficiary of one, the death benefit is included in your estate for the purposes of calculating your estate tax, *even if the insurance is payable to someone else.* Here's an example: Mr. Brown has assets other than life insurance worth $1.2 million. He is also the owner of a life insurance policy that pays $500,000 to his daughter, Anna, on his death. When Mr. Brown dies, Anna gets the $500,000 free of income taxes, but Mr. Brown's estate is considered to be worth $1.7 million. If Anna is Mr. Brown's only heir, the estate taxes on the $500,000 worth of insurance means that she gets about $150,000 less than she would have, which is the increased estate tax that must be paid before she can get anything. Now you know why many life insurance agents don't like to discuss estate taxes.

Is all this avoidable? Happily, it is, with an ILIT. If Mr. Brown were to create an ILIT, and transfer the life insurance policy to his ILIT, it wouldn't be subject to estate taxes, because he wouldn't be the owner, his ILIT would be. The asset protection benefit should also be apparent. The life insurance (and its cash value) isn't subject to the claims of his creditors, because the ILIT owns the policy and the cash value, not Mr. Brown.

At this point, your reaction should be: "Wait a minute! This is too easy! If I can avoid estate taxes and creditors by simply creating an irrevocable trust and transferring the life insurance to the trust, why can't I do it with all my assets?"

The answer lies not in the vagaries of the estate tax, but in the gift tax. Let's assume that Mr. Brown's home was worth $500,000, and that he were to transfer his home to an irrevocable trust. If the transfer were a completed gift, there would be an immediate gift tax based on the value of the home. The gift tax rates are (not coincidentally) the same as the estate tax rates. The result would be that Mr. Brown would be inducing a present tax in order to avoid a future one, which is usually very poor tax planning.

So why is life insurance different? The answer lies in a quirk of the gift tax law. Let's assume that Mr. Brown were to buy a life insurance policy insuring his life that has a $500,000 death benefit. Mr. Brown is the owner and the insured, and he designates his daughter Anna as the beneficiary of the policy. After paying the first year's premium, most of which goes to pay the agent's commission, the cash surrender value of the $500,000 policy is $1,000. Let's assume that the day after he buys the policy, he transfers it to an ILIT. That's when Mr. Brown finds, much to his surprise, that the gift tax isn't based on the $500,000 death benefit, but on the $1,000 cash value. If Mr. Brown had bought a term policy, one having no cash value, the gift tax would be based roughly (but not exactly) on one year's premium.

The result is that life insurance is usually the one asset we can strip out of an estate, avoiding estate taxes, without getting hit with a huge gift tax. As a bonus, the policy is out of the hands of the owner and free from the clutches of the owner's creditors.

Fine. But where's all the complexity? The complexity results from the fact that we don't want to pay the gift tax either, no matter how small.

Most people know that you can make a gift of money or property valued at $10,000 to any person during the year, and not pay gift taxes. Spouses can make $20,000 gifts to any person, and still pay no gift taxes.[3] For example, if Mr. and Mrs. Brown have three children and six grandchildren, they can give away $180,000—$20,000 to each of them—on December 29, 1995, and another $180,000 on January 1, 1996, and pay no gift taxes.

What most people don't know is that the $10,000 gift tax exclusions only apply to *present gifts*. If I hand you a ten-thousand-dollar bill, it's a present gift, but *a gift to a trust doesn't qualify as a present gift*. In order for an ILIT to work, we will be making gifts to the trust. If there's an existing insurance policy, we'll be transferring that policy to the trust. Even if we create the trust and then have the trust buy the policy, we'll still be making annual gifts to the trust, because the trust, which doesn't have any income, will need cash to pay the premiums on the insurance policies it owns. It can only get that cash if someone makes a gift of the premiums to it.

So how do we avoid paying the gift tax when we transfer the policy itself or the annual premiums to the trust? The answer comes courtesy of one D. Clifford Crummey, who in 1968 convinced the Ninth Circuit Court of Appeals that if you write a trust that gives the beneficiaries the right to withdraw money from the trust—regardless of whether they exercise that right—in the same year that you contribute to the trust, it qualifies as a present interest. And because it qualifies as a present interest, the gifts to the trust are tax-free, provided you don't contribute more than $10,000 per

---

[3] In order for spouses to qualify for the $20,000 annual exemption, however, they need to file a gift tax return on Form 709 with the IRS.

year per donee. Since 1968, ILITs have come to be known as *Crummey trusts*, and the beneficiaries' annual withdrawal rights have become known as *Crummey powers*. All this is just paperwork, because Crummey beneficiaries never exercise their withdrawal rights.

There's just one bit of complexity left, which pushes all this over the edge of insanity. The IRS, which generally acquiesces to this scheme, has ruled that you can't draft the beneficiaries' withdrawal rights in the fine print on page 158 of the trust, assuming they'll never learn of their withdrawal rights; you actually have to tell the beneficiaries that they have withdrawal rights. Not only that, the IRS has ruled that it isn't exactly cricket to inform them of their annual withdrawal rights around 10:00 P.M. on New Year's Eve. You must give them adequate notice.

The result is a *Crummey letter,* similar to the one shown in Figure 8–1, that we need to send to every beneficiary every year. These Crummey letters are crazy, because very often the trustee of the trust, who writes the Crummey letters, is also a beneficiary, which means that he or she writes a letter to him- or herself! Also note that our Crummey letters have a space on the bottom for the beneficiary to formally waive his or her withdrawal rights. Because the beneficiaries are often two or three years old, their guardian, who is also the trustee, signs the waiver for the beneficiary. It's all crazy, but it's an essential part of the game if you want to avoid the gift taxes. Don't thank me; thank Crummey.

The Three-Year Rule

There's one final bit of complexity regarding life insurance and ILITs. There's a provision in the tax code that says that if the owner of the insurance dies within three years of the transfer of the policy to the ILIT, the value of the policy is included in the estate for

Mr. John Smith
1111 Santa Monica Blvd. #300
Santa Monica, CA. 90321

Mr. Wallace Brown
1111 Santa Monica Blvd. #300
Santa Monica, CA. 90321

                                    RE: Gift to The Brown Irrevocable
                                    Trust _____

Dear Wallace:

Please be advised that I have received a gift from Sandra Brown to the Brown
Irrevocable Trust. This gift is an amount of cash in the sum of $30,000.00.

You are a beneficiary of this trust. Under the provisions of this trust, you
are allowed to withdraw funds equal to all or a portion of the value of this
gift. You have the privilege of exercising or not exercising your power to
withdraw the funds.

If you choose to exercise your power to withdraw funds, you must do so in
writing delivered to the undersigned within 60 days of this notice. If you
choose not to exercise your power, this gift will be held in trust, which
trust will be for your benefit in accordance with the terms of the trust.

If you choose to exercise your withdrawal rights, please notify me. If you
choose to waive your withdrawal rights, please indicate by executing this
letter in the space provided below and returning this letter to me.

Very truly yours,

John Smith
Trustee, The Brown Irrevocable Trust

I hereby elect not to withdraw any part of the aforementioned gift.

_____   _____

Wallace Brown   Dated

Figure 8–1. **A sample Crummey letter.**

purpose of computing the estate taxes. In other words, if you outlive the transfer by three years, the value of the insurance isn't included in your estate. If you don't, it is. For those persons contemplating the transfer of an existing policy to an ILIT, our considered legal advice is to drive safely and wear your galoshes in the snow.

9

Foreign Asset Protection Trusts

INTRODUCTION

Let's return to Dr. Brown, whom we first encountered in the Introduction (you might want to reread the Introduction at this point).
Since we last met Dr. Brown, we've seen that setting up a Foreign
Asset Protection Trust (FAPT) after a judgment is rendered is likely
to be considered a fraudulent conveyance. It won't work, and Dr.
Brown isn't likely to find an attorney who will help him even if it
could work. In short, it's best to create the trust before you have
any substantial creditors.

Let's return to the happier assumption that Dr. Brown had set up
and funded an FAPT prior to the Smith estate's lawsuit ever having
been filed. What could the estate's lawyer (Mr. Gunn) do? He could
try to collect on his judgment in the Cook Islands. But unlike

Colorado—where Dr. Brown lived—and every state in the United States, the Cook Islands isn't governed by the Full Faith and Credit Clause of the Constitution. The best that Gunn could hope for would be for the Cook Islands to apply the international law concept of *comity*, which allows but doesn't require one country to honor another country's judgments. But the Cook Islands won't honor the U.S. judgment—that's why we selected the Cook Islands as the home of the trust in the first place.

What could Lawyer Gunn do? He could try to relitigate the lawsuit against Dr. Brown in the Cook Islands. In other words, he could try to sue Dr. Brown all over again. Think of it: He'd have to bring all his evidence and witnesses to a strange country that is hostile to creditors. Would it work? Probably not, because the Cook Islands probably doesn't even have jurisdiction over Dr. Brown. Remember: Dr. Brown's money lives in the Cook Islands; Dr. Brown doesn't. Even if Lawyer Gunn were so foolhardy as to try to sue Dr. Brown all over again in the Cook Islands, the courts there probably wouldn't even hear the case.

So what would Lawyer Gunn do? Remember: he's very motivated. He could go back to the judge that presided at the trial that awarded the judgment. His argument would go something like this:

GUNN: Your Honor, we have a $2.3 million judgment against Dr. Brown that we cannot satisfy from any assets Dr. Brown has in the United States. Dr. Brown is, however, the beneficiary of The Brown Family Trust, which he set up in the Cook Islands in the Pacific Ocean. We believe that this trust has sufficient assets to satisfy our judgment. We request that you order Dr. Brown to demand that the trustee, The Southern Pacific Trust Company, distribute sufficient assets from the trust to cover our judgment.

Here's the argument against Gunn's request, made by Dr. Brown's attorney:

SWIFT: Your Honor, there is absolutely no legal basis whereby Dr. Brown can require the trustee to distribute assets to him for the estate's benefit. The trust is an irrevocable trust. Dr. Brown has no power to revoke it or change it. Moreover, the trust is a discretionary trust. Under its terms, Dr. Brown has no power to invade the trust or order any distributions. Under the law of this state, a creditor such as the estate has no right to the assets of the trust greater than Dr. Brown has.

In most states, the law favors Dr. Brown. If the trust was properly drafted, and if the judge follows the law, the estate has no right to order a distribution of assets.

But let's assume the judge doesn't follow the law. Let's assume this judge is like Judge Neely, whom we encountered in Chapter 1. Let's assume this judge is more interested in helping Mrs. Smith's children get their hands on $2 million than in the fine points of the law. But the judge has a problem. A U.S. judge has no jurisdiction over a trustee located in the Cook Islands. The judge has jurisdiction only over Dr. Brown. So the judge orders Dr. Brown to order the trustee to distribute sufficient assets from the trust to satisfy the estate's judgment.

What is Dr. Brown's response? It goes something like this:

BROWN: You want me to order The Southern Pacific Trust Company to distribute $2 million from the trust? Absolutely, your Honor, no problem. Where do I sign? Would you like me to prepare the order, or would you like to prepare it? Better yet, have Mr. Gunn prepare it. I don't disobey court orders. I'll sign anything you wish.

And so an order is prepared directing The Southern Pacific Trust Company to distribute $2.3 million to Dr. Brown for immediate payment to the estate. What does the trustee do with the order when it's received? He or she places it in the round circular file under the desk. The trustee doesn't obey the order. Why? Because the trust prohibits the trustee from making any distributions under the duress of any court order. Long before Dr. Brown was sued, the trustee was made to understand that it would not honor any directive issued directly by any court or as a result of any court order.

What does Lawyer Gunn do now? Hard to say. He seems to be stuck. It may be time to settle for pennies on the dollar.

Let's review what happened. If we assume that Dr. Brown established and funded the trust before the litigation began, there was no fraudulent conveyance; Dr. Brown violated no law. Nor did Dr. Brown violate any court orders. He did everything the judge ordered him to do, even if the judge had no legal authority to do it. Nor did Dr. Brown run the risk of committing perjury by not disclosing to Gunn the whereabouts of his assets. He told Gunn everything.

Did Dr. Brown hide his assets? No, he didn't. Lawyer Gunn knew how much Dr. Brown had and where it was located. He just couldn't get at it. As we shall see later, the fact that Gunn couldn't get at Dr. Brown's assets shouldn't have prevented Dr. Brown from getting at them.

THE BASICS OF FAPTs

Now things are going to get a bit more complicated. We're going to walk through what seems a bewildering maze of tax concepts and creditors' rights laws. It's unavoidable. The FAPT works in large part due to our ability to navigate the shoals between a number of federal tax laws and state creditors' rights statutes.

We should clear up one matter right at the start. An FAPT isn't a form that you can spin out of a word processor. No two are exactly the same. Although every FAPT has certain elements in common with every other one, they all differ to a degree. They differ due to the following reasons:

- *State laws differ.* If you live in California, your trust may be different from the trust created by a person living in Maine. One state may place a restriction on the ability of a trust beneficiary to receive trust income, a restriction another state doesn't have. This may appear strange, because the trust itself will be governed by the laws of the Isle of Man, the Cayman Islands, the Bahamas, or wherever you elect to form the trust. But the rights of your creditors will in part be governed by state law, and we don't want to include a provision in the trust that will benefit creditors. Also, as we saw in Chapter 2, one state may exempt an asset from the reach of creditors regardless of whether we have a trust; we don't need to transfer that asset to the trust to protect it.

  Bottom line: The laws of the state where you live should be thoroughly researched before the trust is drafted.

- *The nature of property differs.* Your assets may consist entirely of stocks and bonds. Another person's assets may consist entirely of an interest in a business. The different nature of two settlors' assets may have an effect on the language of the trust.

- *Different settlors' desires and needs differ.* You may have grown children with substantial assets of their own. They may not have a pressing need for the trust's assets. Another settlor may have small children in need. Your different needs may well produce two very different trusts, especially if you also use your FAPT to effectuate your general estate plan.

Let's clear up one other matter crucial to your understanding of how an FAPT works: Federal tax laws and state creditors' rights laws are rarely consistent and often are contradictory! Here's an example: The tax code may decree that a certain provision of a trust results in the conclusion that the settlor owns the assets of the trust. A state's creditors' rights law may reach the opposite conclusion, that the trust owns the assets. The inconsistency works in our favor. We'll use the most favorable provisions of the tax code and the law of the state in which the trust is created in fashioning the trust.

With that in mind, let's look at a typical FAPT in some detail, bearing in mind that any aspect of the trust is subject to change, depending on your particular needs.

An FAPT Is an Irrevocable Trust

As we've seen, every trust is either revocable or irrevocable by the settlor. An FAPT is irrevocable.

Let's go back to Dr. Brown's attorney's argument against the Smith estate. Attorney Swift claimed that because Dr. Brown couldn't force the trustee to distribute any money to him, Dr. Brown didn't have any interest in the trust superior to that of any creditor. Consequently, the estate shouldn't be able to force the trustee to do something Dr. Brown couldn't do.

Swift's argument is correct. Indeed, his argument is embodied in a number of state laws. Section 15303(a) of the California Probate Code provides:

> If the trust instrument provides that the trustee shall pay to or for the benefit of a beneficiary so much of the income or principal or both as the trustee in the trustee's discretion sees fit to pay, a transferee or creditor of the beneficiary may not compel the trustee to pay any amount that may be paid only in the exercise of the trustee's discretion.

Section 15303(a) says that if the trustee decides that Dr. Brown can't get the money, the creditor can't get the money either.

But what if Dr. Brown can tear up the trust, fire the trustee, and get at the money whenever he wants? That's a very different story. In that event, the trustee's discretion is illusory, because it can only be exercised so long as Dr. Brown permits the trust to remain in existence. The result is that if an FAPT can work at all, it must be irrevocable.

How long should the trust be irrevocable? Long enough. If the trust is irrevocable for only a few years before the settlor can tear it up, creditors will wait. As we saw in Chapter 2, their judgments won't expire. It's best to have the trust be irrevocable for many decades, at least.[1]

An FAPT Is a Grantor Trust

Now we're going to shift gears and talk about taxes—federal gift taxes. The reason for this is that creating an irrevocable trust and transferring assets to it creates a gift tax problem. Fortunately, it's a problem we can easily solve.

An irrevocable trust is, in the eyes of the law, a separate legal entity, just like my Uncle Fred or the General Motors Corporation. It can bring a lawsuit in its own name. It has its own federal identification number, similar to a Social Security number. And it's a separate taxpayer.

If I were to give $100,000 to my Uncle Fred, the IRS would invite me to pay a gift tax. (Remember, the donor of the gift, not the

---

[1] You can't keep a trust going forever. Under the "rule against perpetuities" (which is far beyond the scope of this book), you're prevented from keeping assets in trust forever. But that doesn't prevent you from keeping your assets in trust for as long as you will comfortably need to. The rule may prevent you from keeping the assets in a trust for the lives of your grandchildren, a restriction most people can live with. In any case, many of the countries that are amenable to FAPTs have very relaxed rules against perpetuities.

recipient, is responsible for the gift tax.) As we saw in Chapter 8, I can give $10,000 per year to as many donees as I wish without incurring a gift tax. However, if I give a person more than $10,000 in the course of a year,[2] I'm liable for the gift tax. Gift taxes are very high. The lowest rate is 37 percent (the highest personal income tax rate is only 39%), and the tax on a gift of more than $1 million is 50 percent!

If I transfer assets to an irrevocable trust, it's considered a gift. After all, the trust isn't buying the assets; it's getting the assets for nothing.

How do we avoid the gift tax when the settlor transfers assets into the trust? Easy.

It's a cardinal principle of tax law that the gift tax is due only if the gift is a *completed gift*—that is, if the recipient has the unfettered right to the property after the transfer. If that unfettered right doesn't exist, there is no gift, and no gift tax. But remember this key point: This rule exists only for tax law purposes. For state property law purposes, the recipient (the trustee of the trust) will be the owner of the property, regardless of when and if the gift tax is due.

How do we assure that the transfer into trust is considered an incomplete gift for gift tax purposes? By applying the *grantor trust rules* of the tax code. (We indicated in Chapter 8 that a settlor of a trust is sometimes called a "creator" or "grantor." Don't confuse the dual meaning of the word "grantor." In the present context, "grantor" is used only as a term of art as defined in the Internal Revenue Code.) The grantor trust rules are contained in Sections 671 through 679 of the Internal Revenue Code. Oddly enough, the

---

[2] My spouse and I can give $20,000 to anyone during the year without incurring a gift tax, provided we file Form 709 with the IRS.

grantor trust rules don't specifically address the issue of whether or when gift taxes are payable. Instead, the grantor trust rules define who is responsible for the income tax on trust income. The grantor trust rules determine whether the trust itself or the settlor of the trust is liable for the trust's income taxes. If the trust is a "grantor trust," the settlor pays the income tax. If it isn't, the trust pays the tax. In avoiding the gift tax, we're going to purposely "flunk" the grantor trust rules. The result will be that the settlor of the FAPT will be liable for the trust's income taxes. But it will also mean that any contribution of property to the trust will be deemed to be an incomplete gift, obviating the gift tax.

A trust is a grantor trust if any one of the following tests applies with respect to the trust:

1. The settlor has a reversionary interest in the trust, that is, if trust principal or income reverts back to the settlor at any time. To the extent it can, the settlor—not the trust—pays income tax on the trust's income. If the settlor's interest in the trust is less than five percent of the value of the trust, that interest is ignored.

2. The settlor has the right to use or enjoy trust income or principal without the consent of a person who has an interest adverse to the settlor. A person with an "adverse" interest is a person who is harmed by the settlor's use of trust property, such as another, unrelated, beneficiary.

3. The settlor has certain administrative rights in the trust that he or she can exercise without the approval of an adverse party, such as the power to sell trust property or borrow money from the trust without paying adequate interest or without adequate security.

4. The settlor can revoke the trust. In other words, if the trust is a revocable trust, it will always be a grantor trust.

5. The settlor has the right to receive trust income, or can require the distribution of trust income to him- or herself without the consent of an adverse party.

6. The trust is a foreign trust.

If we flunk any of these tests, the trust is a grantor trust, and the settlor pays annual income tax on the trust's income, as if the settlor had never transferred any property in trust. But being a grantor trust means that for tax purposes only (not for state property law for creditors' rights purposes) the settlor is considered the owner of the property. Consequently, there has been no completed gift. No completed gift means no gift tax.

Which of the tests will we purposely flunk? We certainly won't flunk test number 4. If the trust is revocable, the settlor will be deemed to be the owner of the trust under the property law of most states, permitting creditors to get at the assets. We also won't flunk test number 5. As we saw in California Probate Code Section 15303(a), preventing the settlor from requiring the trustee to distribute assets to him or her is what keeps the creditors at bay.

It may seem that test number 6 is the likeliest test to flunk. But as we shall shortly see, we may want the trust to be deemed a domestic trust, at least until things get very nasty with creditors.

What we will do is flunk test number 3. The trust will include a provision giving the settlor certain administrative rights over the trust's property, including the right to borrow trust assets at less than market interest rates. On occasion, the settlor will exercise those rights. This will result in the trust being a grantor trust for tax purposes without future creditors having any right to trust property.

An FAPT is income tax neutral: It will keep your creditors away, but it won't lower your income taxes. (When used as part of a complete estate plan, an FAPT can substantially reduce estate taxes.) To the extent the property in the trust earns income, that income is taxed to the settlor to the same extent as if the settlor had never transferred the assets at all. There are people in this land who "sell" asset protection plans. One of their sales pitches is that a trust can reduce your income taxes. It can't, and anyone who tells you that it can is pulling your leg.

An FAPT Is a Discretionary Trust

We've covered this already. If the settlor is also a beneficiary of the trust, and the language of the trust requires the trustee to distribute trust property to the beneficiary, any creditor can get the money the beneficiary could. The same holds true if the trust permits the settlor to demand of the trustee a certain amount of trust property every year. To the extent the settlor can demand a distribution, a creditor can too.

An FAPT can be written as a mandatory trust only if the settlor isn't also beneficiary of the trust. For example, if you establish an FAPT and only your children are beneficiaries of the trust, you can provide for mandatory distributions to them. Of course, if any of your children have problems with creditors, those creditors will be able to attach whatever distribution the debtor–beneficiary had coming.

IS AN FAPT A FOREIGN TRUST?

There is no doubt that at least one of the trustees of the FAPT will be an individual or—more likely—a trust company located in a country hospitable to such trusts. (We'll see shortly which countries those are.) The trust will be governed by and be subject to the laws of that country. The one law of the host country we are most interested in being subject to is the refusal of the host country to honor automatically the judgments of foreign nations. At some point, all or a part of the trust's assets will be physically located in the host country.

But that is not to say that the trust will be deemed a foreign trust *for tax purposes*. We may want the trust to be considered a U.S. trust, at least until such time as creditors are hot on the settlor's tail.

The reasons we want the FAPT to be a domestic trust for tax purposes are twofold. The first reason that we may not want the trust to be deemed a foreign trust is that the tax code imposes a 35 percent *excise tax* on the unrecognized gain inherent in any property transferred to a foreign trust. For example, if you transfer property worth $135,000 to a trust for which you paid $35,000 (your tax "basis") there is a $100,000 capital gain inherent in the property. The excise tax owed on the transfer is 35 percent, or $35,000. That's a hefty price to pay just to keep the property out of the hands of a future creditor. Obviously, it must be avoided.

Of course, you need not worry about this excise tax if you don't transfer appreciated property to the trust. If all you transfer is cash, or stocks that you bought recently and that have little or no inherent gain, you have nothing to worry about.

In a recent revenue ruling, the IRS ruled that the excise tax does not apply on the transfer of appreciated property to a trust that is a grantor trust. But that doesn't necessarily solve the problem. If the settlor later gives up the powers that make the trust a grantor trust, the excise tax may then be due. This ruling does not provide sufficient comfort to ignore the excise tax problem.

Even if the settlor is not required to pay an excise tax at the time of the transfer, there is a second reason settlors may wish to avoid the trust's being characterized as a foreign trust for tax purposes. If the trust is a foreign trust, certain reports must be filed with the

IRS. Here's a summary of the reports you will have to file with the IRS if the trust is a foreign trust:

- Form 3520 (Appendix C, "Creation of or Transfers to Certain Foreign Trusts") is an information form (i.e., there's no tax due when it's filed) required to be filed by the settlor of a foreign trust 90 days after a foreign trust is created or a transfer of property is made to it. The form requires disclosure of the name of the trust, the country in which it's located, the name and address of the trustee, and the names and addresses of the beneficiaries. It also requires that you disclose whether the trustee is required to make any distributions to a beneficiary. In an FAPT, the answer to this question will almost always be no. No matter where you or the trustee live, the form is always filed with the IRS office in Philadelphia.

- Form 3520-A (Appendix D, "Annual Return of Foreign Trust With U.S. Beneficiaries") is similar to Form 3520, except that it must be filed annually. It goes further than Form 3520, requiring disclosure of any new beneficiary the trust picked up during the course of the year. It also requires that you disclose how much money the trust made during the year. This form is a tax form, not just an information return. However, if the trust is a grantor trust, the trust won't pay any taxes on the trust's income—the settlor will.

- Form 926 (Appendix E, "Return by a U.S. Transferor of Property to a Foreign Corporation, Foreign Estate or Trust, or Foreign Partnership") duplicates much of the information required by Form 3520. But it also goes further. Its purpose is to collect the 35 percent excise tax on the transfer of appreciated property to a trust. You have to file this form even if the trust doesn't owe any taxes. For example, if you transfer property worth $100,000 to a trust for which you paid $100,000, so that there is no gain inherent in the property, there's no tax to be paid, but you must still file the form. Even if the trust is a grantor trust, so that the trust won't pay any taxes, the form is still required. The form is due on the day that you make the transfer, and is filed in the same IRS office in which you file your personal return.

- Form 90-22.1 (Appendix F, "Report of Foreign Bank and Financial Accounts") is required to be filed by every person who has an interest in a foreign bank account or foreign brokerage account, even if that person doesn't have signature authority over the account. This report dovetails with the question on Form 1040, requiring disclosure of an interest in a foreign account. If you check that box "yes," you need to file Form 90-22.1. The form must be filed by June 30 following any year in which you had an interest in a foreign account.

You might wish to take the position that because you cannot require the trustee to make a distribution from the trust to you, you really don't have an interest in a foreign account. My advice is to file it. Filing it won't trigger an audit, nor can your creditors obtain your form from the treasury. There are penalties that can be assessed if it's determined later that you were required to file the form but didn't.

You won't have to file any of these forms, and there's no possibility that you'll be subject to the 35 percent excise tax, if the trust is not—for tax purposes only—considered a foreign trust. That leads us to the issue of what is a "foreign" trust under the Internal Revenue Code.

The problem—and the opportunity—lies in the fact that there is no clear definition of what constitutes a foreign trust. Section 7701(a) (31) of the tax code provides a model of circular logic, defining a foreign trust as one:

> . . . the income of which, from sources without the United States which is not effectively connected with the conduct of a trade or business within the United States . . .

Fortunately, there is some guidance from the reported cases and from the IRS' own rulings. Here are the factors that are considered in determining whether a trust is a U.S. trust or a foreign trust, *for tax purposes only:*

- *Which country's laws governs the trust?* An FAPT will always be set up and governed by the laws of a foreign country hospitable to asset protection. Specifically, we want to benefit from that aspect of a foreign country's laws that refuses to give any effect to a U.S. judgment.

- *Where are the trust's assets kept?* When we set up and fund the trust, there may be no need to keep the trust's assets in a foreign country. For purposes of convenience, we may wish to keep the trust's cash in a U.S. bank account, transferring the cash overseas at a later date, if the need arises. Consequently, this criterion results in a conclusion that, at least initially, the trust is a domestic trust.

- *Where does the trustee reside?* If there is only one trustee—and there will always be at least one—the trustee will be an individual or trust company located overseas. But what if there are two trustees, one located overseas and one located in the United States? What if there are three trustees, and two of them are located in the United States? If and when creditors come calling, the U.S. trustee will resign, so that no U.S. court has jurisdiction over the trust. Better yet, in order to prevent a U.S. court from prohibiting the U.S. trustee from resigning, the trust document should give the foreign trustee the right to fire all U.S. trustees at such time as any creditor lawsuits are filed.

- *Where is the trust administered?* Initially, the trust may be administered in the United States. When creditors come calling, the trust will have to be administered overseas.

- *Where does the settlor live?* If you are a U.S. citizen, this criterion will always result in the conclusion that the settlor lives in the United States, short of you renouncing your citizenship and moving offshore.

- *Where do the beneficiaries live?* If you establish a trust for your children—or if you yourself are a beneficiary—the beneficiaries will most likely live in the United States.

An FAPT set up by a U.S. citizen will never have solely domestic or solely foreign criteria—the result will be a mix. So how do we decide if the trust is domestic or foreign? From published cases and the IRS' rulings, we know that not all of the previously listed criteria are given the same weight. The location of the trust's assets, the place in which the trust is administered, and the residence of the trustee are given the most weight. The location of the settlor and the beneficiaries are given very little weight.

By naming a U.S. cotrustee when the trust is set up and having at least some of the trust's assets located here, it is possible to take the position that, at least initially, the trust is a domestic trust for tax purposes. This obviates the possibility that the 35 percent excise tax is due when appreciated assets are transferred to the trust, and eliminates the requirement that the IRS' forms described previously be filed. But remember: no two FAPTs are the same. Depending on the nature of your assets and your needs, you may wish that the trust be a foreign trust for tax purposes right from the start.

THE ANTI-DURESS PROVISION

A feature unique to the FAPT is the anti-duress provision. It's not more than a paragraph or two in length, but it could be the key to preserving your assets from creditors.

Let's go back to Dr. Brown, who was forced by Lawyer Gunn to appear in court and answer questions about the nature and whereabouts of his assets. In short order, Gunn knows everything about the trust: how much is in it, where the assets are located, and the identity and location of the trustee. Gunn has no doubt gotten hold of a copy of the trust document (from Dr. Brown) and has read that too. Remember, also, that the trustee is in the Cook

Islands. The only person within the judge's jurisdiction—the only person who can be made to do anything—is Dr. Brown.

Lawyer Gunn assumes—correctly—that Dr. Brown has influence over the Cook Islands trustee, even if the trust document doesn't reveal any such control. So he asks the judge to issue a court order to Dr. Brown. The judge orders Dr. Brown to deliver assets. He directs Dr. Brown to fire the trustee, or he directs the trustee to distribute assets to Dr. Brown, to Gunn, or to the registry of the court. Whatever the judge's order, it can be issued only to Dr. Brown, because he's the only person over whom the judge has jurisdiction.

Let's assume that Gunn gets a sympathetic judge, one so sympathetic that the judge will issue an order to Dr. Brown even though Dr. Brown isn't a trustee or even a beneficiary of the trust, and even though a literal reading of the property law of the state precludes such an order. Let's assume the judge issues an order directing Dr. Brown to instruct the Cook Islands trustee to distribute trust assets to Gunn.

Dr. Brown won't disobey a court order. To do so would certainly risk a fine or even imprisonment for contempt. So Dr. Brown requests the trustee to distribute assets to Gunn. On receiving the request, the trustee knows that this isn't really Dr. Brown's request; this is a request made under duress. The trustee checks the trust document for instructions, and this is what is found:

> The Trustee is directed: (1) to recognize and accept instructions or advice, or to exercise any power, only which are given by or are the result of persons acting of their own free will and not under compulsion of any legal authority or legal process; and (2) to ignore any advice or any directive, veto, order, or like decree of any court or administrative body, where such has been instigated by directive, order, or like decree of any court or administrative body.

In plain English, the trust says that in the event the trustee knows or even reasonably suspects that any request from any person to distribute principal or interest from the trust is made pursuant to the order or direction of a judge or creditor, the trustee *must* refuse to make such a distribution. The trust goes on to say that the trustee shall notify whomever makes the request of the trustee's refusal, specifically citing the Anti-Duress Provision of the trust.

An attorney representing the Cook Islands trustee (not Dr. Brown) appears in court to present the trustee's refusal to the judge. Dr. Brown has disobeyed no court order. He was ordered to request that the trustee distribute trust assets, and the trustee refused. The judge cannot order Dr. Brown to do something that is impossible.

Most creditors quit at this point. But if we are faced with truly motivated creditors, the FAPT goes even further.

THE FLIGHT PROVISION

You never know how truly bloody the battle will be until you have to fight it. And if you'll have to fight a full-scale war, it's best to be prepared. The Flight Provision is the Ultimate Weapon, wheeled out only during the endgame of the bloodiest of wars.

Let's assume that Dr. Brown landed a judge who not only won't follow the law, but also who is very hostile toward him. This judge will do anything to get the money out of Dr. Brown. And so the judge glares down the bench at Dr. Brown and says:

JUDGE: Dr. Brown, I really don't believe that you can't get that money out of the trustee. I really believe that you secretly control him. I order you to deliver the trust's assets to Lawyer Gunn, and if you don't, I'll hold you in contempt of court.

So Dr. Brown again delivers a court order to the trustee. The trustee knows that this second request doesn't come from Dr. Brown; it comes from the judge. The trustee knows that things are getting tight. So the trustee rereads the trust document and discovers the flight provision. The flight provision says that if the trustee believes that there is a reasonable risk that a nonbeneficiary will succeed in obtaining any trust assets, the trustee shall relocate the trust's assets to another country, and the trustee shall not disclose to the settlor the whereabouts of the assets!

Now Dr. Brown, through his lawyer, goes back to the judge with the ultimate defense: "Dr. Brown can't turn over any assets, Your Honor; he doesn't know where they are." One thing a judge cannot order you to do is the impossible.

It should be readily apparent that the flight clause has its risks. For one, the trustee and the settlor (or better yet, the settlor's lawyer) need to work out in advance where the assets are going to go if the flight provision is invoked. If invoked, the assets should be moved to a country that itself has a strong history of preserving assets from creditors and—better yet—has a good bank secrecy law. Another risk is that at least while the war with this creditor is still raging, the settlor will not be able to get his hands on the assets in the trust. As one lawyer said to me, it's kind of like being stuck in a small rowboat in the ocean during a raging storm and having someone remove your paddle. But at least you'll be alive (financially, that is) when the storm is over. As we'll see shortly, you don't dare create a flight provision unless you have the utmost confidence in your trustee.

If a flight provision as draconian as this is not to your liking, the trust should have at least some provision allowing for the removal of the trust to another country. Let's face it: Some of the countries that attract FAPTs aren't as politically stable as the United States. If in the future a hostile government takes over, you and your trustee may wish to remove the trust to a safer haven. The trust document should permit the trustee to do just that.

THE SPENDTHRIFT CLAUSE

We reviewed the benefits of a spendthrift provision in Chapter 8. Just as any well-drafted domestic trust should contain such a clause to keep trust assets out of the hands of trust beneficiaries, an FAPT should also contain such a provision.

WHO'S WHO IN AN FAPT

Let's review where we are.

The *settlor* of an FAPT is the person who desires asset protection. We cannot emphasize enough that for the FAPT not to be deemed a fraudulent conveyance, the FAPT should be created and funded before the settlor knows of the existence of creditors.

The *beneficiaries* of an FAPT are the people whom the settlor wants to eventually receive the assets in the trust. The beneficiaries usually are the settlor's spouse and/or children, but can be any person or entity. A beneficiary can be a business, a charity, or another trust. If the FAPT does not also serve as the settlor's overall estate plan, the beneficiary may well be another trust that previously was established for estate planning purposes. If you have a trust that is part of your will, or you have already set up a "family trust" arrangement that will be funded when you die, that trust should be a beneficiary of your FAPT.

May you be a beneficiary of your own FAPT? Yes, but it's risky. Remember: The trust is irrevocable. If you're named as a beneficiary at the start, you stay as one; the trustee cannot remove you, because he or she is powerless to alter the trust. Consider again Dr. Brown and his attorney when they appeared in front of the judge. It would have been a lot easier to convince the judge that he or she shouldn't have directed any court orders at Dr. Brown had Dr. Brown not been a beneficiary.

Whether the settlor can also be a beneficiary is a function of state law. If state law prevents creditors from reaching a trust's assets if the beneficiary cannot require the trustee to deliver assets to him, the settlor then may also be a beneficiary, but it's still risky.

The *trustee* of the trust will be an individual or trust company located in a foreign country. It's a rare case where the sole trustee will be an individual. If that individual dies, resigns, or decides that he or she is too busy to be the trustee, you may have a real problem. You're best off with an established trust company that specializes in foreign asset protection.

Choosing a foreign trustee is often the most difficult choice a settlor has to make. After all, unless you spend a lot of time in the Cook Islands or the Isle of Man, your prospective trustee isn't someone with whom you have a long-standing relationship. Here's one rule of thumb for selecting a foreign trustee, one which won't please many trust companies trolling for U.S. business:

> Your foreign trustee should never have a presence in the United States.

Why? Because if you ever get in trouble with creditors, a judge unfriendly to you might want to order your foreign trustee to appear in front of him, in order to require the trustee to turn assets over to your creditors. If the trustee has an office in the United States, the trustee will be subject to a subpoena. If the trustee isn't located here, he or she won't be. There are more banks and trust companies out there desiring your business than are worthy of it. Any foreign bank or trust company that touts the fact that they have scores of handy offices scattered around the United States won't do you much good once creditors come calling.

So how do you select a foreign trustee? There's no better way than by obtaining a reference from your attorney, accountant, financial planner, or other advisor who has dealt with that trustee. Armed with a few recommendations, you can contact a few prospective trustees and make your own decision.

The key to the selection of a trust company is how they will act when the chips are down. Anyone can handle assets (for a fee) before the creditors come calling. You need to know what they will do when things get nasty. Will they honor the trust's anti-duress provision? Will they go so far as to honor a flight provision? Or will they cave in at the first whiff of litigation?

Can the settlor also be a cotrustee? If you want to establish that the trust is a domestic trust, you'll need a U.S. citizen to act as a cotrustee. But being a cotrustee of your own trust is even more dangerous than being a beneficiary. If you feel you must be a cotrustee, you will have to resign when things get hot. Better yet, the trust should then have a provision requiring your foreign trustee to fire the domestic trustees. Here again, the extent to which you trust your foreign trustee is critical.

There is one "player" whom we have not yet discussed. The trust should have an "advisor," often called the "protector," and the settlor can fill that role. More on the trust "protector" later in this chapter.

An FAPT must be an irrevocable trust, with a term of at least many years or decades. If the settlor could revoke the trust, a state court judge with jurisdiction over the settlor could order the settlor to revoke the trust, in which event the creditors would get all the assets. It's a grantor trust only for tax purposes. For tax purposes, the assets of the trust are still owned by the settlor. But tax rules have no bearing on state property law or state creditors' rights law. For state law purposes, the trustee is considered the owner of the property.

The trust's provisions aren't uniform from trust to trust, and will vary depending on the settlor's needs and the laws of the state in which the settlor lives. It's preferable, however, that the trust should have no provision requiring the trustee to make any distributions to the settlor, assuming that the settlor is a beneficiary of the trust at all.

WHICH COUNTRY?

Anyone wishing to settle a trust in a foreign country will soon need to make what for many people is a difficult decision—which country? Some years ago, I had a client who had vacationed in the Cayman Islands, enjoyed it, and wanted to return. For him, the decision was easy. But most people have no familiarity with the handful of principal foreign trust jurisdictions.

Before perusing the list of candidates, let's review the criteria that make a country a viable FAPT candidate:

1. *The country should be politically stable.* Panama was once friendly to foreign trusts. Panama then suddenly became very unfriendly to Americans. There's no point in keeping your assets from your creditors if one day you find you can't get at the assets yourself.

2. *The assets you place in trust should be tax exempt.* Most people would consider that incurring a present tax to shield oneself from a future creditor to be a bad bargain. Any country that wants your FAPT must assure you that it won't tax the assets in the trust.

3. *The country should not honor foreign judgments.* A country that will give full faith and credit to a judgment rendered by a U.S. court isn't much of a haven from creditors.

4. *The country should have modern communications.* There is a little speck of a country in the Pacific Ocean called Nauru. A

few years ago, Nauru tried to set itself up as an FAPT haven. The trouble is that the mail gets to Nauru about once a week, and getting through by telephone was no picnic either. If you're going to have your money in a foreign country, it's nice to know that you can get at it readily if you need it. Not too many people chose to settle their trusts in Nauru.

5. *English common law should govern.* This criterion comes as a surprise to many people. The benefit of a country that has a British-type legal system is that it is likely to have a British-type law of trusts, and British trust law is more amenable to secrecy and the desires of the settlor than is American trust law. As we shall see shortly, a country that has a British trust law will provide for the trust *protector,* a concept foreign to American trusts. Countries with a British trust law usually enjoy another advantage: the people there speak English.

With these criteria in mind, let's review those countries that are commonly considered the best FAPT candidates.

The Cook Islands

Located in the South Pacific, due south of Hawaii, approximately 4,000 miles from Los Angeles, the Cook Islands (Figure 9–1) has, over the past few years, become the hands-down leader in the FAPT business. It has become so by enacting a series of laws friendly to FAPTs. It does not recognize foreign judgments. It exempts foreign trusts from taxation, and has a flexible International Companies Act, designed to facilitate foreigners forming corporations there.

The Cook Islands is an independent nation within the British Commonwealth. There was a time when communications to Raratonga, its capital, were difficult. But they have long since solved this

Figure 9–1. The Cook Islands.

problem, and contacting the Cook Islands via telephone or fax is as easy as contacting your local bank.

The Cayman Islands

The Caymans, located 500 miles south of Miami, has been an off-shore haven for decades, largely due to its strict secrecy laws, which make it a crime for any person in the Caymans to disclose banking information. As with the Cook Islands, it does not tax assets in a foreign trust.

The Caymans had a six-year statute of limitations on fraudulent conveyances. If a creditor failed to bring an action to set aside a conveyance within six years of the conveyance, the creditor was out of luck. However, in the Cook Islands' continuing goal of being the premier FAPT haven, the Cook Islands recently enacted a *two-year* statute of limitations on fraudulent conveyances.

The Cayman Islands also is an English-speaking country, being a self-governing British Crown colony.

The Isle of Man

This is one of the oldest FAPT havens. Located in the Irish Sea between England and Ireland, it is a self-governing territory under British protection. It boasts modern communications and easy accessibility from London. Its trust laws are comparable to those of the Cook Islands and the Cayman Islands.

The Bahamas

The Bahamas has been an independent country within the British Commonwealth since 1973. Located in the Caribbean, it recently amended its fraudulent conveyance statute so as to provide for a two-year cutoff, similar to that of the Cook Islands. It exacts no taxes on offshore trusts.

Other offshore FAPT candidates are the Turks and Caicos Islands (located in the Caribbean), Cyprus, and Belize (formerly British Honduras). Notably absent from this list is Switzerland, the one country everyone assumes is the premier asset protection haven. Switzerland's absence proves that one should never confuse asset protection with *secrecy*. Switzerland still has a strict law regarding bank secrecy. But as we have already seen, secrecy is irrelevant if a creditor has the right to inquire of the debtor where all the debtor's assets are located, and to require the debtor to answer truthfully under penalty of perjury. Switzerland is definitely *not* a candidate for FAPTs.

YOUR ACCESS TO YOUR OWN MONEY

If you establish and fund an FAPT, you'll have a vehicle that will assure that your assets are out of the reach of future creditors. It will provide you with the protection that liability insurance provides without the enormous expense of a liability policy. It will provide you with the creditor-avoidance protection afforded by filing for bankruptcy, without the possibility of losing many of your most valued assets to your creditors.

Keeping your assets out of the reach of future creditors is fine. But before any creditors come calling, you'd like to have as free an access to your assets as you do now. You don't want to have to place a telephone call to the Cook Islands every time you want some cash or need to make a stock trade.

You won't have to. It's possible to structure your FAPT so that your access to and control over the assets is unimpaired. It just requires that we employ a little creativity.

THE DOMESTIC LIMITED PARTNERSHIP

Let's again return to Dr. Brown. Let's take a closer look at his assets. We know that he owns a home. Let's assume that he also owns an Aspen ski condo. He also owns publicly traded stocks and bonds, interests in oil and gas leases, and cash, not to mention his personal assets.

There is another asset Dr. Brown owns that we've overlooked thus far. We mentioned that Dr. Brown is one of a number of medical doctors in a professional medical corporation. The medical corporation (Chicago Surgery Associates, P.C.) has its own assets: accounts receivable from its patients, equipment, a contract with a hospital, perhaps even some real estate. Dr. Brown's shares of stock in Chicago Surgery Associates may be a very valuable asset indeed.

We've assumed throughout that in order to avoid his creditors, Dr. Brown would transfer his assets directly to the FAPT. He could, and many settlors of FAPTs do just that. But he doesn't have to. Here's what we'll do to assure that Dr. Brown avoids the clutches of Lawyer Gunn but has free access to his assets until there is a Lawyer Gunn on the scene.

We'll set up a limited partnership for Dr. Brown. The limited partnership will have all the asset protection benefits we discussed in Chapter 5, the principal advantage being that a creditor's remedy is limited to the charging order. The limited partnership will have one general partner, who will be Dr. Brown himself. But unlike the family limited partnerships we visited in Chapter 5, which had only spouses and children as limited partners, this limited partnership will have, as its principal limited partner, his FAPT. Dr. Brown will contribute his assets to the limited partnership, not to the trust. The limited partnership agreement will provide that the general partner—Dr. Brown—will have a one percent interest in the limited partnership, and the limited partners—notably the FAPT—will own the rest.

As shown in the diagram in Figure 9–2, the general partner should own at least a one percent interest in the trust, because there is some legal authority supporting the proposition that you don't have a general partner if he or she doesn't own an interest in the partnership's assets, and you must have at least one general partner in order to have a limited partnership.

The structure outlined in Figure 9–2 affords Dr. Brown with maximum flexibility during the period before serious creditors come calling. But what does Dr. Brown do if things get really hot under the collar? *He dissolves the domestic partnership!* That means that he'll liquidate the partnership's assets to its partners, resulting in 97

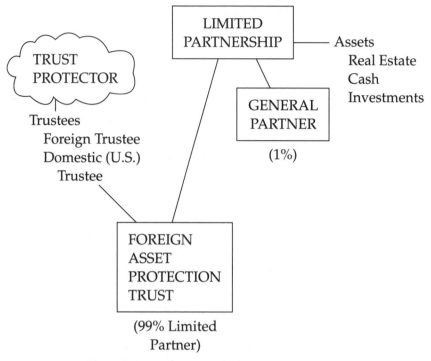

Figure 9–2.   A diagram of a limited partnership.

percent of the assets going to the FAPT. At the same time, he'll resign as a trustee, leaving the trust company in the Cook Islands as the sole trustee.

At that point, we will have removed the assets from the grasp of domestic creditors. If a creditor is motivated enough, we wish him a nice life in the Cook Islands. But we've also created a few problems. Remember that 35 percent excise tax, which is due only when we transfer appreciated assets to a foreign trust? That tax is most definitely due now. Secondly, we now have a truly foreign trust, because all the assets are located overseas, and the only trustee is a foreign person. Filing the IRS forms we reviewed earlier is now mandatory.

Unlike the FAPT, which is formed under the laws of a foreign country, the limited partnership can be formed in Dr. Brown's home state. Let's assume that's Illinois. In order to form the limited partnership, the limited partnership certificate and articles must be filed with the Illinois secretary of state.[3] That's all there is to it. Every year, the limited partnership will have to file a federal income tax return, Form 1065. But the partnership won't be liable for any taxes—partnerships don't pay taxes.

Who owns what after the transfer to the limited partnership? All of Dr. Brown's assets are owned by the limited partnership. That means that the titles to his stocks and bonds need to be changed to reflect that the new owner is the limited partnership. No problem there; completing a form provided by the stock transfer agent or the stock broker will do it. Dr. Brown will also need to have the ownership designation of his oil and gas interest changed, but that shouldn't be difficult either. Two of his assets, his real estate and the stock of his professional corporation, require special consideration.

It shouldn't be too difficult to transfer the titles to Dr. Brown's home and to his Aspen ski condo to the limited partnership: it's just a matter of completing deeds and recording the deeds with the county clerk where the real estate is located.

Here's the problem: Let's assume that there's a mortgage on Dr. Brown's home. (In many states, "deeds of trust" take the place of mortgages.) The mortgage has a "due on sale" or "due on transfer" clause, which permits the mortgage lender—the bank—to call the loan or to increase the interest rate on the loan if the property is transferred. That could be a disaster for Dr. Brown. We avoid the problem by writing the bank and telling it what we intend to do.

---

[3] Some states require that the name of every general and limited partner be filed with the secretary of state. Other states require only a statement that there is at least one general partner and one limited partner.

We inform the bank that the transaction is solely for personal estate planning purposes, and that Dr. Brown will continue to make the mortgage payments on the real estate, just as he always has. We invite the bank to respond if there's a problem with the proposed transfer.

All of this assumes that we want to transfer the real estate to the limited partnership in the first place. We may not want to, because we may not need to. As we saw in Chapter 4, most states provide for a homestead exemption, which to a greater or lesser extent places a debtor's interest in the home outside of the reach of his or her creditors.

If your creditors can't get at the interest in your home that's covered by the homestead exemption, there's no need to convey that interest to the limited partnership. But let's say that the equity in your home exceeds the homestead exemption granted under state law. What do we do? That depends. If the homestead exemption is represented by a dollar amount of equity, it's possible to borrow on the equity in the real estate, contributing the cash to the partnership. If the homestead is calculated like that of Kansas, that is, it is based on acreage, it's just as easy to divide the property, conveying only part of it to the partnership, holding aside an amount of acreage equal to the homestead.

All of which says that Dr. Brown will probably want to transfer the Aspen ski condo to the limited partnership. Depending on the value of his home and the extent of his state's homestead exemption, he will probably keep all or a part of his home outside of the partnership.

Dr. Brown's stock in Chicago Surgery Associates may present a more difficult problem. The reason is that state law may prohibit anyone but a licensed medical doctor from owning the stock of a medical corporation. It may also prohibit anyone but an attorney from holding stock in a law firm or anyone but an accountant from holding stock in an accounting firm. If that's true, then the limited partnership may be precluded from owning the stock.[4]

What to do? The answer is easy if Dr. Brown is the only owner of the corporation. If that's the case, he should create another corporation solely for the purpose of owning physical assets such as equipment and real estate. Contracts, such as the medical corporation's contracts with the hospital, should, if permitted by the contracts, be assigned to the new corporation. The stock of the new corporation would then be assigned to the limited partnership. The medical corporation would be granted the right to use the equipment and real estate by entering into a lease with the new corporation. If and when creditors come calling, they couldn't get their hands on the medical corporation's assets, which are owned by the limited partnership, which is in turn 97 percent owned by the FAPT. All they could get their hands on is the stock of a medical corporation that owns very little in the way of assets.

It's more difficult if Dr. Brown isn't the only shareholder in the medical corporation. In order to make it work, he would have to convince his fellow doctors that it's wise not to place all of the eggs in one basket; that they too would be better off spinning the assets of their medical corporation off into a new corporation.

WHO CONTROLS THE LIMITED PARTNERSHIP?

Let's assume that Dr. Brown transferred to the limited partnership all of his stocks and bonds, most of his cash, his Aspen ski condo, and all of the equity in his home except that part exempt under

---

[4] If that's true, it presents an interesting, and as yet unresolved, question. If no one other than a licensed medical doctor can own the stock of a medical corporation, could a creditor ever attach the stock?

the state homestead exemption. He owns one percent of that limited partnership; his FAPT (97%) and his children (2%) own the rest.

Let's now assume that Dr. Brown wants to sell the Aspen ski condo. Let's also assume that he spots a new investment, and wants to sell the certificates of deposit (CDs). How does he do it?

As easy as he could have before he transferred the assets to the limited partnership. Few things in law can be said with absolute certainty, but one thing that is certain is that the only person who operates a limited partnership is the general partner. With some very limited exceptions, the only person permitted to make decisions for a limited partnership is the general partner. That means that Dr. Brown can sell the partnership's ski condo if he wants to without obtaining the limited partners' approval. He can sell the CDs in the same manner, making whatever investment he desires with the proceeds. The limited partnership won't need to wire any money to or from the Isle of Man or the Cook Islands or wherever the FAPT resides. The limited partnership will have a local bank account right where Dr. Brown can use it.

DOES THE LIMITED PARTNERSHIP DISTRIBUTE ITS EARNINGS?

One of the powers that the limited partnership agreement can provide to the general partner is the right to either withhold earnings or distribute them. The limited partnership agreement may also require the general partner to distribute earnings. To this extent, a limited partnership is like a trust: you're not limited as to what you can do.

Whether the general partner will be required to distribute earnings will vary, depending on the types of assets contributed to the partnership, the needs of the general partner (who is the settlor of the trust), and the country in which the trust is located.

There shouldn't be a problem if the partnership holds no income-producing assets, such as dividend-paying stock or interest-bearing bonds. But if the partnership does hold such assets, a number of problems arise. First, income distributed to the general partner is reachable by creditors. Because the general partner will be subject to a court's jurisdiction, as will the limited partnership itself (remember: it's a domestic limited partnership), a local court could order the general partner to turn over his interest in partnership distributions. Because this is only one percent of partnership income, it shouldn't matter that much.

There's a second problem. Partners are taxed on partnership income, regardless of whether it's distributed. We said earlier that a FAPT is tax neutral; it won't help to reduce your tax bill. But there's a problem. As we saw in Chapter 5 when we discussed "phantom income," it's a cardinal rule of partnership tax law that partners in a partnership are taxed on their share of partnership income, regardless of whether that income is distributed. If the general partner's one percent interest—or the FAPT's 97 percent interest—is taxed, but the partnership hasn't distributed any income, the partners are subject to taxation, without the requisite cash to pay the tax!

A way out of this conundrum is to require the trustee to distribute cash sufficient only to pay any tax. But this amount could be reached by creditors. In certain states, an amount equal to the amount the trustee is required to distribute is reachable by creditors, even if nothing is distributed. This is especially true if the settlor of the trust is also a beneficiary. This problem underlines what we said before: An FAPT isn't a standard form. Each must be tailored to the settlor's particular needs, assets, and location.

A NEW PLAYER: THE TRUST'S PROTECTOR

We saw in Chapter 8 that a trust has three "players": the settlor, the trustee, and the beneficiary, and there may be more than one of each. But if the trust is established in a country that has a British-type trust law, there will be one more player who, although very important, is often not named in the trust—the trust advisor, who is sometimes referred to as the trust "protector." The concept of a trust protector is firmly embedded in British common law, although trust advisors or protectors are rarely used in the United States.

A trust protector's duties usually are not spelled out in an FAPT. Instead, the settlor gives the trustee a side letter when the trust is created, spelling out the identity of the protector, his duties, and any other desires the settlor has. The side letter is often called a *letter of wishes.* Because the protector's role is not spelled out in the trust document, the instructions in the side letter are not legally binding. But in those countries that we discussed as the principal FAPT candidates, the trustees are familiar with the protector concept, and generally will honor a letter of wishes.

Here are some things that should go into a letter of wishes:

- If the trust authorizes but does not require the trustee to make distributions of trust property, and if the settlor is him- or herself a beneficiary of the trust, the letter of wishes should instruct the trustee to make no distributions after receiving notice from the protector that a creditor has or is about to obtain a judgment against a beneficiary. The letter can also say that distributions should be resumed only on advice from the protector.

- The protector may advise the trustee to resign in favor of an alternate trustee in the case of a certain event. If the foreign trustee has the power to fire a domestic trustee, the letter should inform the trustee regarding the type of advice that will be provided regarding when the trustee should exercise that right.

• Many settlors use their FAPTs as their basic estate planning document. Many settlors have personal reasons for not wishing to disclose in any document that might fall into unfriendly hands who the settlor's intended beneficiaries are and how much each will be entitled to get in the event of the settlor's death. For these settlors, the letter of wishes can form the ideal estate planning vehicle.

The settlor can be the trust's protector. However, if this is so, the letter of wishes should designate an alternate protector, with the request that the trustee follow the advice of the alternate protector after the original protector—the settlor—resigns.

It's important that the letter of wishes be phrased only in terms of the desires and wishes of the settlor. If the words of the side letter read as requirements, a court friendly to creditors could interpret the letter as being part of the trust, and that the commands in the letter make the trust revocable at the election of the settlor. If the trust is deemed to be a revocable trust, a judge unfriendly to the settlor could command the settlor to amend it favorably to a creditor.

CONCLUSION: A TALE FROM REAL LIFE

If you spend a few days in a law library scouring all of the reported cases dealing with FAPTs, you'll find that there are very, very few. Here's why:

In 1985, shortly before I had been fully introduced to FAPTs, I met with a client on a business deal. Apropos of nothing we were discussing, he told me that a neighbor of his owed him about $80,000 and wouldn't pay. Almost by instinct, I reached for my legal pad and prepared myself to get all the data needed to sue on behalf of my client.

"Don't bother, Bob," my client said. "I hear he's put all his assets in a trust in the Turks and Caicos Islands."

I had no idea where the Turks and Caicos Islands were, but I wouldn't be deterred. I convinced my client to permit me to do some digging.

My digging consisted of calling every lawyer in the Turks and Caicos Islands. Because the Turks and Caicos Islands is an FAPT haven, there are a surprising number of lawyers there, considering the country consists of two specks of sand in the Caribbean. Speaking to every lawyer there taught me that having a U.S. judgment would do me no good, because the Turks and Caicos Islands doesn't recognize foreign judgments. Even if we brought suit in the Turks and Caicos Islands, our chances there would be less than sterling, and even if we managed to win, the assets would probably have been moved somewhere else (the Isle of Man?) as I got closer to them. Having succeeded in doing nothing but running up the phone bills to the Turks and Caicos Islands, I gave up.

All the law books reveal no case involving my client and his debtor. Had the debtor kept his money in the United States, there might today be a case for all to see. But because we gave up, there is no case.

That's why there are so few cases involving FAPTs.

10

Firing Big Bertha: Filing Bankruptcy to Protect Your Assets

INTRODUCTION

It is often the case that, for whatever reason or series of reasons, none of the asset protection techniques we have thus far discussed are available or will work. Even if an asset protection technique is available to you, you might reject it as being too expensive. The day might come when you need to consider the possibility of a bankruptcy petition.

Bankruptcy is as old as the republic. Indeed, the United States Constitution grants to the Congress the sole authority over bankruptcy laws. All bankruptcy matters are governed by federal laws and thus are uniform throughout the country, with the exception of laws regulating which assets are exempt from creditors—those assets are subject to state laws.

Bankruptcy isn't new, but what is new is the attitude toward it. It used to be that bankruptcy carried a stigma with it, and people felt ashamed to do it. The stigma kept bankruptcy filings to a minimum. People often labored for years to pay off creditors that they could have avoided with the stroke of a pen. In recent years, however, the stigma has receded, if not totally vanished. Many people would still rather die than file a bankruptcy petition, and many others will swallow hard before they do, but the majority of people accept bankruptcy for what it is—the tool whereby an innocent but unfortunate debtor is permitted to wipe the slate clean and start over. The necessity of a bankruptcy system to a productive economy is manifested by the former Communist countries that have felt the need to enact new bankruptcy codes.

MAKING THE DECISION

The moral stigma may have vanished, but no one should file a bankruptcy petition without first considering the risks, the downsides, and the alternatives. It is never a decision that should be made casually.

There are many reasons why a person who feels burdened by debts should not file for bankruptcy. First, the burden might not be as great as you might think. Merely because you have one creditor hounding you is no reason to take the plunge into bankruptcy. Second, you might not need to file for bankruptcy for a variety of reasons. Merely because you have a series of creditors hounding you doesn't mean they're ready to take the next step and sue you to recover their debts. Once they find they cannot collect, they might decide to merely write them off. That will harm your credit, but that's all. You also might not need to file for bankruptcy because your assets are exempt from creditors due to state exemption laws.

For example, if your principal asset is your home, and a state homestead exemption is broad enough so that your creditors cannot get at the home, there's no need to file for bankruptcy.

It's also possible that bankruptcy might not benefit you. Certain debts, such as alimony and child support, cannot be extinguished by a bankruptcy filing. If all you owe is $200,000 in back alimony to your ex-spouse, don't even think about bankruptcy.

A final reason that we might not need to file a bankruptcy petition is that the threat of a bankruptcy might be all that's required. Here's an example.

Many years ago I represented a Mr. Goldstein,[1] a successful furrier. In the days before environmental fanaticism, you could make real money manufacturing mink coats, and Mr. Goldstein did. One morning he opened his small factory and found that many of the furs were gone. Mr. Goldstein called me and we set out to narrow the suspects. Later that day, we found that cash in the till and checks from customers also were missing. By the following morning, the mystery was solved. Mr. Goldstein's partner didn't show up, but he had left a note. It turns out that the partner had been stealing from the business for some time to cover gambling debts.

On that day, Mr. Goldstein's little fur business owed hundreds of thousands of dollars to scores of fur brokers, jobbers, and other furriers, and had no cash to pay. All of these creditors were unsecured, and we could have washed them out with the stroke of a pen. But the fur business was then a very tightly knit world, and a bankruptcy would have been embarrassing and damaging. So Mr. Goldstein and I began pounding the pavement, going from creditor to creditor. Each of them had known Mr. Goldstein for years, and most admired and respected him. We played a little

---

[1] The name is fictitious.

game of "good cop–bad cop." Mr. Goldstein begged each creditor to accept anywhere from 20 to 40 percent of the debt, paid out over a period of many months. I played the heavy, reminding each creditor that if they failed to go along, they would get perhaps five cents on the dollar in a bankruptcy. In short order, they all went along with the plan. Mr. Goldstein stayed in business without the necessity of a bankruptcy filing. The lesson I learned was that, very often, shoe leather works better than legal brilliance.

Mr. Goldstein was lucky. Had he not enjoyed the respect and empathy of his creditors, they might not have gone along with the plan. In that event, a bankruptcy filing might have been the only alternative.

CHAPTER 7 AND CHAPTER 13

The Bankruptcy Code is divided into various chapters. Unless you run a municipality that's insolvent, you'll never encounter Chapter 9. The only chapters you'll ever likely encounter are chapters 11, 7, and 13.

Chapter 11 involves the reorganization of a business. Unlike Chapter 7 and Chapter 13, which result in the *discharge* of the debtor's debts, Chapter 11 doesn't result in a discharge. It allows a business debtor to get a breather from its creditors while it files a *reorganization plan* that a debtor's creditors (and the bankruptcy judge) may or may not accept. It often results in the relief from payment of many unsecured debts, if that's what the plan says. But a majority of Chapter 11 plans don't work. The result is that the debtor, having spent a considerable amount of time and money on the reorganization plan, is either tossed out of the bankruptcy court or has his or her bankruptcy converted into a Chapter 7. We won't dwell on Chapter 11 here.

Chapter 7 is sometimes called a *straight bankruptcy*. What follows is a very rudimentary sketch of how it works.

You initiate a Chapter 7 bankruptcy by filing a *petition*. The petition lists all your secured and unsecured debts and your assets. You also list all your assets you deem to be exempt from the clutches of your creditors. We saw in Chapter 2 that every state has its own list of assets that are exempt from creditors. The Bankruptcy Code has its own list. However, each state is free to supplant the Bankruptcy Code list with its own, and 34 states, including California, New York, Ohio, Illinois, and Florida, have done so. If you live in one of the 34 states, you get your choice of the state exemptions or those listed in the Bankruptcy Code, whichever is more favorable to you. Depending on where you live, the fact that your state has opted out (or hasn't) could be beneficial or detrimental to you.

Could you change your state of residence prior to filing a bankruptcy in order to avail yourself of more generous state exemptions? You could, but for the plan to be successful you would have to be *domiciled* in your new state for at least 180 days prior to the filing of the petition, and you would have to actually reside in the new state for at least 91 of those 180 days. In order to establish a domicile, you must do all those things that usually attend citizenship in a state, such as changing your car registration and voting registration. It's a lot of work, but it could be well worth it. In any event, you should never file a bankruptcy petition without knowing exactly what exemptions are available to you.

The final section of your bankruptcy petition is a statement of affairs, which is a series of questions about you and your finances. The statement of affairs is important for a number of reasons. If you made any gifts to family members during the 12 months preceding the petition, the bankruptcy trustee could avoid that transfer as being a fraudulent conveyance. If you paid any of your creditors within the 90 days prior to filing, the trustee could ignore that payment (and recover the money from the creditor you paid) as being a *preferential transfer*. Very often, part of careful bankruptcy planning means waiting to file, so as not to run afoul of these rules.

The moment a Chapter 7 petition is filed, the *automatic stay* against every actual and potential creditor goes into effect. From that moment on, no one can bring a lawsuit against the debtor to recover on any debt, and any lawsuit previously filed is stopped in its tracks. Mortgages, deeds of trust, and other liens may not be recorded, and foreclosure proceedings are halted, even if the real estate is about to be sold at auction. Moreover, all collection efforts, including as little as contacting the debtor asking for payment, are prohibited. Anyone who contacts a debtor seeking payment while knowing that a bankruptcy has been filed is liable for contempt of court. Interest on debts stops accruing.

That's not to say that the automatic stay lasts forever. A secured creditor who can prove to the court that there's no chance the debtor will be able to pay can ask the court for relief from the automatic stay. The result is that secured creditors can then start or continue the process of foreclosure.

The goal of every Chapter 7 is a discharge. When a petition is filed, the bankruptcy court appoints a trustee, whose duty it is to see that whatever nonexempt assets remaining are applied to paying off every creditor who filed a *proof of claim*. Technically, the trustee owns all of the debtor's assets as of the date of the filing, not the debtor.

The principle advantage of Chapter 7 is that the trustee has available for distribution only those assets the debtor owned on the date of the filing of the petition. Any earnings or wages that the debtor comes into after filing belongs to the debtor, and is not available for the creditors. For example, if you file a bankruptcy petition on a Monday saying you have $200,000 in debts and only $4,000 in assets, and on Tuesday you win $1 million in the Irish Sweepstakes, you get the $1 million, not the trustee and not the creditors. The only exception to this rule is that a trustee can get his hands on sums the debtor inherits or receives by way of a divorce settlement within six months of the filing of a petition. These exceptions exist only on paper, because anyone with a clear head can time the receipt of a divorce settlement or an inheritance so that it's not received within six months of filing.

The principle disadvantage of Chapter 7 is that not all debts can be discharged. The principal nondischargeable debts are those that arose due to the debtor's fraud, "willful and malicious" conduct to another, or breach of a fiduciary duty. Here's an example: Let's assume Mrs. Green sues Mr. Biggs, her stockbroker, claiming that he lost all of her money. She not only alleges that he was negligent, she also claims that he defrauded her, not telling her that he was a part owner in the Costa Rican diamond mine in which he invested most of her money. Mrs. Green wins the lawsuit, the jury awarding her $10 million. But the jury found only that Biggs was negligent, not fraudulent. Biggs can march straight down to the courthouse and wash out the negligence judgment in bankruptcy. But if the jury had also found that Biggs had defrauded Mrs. Green, filing under Chapter 7 would do Biggs no good, because Mrs. Green's lawyer would argue—probably successfully—that the jury verdict is not dischargeable in the bankruptcy.

Using Chapter 7 is like firing a cannon that fires only one shell and that takes forever to reload. If you get a discharge in Chapter 7, you cannot file again for six years.

Most people have a rough idea of how Chapter 7 works. People are less familiar with Chapter 13, only because it's newer. It has certain advantages over Chapter 7, but also carries with it some limitations.

Chapter 13 is sometimes referred to as a "Wage Earner Plan," but that is something of a misnomer. You need not receive a paycheck in order to qualify for Chapter 13; all you need is some form of regular income, even if it's from your ownership of a business. Unlike a Chapter 7, however, which places no limit on the amount of debt you can wash out, you're limited in a Chapter 13 to $250,000 in unsecured debt and $750,000 in secured debt. Moreover, whereas corporations, partnerships, estates, and trusts can use Chapter 7, only a natural person (or a married couple) can use Chapter 13.

Chapter 13 operates the same way as does Chapter 7 in that you initiate it by filing a petition, and the second you file the petition the automatic stay goes into effect. But that's where the similarities end. Fifteen days after you file the petition, you must file a plan saying how much you can pay your creditors over the next few years, usually three but never more than five years. The plan must devote all your *disposable income* toward your creditors. But disposable income is defined in the Bankruptcy Code as being that which isn't necessary for "the maintenance and support of the debtor or a dependent of the debtor," and if the debtor owns a business, disposable income is only that which is left over after "the payment of expenditures necessary for the continuation, preservation, and operation of the business." In short, the plan may leave very little for the creditors. The only limitation is that the plan cannot allot to the unsecured creditors less than they would have received had you filed under Chapter 7. That's not much of a limitation, because unsecured creditors generally get very little in a Chapter 7 filing. Finally, the plan must provide that certain "priority" claims, such as alimony and taxes, are paid in full.

Once the Chapter 13 plan is filed, your creditors get a chance to object to it. They can allege that the plan was filed in bad faith, meaning that you really can pay them more than you say you can. Most Chapter 13 plans are accepted ("confirmed" in the jargon of the Bankruptcy Code) and sail through without any objections from any creditors. In fact, many debtors who go through Chapter 13 are surprised at how easy it is. One reason is that even though unsecured creditors have the right to object, they have no right to refuse to go along if the plan is confirmed. Secured creditors, however, need not go along. They have a right to have the property that is covered by their security interest returned to them, or be paid the full amount of their debt.

The one secured debt that most people are concerned about is the mortgage on their residence, and here Chapter 13 affords a considerable benefit. Many people, when they get into trouble with their creditors, fall behind on their mortgage payments. Foreclosure is threatened or has already begun. Unlike Chapter 7, a debtor in Chapter 13 has the right to cure any default in the payment of the secured debt, obviating the foreclosure. In Chapter 7, a secured creditor who obtains relief from the automatic stay can proceed with foreclosure outside of the bankruptcy. This ability to cure a default makes Chapter 13 a favorite haven for debtors faced with the loss of valuable real estate.

The principle difference between Chapter 7 and Chapter 13 is that, whereas the trustee under Chapter 7 has no right to your income after the filing of the petition, he or she does under Chapter 13. In fact, the Chapter 13 plan is based on your assessment of how much you think you will earn during the three to five years that the plan will be in effect. Moreover, you must fork over to the trustee all the income that the plan says constitutes your "disposable income," which the trustee uses to pay your creditors. If your income goes up during the period of the plan, there's more available for your creditors.

The principle advantage of Chapter 13 is that the discharge provisions are broader. In our previous example, had the jury found that Biggs had defrauded Mrs. Green, Biggs would be able to wash out the debt in a Chapter 13, although discharge of a fraudulently incurred debt would not be possible under Chapter 7. Even tax penalties and student loans, not normally dischargeable under Chapter 7, are dischargeable under Chapter 13. The only debts that are never dischargeable in Chapter 13 (or Chapter 7) are alimony, child support, and personal injury awards resulting from drunk driving.

Unlike Chapter 7, you're not limited to one Chapter 13 filing in six years, and you can use Chapter 13 even if you have obtained a prior Chapter 7 discharge, provided that your Chapter 13 filing is not considered one made in bad faith.

Is Chapter 13 "better" than Chapter 7? For some people it is, for others it isn't. Each person contemplating bankruptcy must first see if he or she qualifies for Chapter 13, and if so must weigh the benefits and limitations of each. There are no rules of thumb.

ARE TAXES DISCHARGEABLE IN BANKRUPTCY?

Most people, even many lawyers, assume that if anybody must be paid, it's the IRS. It therefore comes as a shock to many people to learn that income taxes may be discharged in bankruptcy.

In order to discharge income taxes in a Chapter 7, you need to jump through a number of hoops. The first is that at least three years must have elapsed since the tax return first became due. For example, your income tax return (Form 1040) for calendar year 1990 came due on April 15, 1991. If you wanted to discharge 1990's taxes, you needed to wait until April 15, 1994, to file your Chapter 7 petition. If you filed Form 1040 early, you still need to wait until three years from the due date, April 15, 1994.

The second hoop involves people who filed late. In the above example, if you didn't file your 1990 tax return until January 15, 1993, you needed to wait two years—until January 15, 1995—to file your Chapter 7 petition.

These two rules point up one fact: You can never discharge income taxes in Chapter 7 if you never filed a return.

The third hoop is easiest to jump through. In order to discharge income taxes, there may not have been an IRS *assessment* against you within the 240 days preceding the bankruptcy petition. An assessment is the action on the part of the IRS that says you owe the tax. The IRS never sends you a certificate saying you've been assessed. But if you filed a tax return that says you owe a certain amount, or if the IRS has started going after your assets, you can safely assume that there's been an assessment. But if you're still in the audit stage for a given tax year, there may not yet be an assessment, which means your bankruptcy filing, at least for that tax year, may be premature.[2]

If you jump through all these hoops, are you home free? Yes and no. Your income taxes will be discharged. But if prior to the bankruptcy filing the IRS had gotten around to filing a Notice of Federal Tax Lien against your property in a given county, the bankruptcy doesn't remove the lien. It means that, at least in that county, you can't sell the assets covered by the lien without first paying the tax.

Note that we've referred here only to *income* taxes. If you're on the hook for *employment* taxes (the taxes that you're supposed to withhold from your employees and turn over to the IRS), there's no way you can discharge these obligations in bankruptcy; the Bankruptcy Code specifically prohibits it.

PREBANKRUPTCY PLANNING

A bankruptcy may help, but it will help a lot more if you plan in advance.

---

[2] You can find out if and when there has been an assessment by going to an IRS office and ordering your *transcript of account*. If discharge of a tax debt is a concern, you should never file a bankruptcy petition without first ascertaining if and when you were assessed.

We've already seen that there are certain transfers that, if they occur within one year of the filing of a bankruptcy petition, can be ignored by the bankruptcy trustee. Let's assume that prior to filing a bankruptcy petition, you decide to form a family limited partnership, making gifts of limited partnership interests to your children and grandchildren. The interests you give away should be outside of the reach of the trustee, because you no longer own them. But if you don't wait a year before filing the petition, the trustee might well go after those partnership interests.

Similarly, the trustee can ignore, as preferential transfers, any payments made to creditors within 90 days of the bankruptcy filing. There are certain classes of creditors you might well wish to prefer over others. For example, you might have to pay certain suppliers if you need them to stay in business. You might feel a moral obligation to pay the family doctor. But if these creditors are paid within 90 days of the filing, the trustee can demand that these creditors return the money to him. That could be devastating to your business. If you have paid off certain vital creditors, you should wait 90 days before filing.

The most basic prebankruptcy planning involves the conversion of nonexempt assets to exempt assets. Let's assume that your state has a generous homestead exemption, such as California's ($50,000 for a single person, $75,000 for a married couple, and $100,000 for the elderly) or Florida's (unlimited). Let's also assume that you don't own a residence, but have $100,000 in stocks and bonds. Deciding to rent a home rather than own one may have been a smart investment decision, but it's poor bankruptcy planning. The existence of $100,000 in liquid securities is the same as free money for the trustee, because there's no exemption covering the securities. If you took the $100,000 and bought a residence, you would come through the bankruptcy with a $100,000 asset, and the trustee would get less.

Let's assume that you do own a home, but your equity is greater than the allowable homestead exemption. That means that the trustee could force the sale of your home in order to pay off creditors. What to do? Consider borrowing on the equity in the home up to the level of the homestead exemption, reducing the equity to that level. With the cash available from the refinancing, you could pay off certain creditors you need to pay. In fact, with the cash and the threat of bankruptcy, some of them might be willing to settle for less.

Here's another example. If you own a life insurance policy with a large cash surrender value, you can be assured that the trustee will get that cash value and distribute it to your creditors. If, however, you borrow on the policy, there's little the trustee can do. However, be sure that you wait a full year after borrowing the money before you file the bankruptcy petition.

If you received any proceeds as a beneficiary of a policy that insured someone else's life, you need to wait six months before you file a bankruptcy petition. That's because, under the Bankruptcy Code, your bankruptcy estate includes any proceeds received within six months of the filing of a bankruptcy petition.

Throughout this book, we've tried to avoid touting the invaluable services of lawyers. But here's an exception, one last iron-clad rule:

> Never file a bankruptcy petition without first seeking professional advice.

11

How to Fight the IRS

INTRODUCTION

Let's assume that you arrive home from work one day to discover a letter from the Internal Revenue Service (IRS). Unless you're expecting a tax refund, your instincts tell you that this can't be good news. Your instincts are confirmed quickly. The letter informs you that you owe $47,541 in back taxes. Moreover, the letter informs you that you have 30 days to pay, and threatens dire consequences if you don't. Let's assume that you have a hefty bank account, a home with substantial equity, and a profitable business. Can they take it all away 31 days from now?

Sound farfetched? I receive calls like this all the time in my law practice. But what's the answer?

The answer is that, with the information provided, we don't yet know. The missing datum is just what it is the IRS sent. If the letter is a "30-day letter," the IRS can't yet do anything. If the letter is a "90-day letter," they still can't do anything, but they're closer. If the letter is a "Notice and Demand for Payment," they're still a few months away from being able to do anything, but you've already waived precious defenses. If the letter is a "Notice of Intent to Levy," it means you've been practicing denial with respect to the prior mail you've received, and they're very close to seizing your assets.

The IRS has a panoply of weapons at its disposal, but its greatest strength is that few citizens know how the IRS works, and the result is that most people who have to deal with the IRS do so in the dark. Congress tried to ameliorate the unfairness in 1988, when it enacted the Taxpayer Bill of Rights. One of the provisions of that act is that the IRS is required to tell you—at every step along the way—what your rights are. But IRS officials do very little to shed light on what a taxpayer's rights are, knowing that your ignorance of how the IRS works is their biggest weapon.

In this chapter, we're going to shed a little light on how the IRS operates. We'll also focus on your two best—and least known— weapons in your arsenal, the Installment Payment Agreement and the Offer in Compromise. But before we look at some of the trees, let's take a bird's-eye look at the forest.

THE BIG PICTURE

Most people don't know very much about how the IRS operates. As a result, they don't know what rights they have. This general ignorance is due partly to people not wanting to develop too much experience in dealing with the IRS. But the principal reason is that until very recently the IRS was quite content in keeping their procedures as murky as possible—it provided them with a distinct advantage over every taxpayer "client."

Take a look at Figure 11–1. It all looks pretty complicated at this point. The chart should make one fact fairly apparent. Every step in the process leads toward—and away from—the assessment. The IRS' assessment of someone's taxes is the key concept in understanding how the IRS works, and how we will have to deal with it. If you don't understand the concept of the assessment, you can never learn how to deal with the IRS. But once you understand the concept of the assessment, everything else will begin to fall into place.

The Assessment

What is an IRS Assessment? It's the official act on the part of the IRS that says that you owe them a particular amount of money. The act of assessment is vitally important for two reasons:

> Reason #1: Many things may have to happen before the IRS is permitted to make an assessment.

and:

> Reason #2: Until there has been an assessment, you don't owe the money.

All of which means that the IRS can't take your house, your bank account, your wages, or your property until there has been an assessment, because until there has been an assessment, you don't owe the money. It also means that one of the strategies we may employ is to delay the date when the IRS may make an assessment for as long as possible.

Consider the following hypothetical example, one that occurs many times every day. Mr. Brown completes his Form 1040 individual

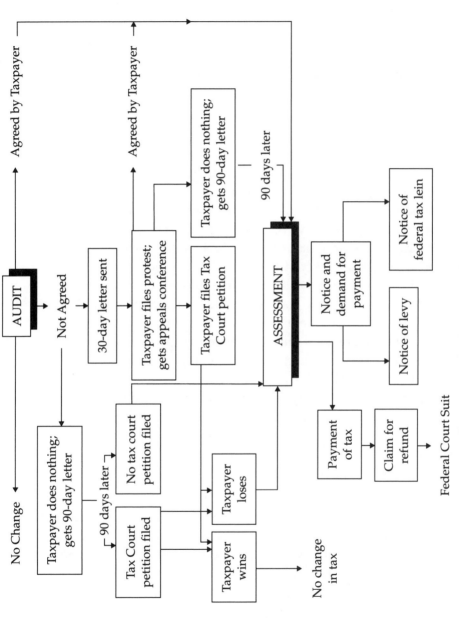

Figure 11–1. Tracking a typical tax case.

tax return and signs it. The return indicates that Mr. Brown owes $10,000. Mr. Brown encloses a $10,000 check with the tax return. When the IRS receives the return and the $10,000 check, do they assess Mr. Brown for $10,000? Yes! Why? Because unless and until there has been an assessment, Mr. Brown doesn't owe the money.

If you've ever been in an IRS office, you may have noticed that it was divided into (at least) two areas. One area was marked "Examinations," which is the IRS' term for audits. The other area was marked "Collections." What distinguishes the two areas? Examinations is the division of the IRS you deal with before you owe the money. You deal with Collections only after it is established that you owe the money. You deal with Examinations before there has been an assessment, and with Collections after an assessment. The strategies and tactics we'll need to employ in dealing with Examinations are vastly different than those we'll need to employ with Collections. If you have ever had to deal with both branches of the IRS, you may have noticed that the people who work for Examinations are very different than the people who work for Collections. The people at Collections don't know much tax law; they don't have to. By the time you land in their clutches, Examinations has already determined that you owe the money. All Collections cares about is collecting it. The good folks at Examinations know lots of tax law, but they really don't care about how the IRS is going to get the money from you. Different people, with very different missions, requiring very different treatment.

If an assessment is such a key part of the puzzle, just what is it? Part of the secrecy and mystery that the IRS lives and thrives on is that this very important procedure is something that is almost never seen by anyone outside of the IRS. The assessment is actually nothing more than the official act of some bureaucrat at the IRS recording the fact that you owe the money. Months—even years—may elapse before that simple act may occur. If you're successful in challenging the IRS at any one of a number of steps along the way, that simple step of recording that you owe the money may never happen.

It may take years before the IRS is permitted to assess you, but it may require only days after that. Take the case of Mr. Brown, who filed a tax return showing a $10,000 tax. What does the IRS need to do before they can assess Mr. Brown $10,000? Nothing. Because Mr. Brown has admitted that he owes the $10,000, the IRS doesn't have to prove anything to establish his tax liability. They can assess immediately. If Mr. Brown had not included a $10,000 check along with his tax return, nothing would have prevented the IRS from sending the file to the friendly folks at the Collections Division.

The Statute of Limitations on Assessments

If you don't owe the money until there's been an assessment, can the time run out on the IRS' ability to make an assessment, meaning that you'll never have to pay the tax?

Yes! Generally, the IRS has three years from the day you file your tax return to decide that you owe more money than you said you owed and to do all the other things they are required to do and make an assessment. If those medical expenses you took on your tax return really weren't deductible, they have three years from the day you filed that return to catch it, or you're home free. The three years ends on the date that the tax return is postmarked, not on the date the IRS receives the return. It may sound trivial, but it can be crucially important in those cases in which the IRS is racing to make an assessment before the clock runs out.

There are a few exceptions to this three-year rule. If you file your tax return early (i.e., before it's legally due) the three years starts to run on the day after the day the return is due. Here are two illustrations:

Example #1: Mr. White gets an automatic extension to file his 1990 individual income tax return until August 15, 1991. The IRS has until August 15, 1994, to assess Mr. White for any more taxes for 1990.

Example #2: Mr. Black files his 1990 individual income tax return on January 2, 1991. The IRS has until April 15, 1994, to assess Mr. Black for any more taxes for 1990.

If you file your return late (in IRS jargon, a "delinquent" return), the three-year meter doesn't start to run until the day you file the return.

Example #3: Mr. Green doesn't file his 1990 individual income tax return until November 15, 1991. The IRS has until November 15, 1994, to assess Mr. Green.

What if you never file your tax return? It means that the statute of limitations never starts to run against the IRS. But it gets worse. If you never file a return, the day will come when the return will be late (April 15 of the following year). It's not likely they'll catch up with you that soon, but technically they could, and on that date they're permitted to make the dreaded assessment, kicking you into the Collections Division.

What happens if you file your tax return, and then later amend it, by filing an "Amended Tax Return," Form 1040X? There's no change in the statute of limitations. The IRS still has the same three years from the date you filed the original return, even if the amended return reports a lower tax liability than the original return. The reason for this is that there is no provision in the Tax Code for an amended return in the first place, so the filing of an amended return can't change the rule.

There are some other exceptions to the three-year rule. The first exception involves those rare instances in which the IRS believes that the tax return is false and fraudulent, made with the "intent to evade tax." In that event, they can assess any time after the return is filed. But in that case, the burden of proof is on the IRS to prove that the return was filed with bad intent. This is an important switch on the usual rule that puts the burden of proof on the taxpayer to prove that the tax return is correct.

Another exception to the three-year rule occurs if you fail to include more than 25 percent of your gross income on the return. In that case, the IRS has six years to make an assessment. Note that the three-year limitation is extended to six only if you understate your gross income, not your taxable income or taxes, by more than 25 percent.

> Example #4: Mr. Wolf had $100,000 in gross income from wages in 1990, and files his tax return for 1990 on April 15, 1991. He fails to report $30,000 in gambling winnings. The IRS has until April 15, 1997, to assess Mr. Wolf for 1990.

> Example #5: Mr. Bear had $100,000 in gross income from wages in 1990, and files his tax return for 1990 on April 15, 1991. He takes a $60,000 deduction for a yacht he bought, which the IRS determines is nondeductible. The IRS has until April 15, 1994, to assess Mr. Bear for 1990.

As is often the case in the field of tax law, there is an "exception to the exception," that is, a circumstance in which the underreporting of more than 25 percent of a person's gross income will not increase the statute of limitations to six years. The three-year period is not extended if you include a statement with the tax return telling the IRS about the gross income you didn't include on the tax return, and why you didn't include it.

I wouldn't advise using this procedure, unless you're absolutely certain that your return is so squeaky clean that a team of auditors couldn't find any additional tax. Attaching a statement to your return which tells the IRS why you made 25 percent more money and why you haven't included the money on your return is a pretty good way to assure that an IRS Examiner is going to spend the better part of one morning poring over your return.

A Good Rule to Live By

We just saw that until you file your tax return, the statute of limitations on assessments doesn't begin to run, and that if you never file a return, they have forever to assess you.

This is a good place to mention the *Rule to Live By* (which is also a good strategy): *File Your Tax Returns!* Most people do, but many people don't. The reasons they don't are many and varied, and most people who don't file tax returns aren't criminals. Some people, for whatever crazy reason, think that they don't have to.

Many people just can't get themselves to file a tax return. This is true even though they owe no taxes. In fact, the failure to file a tax return often results in a person not getting a refund that would be owed if the person would only file the return and claim the money.

A former lieutenant governor of Colorado saw his career go up in smoke when it was revealed that he had let a few years go by without filing any tax returns. An accountant had prepared the returns for his signature, but the lieutenant governor never signed them. Every day, he opened his desk drawer and saw the unsigned returns. But he just couldn't get himself to mail in the returns. And with every passing day, filing the returns became harder to do.

The worst reason not to file a tax return is, "I haven't got the money." If you don't have the money, file the return anyway. After you do, we'll have to start dealing with the Collections Division to stretch out and, with some luck, lower the tax burden. But at least we'll avoid a "failure to file" penalty, which can be as much as 25 percent of the tax owed. We'll also avoid the possibility that the IRS will take drastic action (such as levying on wages) if they find out for themselves that a return is due.

Here's an important rule of thumb regarding IRS psychology: The failure to pay taxes doesn't bother them nearly as much as the failure to file. They know that the tax laws are very complex and that no one—including them—knows exactly what's owed and what isn't. Unless they smell fraud, they understand that taxpayers get aggressive, or become forgetful, or momentarily lose the ability to add a column of figures, especially when their own money is involved. But if you never file a tax return (or stop filing returns), they start to feel that you don't love them anymore, and they get lonely for you.

They would like to hear from you, and the only way to get your attention is to do something more drastic than they otherwise would, such as taking your house.

What should you do if you haven't filed tax returns for many years—or ever? Is it criminal? Can they arrest you? Yes and yes. But if you visit them and tell them that you haven't filed a tax return in 20 years and that you've been waiting to hear from them, they'll overcome their initial embarrassment and tell you to file the returns for the years you've missed. They won't call in the boys from Criminal Investigations Division (CID) if you visit them before they visit you. In fact, the best strategy would be to prepare all the prior years' tax returns before you visit them.

Every so often I have a client who hasn't filed a return in many years, if ever. If they're in my office, something has jolted them into reality. I always tell them that it isn't as bad as it may initially seem. They may have forgotten about those years in which their income was overwithheld, for which they will be entitled to a refund, which may reduce the interest and penalties. There may even be an explainable reason why they haven't filed that might result in a complete or partial waiver of the penalties. No matter what your history—*File!*

A WALK THROUGH THE MAZE

Take a look again at Figure 11–1. We'll cover every step along the way in more detail later, but for now we just want to take a look at the "big picture." In walking through the process, we'll assume that you have filed a tax return on time. As we follow each step, remember that until there has been an assessment, you don't owe any money, but that after there has been an assessment, you do. Before there has been an assessment, the IRS really can't do anything to you. After an assessment, they can.

IRS Audits

Most tax returns aren't audited, but let's assume that yours is. You may undergo a Correspondence Audit, an Office Audit, or a Field Audit. The audit will be conducted by an examiner, who works in the Examinations Division of the IRS. The examiner isn't interested in collecting taxes from you; he or she is interested in determining the correct amount of tax—that is, comparing your return with the requirements of the tax law and making sure that the two conclusions jibe.

The examiner may decide to close your case without adjustment. This is referred to as a "No Change" audit. This means that you've convinced him or her that the tax you reported on your return is the correct amount.

But the examiner may decide that you owe more tax, that is, he or she will make adjustments. If this is done, a report of the adjustments made will be sent to you. Since the enactment of the Taxpayer Bill of Rights, the examiner must provide you with an explanation of the adjustments made.

At this point, you're presented with the first of many options you may have along the way. You'll have to decide whether you agree or disagree with the examiner's adjustments. You may also agree in part and disagree in part if you want to concede one or more but not all of the adjustments made.

If you agree with the adjustments, you'll be asked to do so in writing. Your consent will include a consent to an immediate assessment. With that, most (but not all) of the rights you may have to fight the tax will be waived. You won't be allowed to take an appeal of the examiner's adjustments within the IRS. More significantly, you won't be allowed to contest the adjustments in the Tax Court. What's worse, if you do agree to the adjustments but don't and/or can't pay the increased tax, the IRS will make an assessment. At that point, you'll owe the money. The Examinations Division will promptly send the file to the people at Collections, who will do their best to collect it from you.

Let's assume you don't agree with the examiner's findings. Remember that the examiner's adjustments are not an assessment; they're just the examiner's opinion of what is the correct tax. At this point, there hasn't yet been an assessment. Can the examiner make an assessment? No, not yet, and maybe not for a long time to come. At this point, can the IRS do anything to collect the tax reflected on the adjustments? No. You don't yet owe any money.[1]

Remember that if the examiner only gets around to your file after three years from the date you filed your return, there is nothing that the examiner can do, because by then it's too late for an assessment to be made.

IRS Appeals

If you don't agree, the examiner will send you a 30-day letter. This is a letter telling you that you have 30 days in which to appeal the

---

[1] Two notable exceptions to this rule are "Jeopardy Assessments" and "Termination Assessments," which are basically the same thing, differing only in the time of year that they are made in relation to the due date of the tax return. Jeopardy and Termination Assessments may be made by the IRS any time that the IRS feels that they are in danger of permanently losing the ability to collect the tax. They are usually reserved for criminals and others in flight. As one famous case revealed, a woman apprehended at the airport with a one-way ticket for Switzerland with enough cash stuffed in her bodice to make her appear very pregnant is a good candidate for a Jeopardy Assessment.

examiner's findings within the IRS. An Appeals Conference really isn't an "appeal," and requires its own unique strategies. The IRS is not required by law to give you an IRS Appeal, but they almost invariably will, with one exception: Because the three-year clock on assessments doesn't stop while you're in an IRS Appeal, the IRS won't give you an appeal if the clock is about to run out, unless you voluntarily agree to extend the statute of limitations on assessments.

No one is required to take an IRS Appeal, and there are numerous cases where the best strategy is not to appeal. If you don't want to appeal the examiner's adjustments, you can put the 30-day letter in the trash. If you ignore the 30-day letter, you'll soon get a 90-day letter from the IRS. More on that shortly.

If you decide to appeal, you initiate the appeal by sending a protest letter to the IRS, officially protesting the examiner's adjustments, stating your reasons that the examiner's conclusions should be reversed.

After the IRS receives the protest, they will schedule an Appeals Conference between you (and your attorney and/or CPA, if any) and an Appeals Officer. There are two likely outcomes of an Appeals Conference. The most likely outcome is that you will settle the case. You will agree to pay more than you reported on the return, and the IRS will accept less than the examiner concluded was due on the adjustments.

But the other possibility is that you won't be able to settle the case, in which event the examiner's adjustments will stand. Can the IRS now make an assessment? Do you now owe them any money? No, and maybe not for a long time to come.

If you can't settle the case on appeal, the Appeals Office will send you a Notice of Deficiency, which is more often referred to as a 90-day letter.

The 90-Day Letter

This is the most important piece of mail you can ever receive from the IRS. The IRS is thoughtful enough to send it certified. Very often, clients come into my office with a small mountain of correspondence from the IRS. Often the mail is unopened, because the client has been practicing denial. The first thing I do is hunt through the junk, looking for that important 90-day letter. Here's why: The 90-day letter says that you have 90 days to file a petition with the United States Tax Court contesting the examiner's adjustments, asking the Tax Court to determine just how much tax you owe. The 90-day letter also says that if you don't file a Tax Court Petition within 90 days, the IRS will assess you for the amount that the examiner said you owe. If the 90-day period (150 days if you are out of the country at any time during the 90-day period) passes without you having filed a Tax Court petition, the IRS can assess you for the tax they claim is due and start enforced collection proceedings.

The 90-day letter also stops the clock on assessments, but only for 90 days. If you don't file a Tax Court petition within 90 days, the IRS can assess and start collecting on the 91st day. But if you do file a petition with the Tax Court, the clock on assessments stays stopped until the Tax Court has made a determination. That is a process that can take months or years.

The 90-day letter is also important in that it is the document that confers jurisdiction on the Tax Court to hear your case. Even if you're dying to go to the Tax Court, you cannot get there unless and until you've first received a 90-day letter.

Just to make matters more complicated, it's possible to reverse the steps we have just discussed. In the usual case, the taxpayer files a protest to a 30-day letter, has an appeal within the IRS, receives a 90-day letter, and then goes to the Tax Court. But it's possible to have an IRS Appeal after you have received a 90-day letter, and after you have filed a petition in the Tax Court.

The Tax Court

Let's assume that you decide to litigate against the IRS in the Tax Court. While you're in litigation against them, they cannot make an assessment, which means that you still don't owe them any money. One of the truly remarkable features of our system of tax controversies is that a taxpayer is permitted to have his or her case heard before an independent tribunal without first having to pay the tax. What if you lose your case in the Tax Court? Can the IRS then make an assessment and start collecting the money? Not exactly. You have the right to appeal the Tax Court's decision to one of the eleven Federal Appeals Courts. You could even appeal that decision to the United States Supreme Court. Unlike the Appeals Court, which has to take your appeal, the Supreme Court does not, and very rarely does. It's only after your appeal rights have expired that the IRS finally can take that rarely seen action of recording an assessment against you. Only then do you owe the money.

At any step along the way, you can change your mind and pay what the examiner says you owed. You also could have agreed to the examiner's adjustments, or failed to file a Tax Court petition in response to the 90-day letter, both of which would have resulted in an assessment. Is the ball game over? Not at all.

You have the right to make a claim for a refund of what you paid. If the IRS denies that claim for refund, you have a choice of suing the IRS for a refund either in the United States Claims Court or in the local Federal District Court. One big advantage of suing in the District Court is that you have the right to a jury trial. Think of it! Arguing before your neighbors why the IRS is all wet.

CUTTING A DEAL

The Installment Payment Agreement

Let's assume that the IRS finally gets around to assessing the tax. At that point, the Examinations Division sends your file to the Collections Division. The best way to view the Collections Division is as a collection agency that has only one client—the IRS. The folks who work for the Collections Division—*Revenue Officers*—are bill collectors, pure and simple.

A revenue officer (RO) can't take forever to collect money, but almost forever. The statute of limitations on collections is ten years from the date of assessment. If you can dodge the RO for ten years (or not have any income or property from which to pay the tax), you're home free.

The sad truth is that most people deal with the Collections Division from a position of weakness. The odd thing is that the more assets and/or income you have, the dicier your negotiating position with the IRS becomes, and the less assets and/or income you have, the stronger your negotiating position is. Because most people don't want to have the prospect of IRS liens and levies hanging over their heads for ten years, the first avenue that is usually explored is an Installment Payment Agreement with the IRS.

An Installment Agreement (see Appendix G, Form 433-D) is a contract you enter into with the IRS. It doesn't relieve you of any tax that's been assessed; it just stretches out for a period of months or years the time you have to pay. During that time, the IRS won't undertake any collection activities, provided that you abide by the agreement, that is, you keep paying. The IRS may terminate the agreement if there's a substantial change in your financial position during the payment period. They will learn of the change by requiring you to file updated financial reports, and may terminate the agreement if you fail to do so.

Not only doesn't an Installment Agreement lower the tax bite, it increases it, because you're charged interest on the outstanding debt. In that respect, the IRS becomes your banker. For many years, there was no legal basis for Installment Agreements, and their use varied from IRS district to district. But Congress amended the Tax Code so as to formalize the use of Installment Agreements, in the hope that they will be used more frequently and with greater uniformity. But there's still no guarantee that anyone can get an Installment Agreement with the IRS, and as we shall see shortly, certain people can't qualify.

The Collection Information Statement. In order to enter into an Installment Agreement, two things are necessary: (1) You must be current in filing your tax returns with the IRS; and (2) You'll first have to complete either IRS Form 433-A ("Collection Information Statement for Individuals") or IRS Form 433-B ("Collection Information Statement for Businesses") (see Appendix G). If you operate a business, you must file both forms.

It's impossible to overstate the importance of these two forms. They are used by the RO for two purposes: to determine if the IRS wants to enter into an Installment Agreement with you, and if so, on what terms. Your financial future can depend on how they read these forms; they should be completed with great care.

Many people who aren't represented by CPAs or attorneys have the RO complete the forms for them. That's a terrible mistake. You should complete the form at your convenience, presenting it to the RO at the first meeting, even before you've been asked for it. I've seen the startled look on an RO's face when we whip out the completed form and hand it to him or her about two seconds after my client and I have warmed our chairs. It shifts the dynamic of this all-important meeting from the RO to you. It also shows the RO how serious you are about concluding a deal and getting the taxes paid.

Take a few moments to peruse Forms 433-A and 433-B (Appendix G). Note that you'll need to provide information regarding your assets and your income. The forms need to be completed truth-fully—under penalty of perjury—but they do call for your best estimates of the values of property and your average monthly expenditures. That means that you do have some leeway in com-pleting the forms. If the RO completes the form by asking you oral questions, you have no leeway.

The disclosure of your assets and liabilities will be the most signifi-cant factor in determining whether you get an Installment Agree-ment at all. If the assessment is for $30,000 and your Form 433-A shows you own General Motors stock worth $50,000 that you could sell and reduce to cash in a week, the chance of your getting an Installment Agreement is zero; the RO will demand that you sell the stock and give him or her the cash.

But if the stocks that your Form 433-A discloses aren't listed as tradable securities, they may have little or no market value. ROs often aren't very sophisticated, and your RO may not know the difference between shares sold on the New York Stock Exchange and those traded broker to broker (on the "pink sheets"), where there may be few if any buyers. If the securities you own truly can't be sold, it would help to bring to the meeting a few letters from brokers, explaining that there is no market for the stock.

It can't hurt to do some asset planning before you complete Form 433-A. Any listed stock, CDs, or mutual funds are red flags for the RO, and ROs are trained to look for them. However, they tend not to be so sophisticated when it comes to other investments, such as life insurance.

Note that Forms 433-A and 433-B differ from an accountant's bal-ance sheet in that the IRS forms ask about the current market values of your property, although an accountant's balance sheet discloses only the "historical" cost of your assets—what you originally paid for them. In fact, the RO isn't interested in the fair market value of your assets; he or she is interested in their liquidation value, that is, how much cash your assets could fetch if they were sold.

Let's assume you bought a house two years ago for $300,000 and have a $275,000 mortgage. It's not likely that the RO is going to be too interested in it. If the RO doesn't enter into an Installment Agreement with you, he or she could file a federal tax lien on the house. The RO could seize the house, but by the time foreclosure costs have been paid, there might not be anything left to pay the tax. The RO might also have jeopardized your ability to borrow on the house in a year or two, if it appreciates in value, because you've already been thrown out of your house.

Moreover, there's little need for the RO to foreclose. With every passing year, as you pay off the mortgage, it means that there will be more for him or her when you ultimately sell or he or she later forecloses.

But the situation is different if there's only a $225,000 mortgage on the property. With $75,000 in equity, rather than give you an Installment Agreement, he or she might insist that you take out a second mortgage on the property and give him or her the loan proceeds. The RO might also decide that he or she could sell the house and clear enough cash after the payment of costs to pay off a substantial part of the assessment. If either of these scenarios is a possibility, you need to come prepared. You might provide the RO with letters from a few local lenders saying that you don't have sufficient equity in the house or enough creditworthiness to get any kind of loan on the house. You might also provide a letter from a local realtor saying that even though you bought the house for $300,000, it's now worth only $275,000. That letter will be the justification for the $275,000 "current value" figure you put on the form.

If you do have substantial equity in your home or other real estate, you might want to borrow on it to avoid the filing of a tax lien.

In that case, the existence of the equity becomes your leverage to avoid the filing of a lien. You tell the RO, in so many words, that if he or she holds off on the filing of a lien, you'll be able to get a loan on the property and pay the tax, but that if he or she goes ahead with enforced collection, you'll never be able to borrow any money and the taxes won't get paid.

If the RO is amenable to an Installment Agreement, the terms will be determined by the income and expense items on the form. Basically, the RO wants to know how much you earn every month and what your bare minimum living expenses are. He or she wants the difference. There are certain "expenses" that won't be allowed. For example, if you pay $50 per month for a TV set, the attitude is that there's no way the RO is going to stand in line behind the finance company that sold you the set; he or she would rather you stopped paying the finance company. The RO certainly won't allow the debt you owe your Uncle Charlie, regardless of how valid the debt and how quickly Uncle Charlie will sue you once you stop paying.

Unfortunately, the IRS may not allow all of your legitimate expenses. For example, if your monthly mortgage payment is $2,500, there's no way an RO will give you credit for the whole amount. The prevailing attitude is that if you want an installment agreement, you should first move into less expensive housing. That's why not everyone qualifies for an Installment Agreement.

Most people underestimate their legitimate allowable monthly expenses. For example, your property tax bill may come due only once or twice a year. But you shouldn't forget it when filling out the form. Remember: The smaller the difference between your monthly income and expenses, the lesser will be the amount you'll have to pay the IRS every month.

What if you have no assets that the IRS could go after and no income left after paying all your necessary monthly expenses? Indeed, you may have no income at all, which is why you're sitting in front of an RO in the first place. If the RO sees no assets or income he can go after, he may decide to "53 the file," which is IRS parlance for closing the case. It doesn't relieve you of the tax, it just means that the IRS isn't going to try to do anything for now. (Remember: They have ten years from the date of assessment to collect the money.) Does the prospect of having to "53 the file" anger the RO? Not at all! The RO's main goal is to close cases, and "53ing the file" is a perfect way to close another case and move on to somebody else.

Here's one fact the IRS doesn't advertise: If you promise to pay the tax liability *within three years,* it doesn't really matter what your Form 433-A and/or Form 433-B reveal; the IRS will accept almost any installment agreement that gets the tax paid in that period. Remember, however, that interest keeps running during the three-year period. That could add upwards of another 30 percent to the overall bite.

Offers in Compromise

There's an old saying: "You can't get blood from a turnip." That old saying finds expression in the Internal Revenue Manual, which instructs all ROs to consider an Offer in Compromise when:

> It is unlikely that the tax liability can be collected in full and the amount offered reasonably reflects collection potential . . . The goal is to achieve collection of what is potentially collectable at the earliest possible time and the least cost to the government.

An Offer in Compromise (see Appendix G, Form 656) is a contract you enter into with the government for the payment of a lesser amount of tax, interest, and/or penalties than you otherwise would owe if the IRS were to get 100 cents on the dollar of their assessment. That's what distinguishes an Offer in Compromise from an Installment Agreement, which only stretches out, but doesn't reduce, the amount of tax, interest, and penalties.

However, because an Offer in Compromise reduces the amount you otherwise would owe, they don't throw Offers in Compromise at everyone. In fact, you'll qualify for one only if you fall within an unusual set of circumstances. The IRS will enter into an Offer in Compromise only if they determine that there is either "doubt as to liability" or "doubt as to collectibility."

Let's first consider "doubt as to liability." How can the IRS doubt your liability for the tax, as there's already been an assessment? Don't you already owe it? Yes, you do. But that doesn't necessarily mean that the Tax Court ruled that you owe it. You may simply have ignored the 90-day letter and allowed 90 days to run, at which point the IRS could—and did—make an assessment. But that doesn't mean you still can't pay the tax and sue for a refund. If the tax assessed is the "Trust Fund Recovery Penalty,"[2] you won't have to pay anything more than a nominal amount to get your case into Federal Court. If the examiner's adjustments do not stand up under the cold scrutiny of a judge, there's doubt as to liability.

"Doubt as to collectibility" is just what it says. Even though the IRS has ten years to file liens, levy on wages or bank accounts, and/or seize real estate and other property, they might still not get the assessment paid. If you owe $100,000 in back taxes, and you're not working, don't own a home with any equity, or have any other property, what's the point of chasing you for ten years? Remember the first rule:

> An RO's primary goal is to close cases, not to collect taxes.

---

[2] Formerly known as the "100 percent penalty." If the IRS cannot collect employment taxes from a defunct or insolvent business, they go after the owners and operators of the business.

An Offer in Compromise starts out with the taxpayer making an offer to pay some of the tax now in exchange for the IRS agreeing not to go after the rest. Once the taxpayer pays the agreed-upon amount, the IRS releases any liens or levies it may have previously imposed.

How much do you have to offer for the IRS to go along? It's hard to say. As an absolute minimum, you must offer an amount at least equal to the net equity of your assets as disclosed on your Form 433-A. For example, if your Form 433-A reveals that you have $10,000 in equity in your home and another $5,000 in equity in your car, you must offer at least $15,000 for the IRS to even consider the offer. This reveals that, if anything, Form 433-A is even more important when making an Offer in Compromise than when making an Installment Agreement.

The most important part of Form 433-A is Section V, which asks you to list your monthly income and expenses. If Section V reveals that your allowable expenses are $300 per month less than your monthly income, the Revenue Officer will multiply that net amount by approximately 50 to arrive at an additional amount you should offer. In this case, he'll require you to offer an additional $15,000 (300 × 50). They have very sharp pencils. That's why completing Form 433-A with extreme care can make the difference between getting an offer accepted and having it either rejected or not even reviewed at all.

There's an inherent contradiction in most Offers in Compromise. If you have cash or assets to offer the IRS, why haven't they already gotten their hands on them? Is it because they can't find the assets, or because you're offering assets that aren't yours?

A typical Offer in Compromise goes like this: "I don't have any money or assets to pay the $100,000 in taxes I owe, but I think I can borrow $30,000 from my Uncle Louie. Take $30,000 or chase me forever." Another typical Offer in Compromise goes likes this: "I own property as a tenant by the entirety with my wife. Under the property laws of our state, you can't seize it, because only I owe the tax. But if you let me sell the property I can realize $30,000 from the sale. I'll pay that to you if you drop your claim for the other $70,000."

Making the Offer

Offers in Compromise are filed with the service center that made the assessment. The form asks if the offer is being made because of doubt as to liability or doubt as to collectibility. If it's the former, the Examinations Division will consider the offer, because they're the people who know the tax laws. If it's the latter, the Collections Division will consider it. In either event, you can figure on it taking six months before the offer is accepted or rejected.

If the offer is based on doubt as to liability, you must submit a detailed explanation as to why you don't owe the tax, similar to the protest you file when you get a 30-day letter. If the offer is based on doubt as to collectibility, you should furnish a detailed statement explaining why you don't think the IRS will be able to collect the full amount of the tax in the ten years that they have to collect it. If you own assets that are available to you but not to the IRS (for example, your spouse owns the property), you need to spell that out. Most importantly, you need to complete Form 433-A.

Most ROs will demand more financial information than is required by Form 433-A. For example, you may be asked to submit a current appraisal of real estate, if real estate is a key component of your financial statement.

Making an Offer in Compromise carries with it certain promises you must make to the IRS. If they agree to the offer, you'll be required to file and pay your taxes timely for the next five years. If you don't, they can tear up the deal. You also agree that if the IRS owes you a refund, you agree to waive it.

The Offer as a Delaying Tactic

The Internal Revenue Manual provides that enforced collection efforts—liens and levies—will be stopped while the IRS is considering an Offer in Compromise unless they feel that the offer is a delaying tactic. Nonetheless, an Offer in Compromise is a good way to buy time. Obviously, you don't want to let the RO ever think that you're not serious about the offer, or that you're employing a delaying tactic.

More than as a delaying tactic, an Offer in Compromise serves another purpose. When you're dealing with the Collections Division, it doesn't hurt, and in fact usually helps, to get your case kicked up to the highest possible level. Making an Offer in Compromise is a good way to get your file off the desk of a particularly doltish RO and onto someone else's desk.

What if the Offer Is Rejected?

If the offer is accepted, it becomes public record. That used to present a problem to the IRS if the taxpayer was a famous person, because the IRS didn't want the news to get around that they had accepted less than 100 cents on the dollar. It appears, however, that the potential for adverse publicity no longer impedes the ability to get an offer accepted.

If the RO rejects the offer, you do have the right to appeal the rejection of the District Appeals Office. Unless the rejected offer is the absolute final amount you're able or willing to pay, making another offer may be a more productive use of your time and resources than an appeal of a rejected Offer in Compromise.

Collateral Agreements

Until recently, the IRS required you to enter into a Collateral Agreement whenever you entered into an Offer in Compromise. A Collateral Agreement obligates you to give the IRS an agreed-upon percentage of your income in each of an agreed on number of years. If you default, the original assessment pops back up. Taxpayers who entered into Collateral Agreements were required to submit Form 3439 ("Statement of Annual Income"), the proof of their income every year, directly to the Collections Division. The IRS no longer requires a Collateral Agreement, but you might consider offering one if it's needed to nail down an Offer in Compromise.

THE OMBUDSMAN TO THE RESCUE! (MAYBE)

Let's assume you can't cut a deal with the RO, and he or she is close to seizing some of your property. Let's also assume that the RO can't be made to see that the IRS will be better off giving you some breathing space so that you can pay more of the tax later.

We noted earlier that when you're dealing with the Collections Division, it can't hurt to kick your case up the pecking order as high as you can as fast as you can, so that someone other than the clod you're dealing with gets to review your case. Since 1988, the Tax Code has included a formal way to go over the head of your RO.

In 1989, as part of the Taxpayer Bill of Rights, Congress created the Office of the Ombudsman within the IRS. "Ombudsman" is a Norwegian word and refers to the government official whose job it is to represent the government's "clients," that is, the citizens who deal with the bureaucracy. If the bureaucrats act particularly venal, the Ombudsman is supposed to intercede on the citizen's behalf.

Taxpayer Assistance Orders

That's how it's supposed to work with the IRS. If the Ombudsman determines that an action that the IRS has taken or is about to take has or will create a significant hardship, then the Ombudsman may issue a Taxpayer Assistance Order (TAO) reversing or delaying the action that has or is about to take place. The action that is most likely to cause a "significant hardship" is a levy on wages.

12

A Final Review

It's easy to lose the forest for the trees. By getting too caught up in the technicalities and the minutiae, we can lose sight of the big picture. So let's review, concentrating on how all the pieces fit together.

THE PREREQUISITE OF A JUDGMENT

Before a creditor can obtain your assets, the creditor must first bring a suit against you. He or she must succeed in proving that you are liable, and that success allows the creditor to obtain a judgment. Even if the creditor has a secured debt, such as a mortgage, the creditor must first bring a suit to foreclose on his or her security. Without a judgment, the creditor is nowhere.

If you're the debtor and a judgment is entered against you, the judgment is in your name. Of all the property in the world, the creditor can go after only those assets that are in your name. In certain instances, the creditor can go after property that isn't titled in your name if the creditor can prove that you, the debtor, own an interest in it. For example, if you live in a community property state, an asset may not be in your name, but if it's community property, you own half of it, and the creditor can take it all. We can solve that problem by removing residents of community property states from the community property law by signing and recording a transmutation agreement. But generally, a creditor can only go after assets that are titled in the name of the judgment debtor.

But if assets aren't titled in your name, the creditor has lots of problems. A lien that attaches to all of the assets of the judgment debtor won't attach to property not titled in the name of the debtor. If the creditor has a judgment, he or she can instruct the sheriff or the marshal to take all the property that the judgment debtor owns. But the sheriff isn't likely to take assets that somebody else owns, and there's no way that the sheriff is going to try to sort out which property not titled in the judgment debtor's name is really owned by the debtor.

Result: The hallmark of asset protection is to have as little property as possible titled in your own name, and as much as possible that is titled in the name of someone else. But that "someone else" must be a "person" over whom you have some control or influence, whether that "person" is your spouse, a trust, a limited liability company, a family limited partnership, or a foreign trust that combines the best features of two or three of these "persons."

THE FRAUDULENT CONVEYANCE TRAP

Transferring assets from yourself to someone (or something) you control isn't as easy as it sounds. If you do it too late, a transfer that leaves a creditor holding the bag is likely to be deemed a fraudulent conveyance. If it is a fraudulent conveyance, a creditor can ignore the transfer and go against the transferee. One of the principal advantages of a Foreign Asset Protection Trust (FAPT) is that most of the sting associated with a fraudulent conveyance is removed. If you "flunk" the tests to determine if there has been a fraudulent conveyance, it means that the creditor can sue the transferee. But that's small consolation to the creditor if the transferee is a trust company located in the Cook Islands. If the creditor does sue the transferee, he or she will have to haul all of the evidence and witnesses 4,000 miles away, to a land that gives no credence whatever to U.S. judgments and that has its own very limited fraudulent conveyance law.

Unfortunately, most people don't think of asset protection until it's too late; in other words, until transferring an asset would likely be a fraudulent conveyance. When is it "too late?" After a lawsuit is threatened is probably too late. After a lawsuit is filed is certainly too late.

Even if you're one of the few with the foresight to protect your assets before creditors come calling, a transfer can still be deemed to be fraudulent if it carries with it too many Badges of Fraud. That means that the transfers must be open and aboveboard. No matter what we do, we'll do it on the assumption that our creditors will one day learn of it, because they'll have the right to ask. It also means that we won't transfer everything. We'll leave enough so that we're not insolvent after the transfer. It's hard to explain why you transferred so many assets that you couldn't pay your bills; people might conclude that you transferred the assets in order to defeat your creditors.

The best way to prevent a transfer from being considered a fraudulent conveyance is to show the creditor (and the judge) that you received something in return. Thus, the transfer of assets into a corporation might make it far more difficult for a creditor to get his hands on the assets, but the transfer shouldn't be considered fraudulent. After all, you received something in return—the corporate stock. The same should hold true of a transfer of assets to a limited liability company (LLC) in exchange for an LLC membership interest, or the transfer of assets to a family limited partnership in exchange for a partnership interest.

STATUTORY EXEMPTIONS

Certain assets come wrapped in their own asset protection plan. If you're fortunate enough to be a beneficiary of a "qualified" profit sharing plan, all of the cash that's in that plan is safe from the clutches of your creditors. If you're lucky enough to live in a state that has a generous (or, in the case of Florida and Texas, unlimited) homestead exemption, you don't need to worry about a creditor selling your home on the auction block to satisfy a debt.

Aggressive asset protection planning means more than hoping passively that more rather than less of your wealth will be shielded by statutory exemptions. We need to ascertain what the exemptions are and maximize their use. An exemption unused is an exemption wasted, and is free money to a creditor who can get at unshielded assets. Maximizing your exemptions should never be considered a fraudulent conveyance, because you're not transferring your assets to anyone else.

EVERYONE IS DIFFERENT

It should be obvious by now, but we'll restate it for emphasis: The asset protection plan that is appropriate for one person may be completely inappropriate for someone else. Let's review just some of the variables that come into play in selecting an asset protection plan:

- *Single or married?* A married person has the ability to shield assets in the name of his or her spouse, provided that the spouse doesn't have exposure to creditors. Obviously, a single person has no such ability.

- *Community property or separate property state?* If you're married and asset protection is your goal, it becomes very important to determine whether you live in a separate property or a community property state. If your state has community property, a transmutation agreement removing you from the purview of the community property law should be considered. If your home state has separate property, it most likely recognizes tenancy by entireties for real estate. But does it recognize tenancy by entireties for personal property?

- *Stable marriage?* If you've been married ten weeks, you might not transfer your assets to your spouse as readily as someone who has been married ten years.

- *How large is the estate?* You might be enamored with the thought of setting up a trust in the Cayman Islands and visiting your trustee once or twice a year. You might be less enthralled with a foreign trust after you learn what the trust will cost, first to set up and then to maintain every year. We try to dissuade anyone with an estate worth less than $1 million from setting up a foreign trust.

- *What are the assets?* Assume two unmarried people, John and Joe, both aged 32, both residing in Rhode Island, and both having an estate worth exactly $2 million. So far it sounds as if the asset protection planning we'll do for them will be fairly similar. Let's add one fact: John's $2 million estate is entirely cash. Joe's $2 million is entirely real estate. Real estate differs from every other asset in one respect: It's immovable. You can move cash, a stock portfolio, or even a business to the Isle of Man. But you can't move the real estate. We can change the titles, so that the ownership moves to the Isle of Man, but we'll never move the real estate itself.

- *What are the exemptions?* Let's change one fact. Joe doesn't live in Rhode Island. He lives in Florida, a state with an unlimited homestead exemption. If Joe builds a home on his real estate, he may not need any further asset protection.

We've just listed six obvious variables. There are countless more. When you realize that there are two possible marital conditions and 50 states, that's at least 100 permutations right there. Within the six variables listed above, there are at least 600 different permutations, resulting in 600 different asset protection plans.

If everyone is different, how is it that people can sell family limited partnerships through the newspaper, or market foreign asset protection trusts through seminars? The answer is that they can't, unless they're more interested in selling off-the-shelf "products" than they are in assisting their clients.

DO IT EARLY (ONE LAST TALE FROM REAL LIFE)

A few years ago, a man appeared in my office eager to set up an FAPT. If I could have fished one out of my desk drawer and typed in his name, he would have signed it on the spot. He had been referred to me by his friend, who already had one, and he wanted one too. Here's why he was so desperate to move his assets offshore.

He owned two shopping centers. One had a $1 million mortgage, but was worth nothing. Its value had plummeted from more than $1 million (his purchase price) to nothing due to a little environmental contamination problem that caused all the tenants to move out and that rendered the property unsalable at any price. He literally couldn't give it away, because anyone accepting this "gift" might find him- or herself paying far more in required cleanup costs than could ever be recouped.

His second shopping center was just the opposite. It was also worth about $1 million, but it had no mortgage. It was free and clear.

Because the tenants had moved out of the first shopping center, he couldn't service the mortgage, which meant that the bank had already begun foreclosure proceedings. He didn't care about that, because he would be delighted to give the bank the property. He was concerned about the $1 million judgment he'd be faced with after the bank foreclosed the worthless property. Where would they then turn? To the second shopping center. That's why our friend was starting to think seriously about the Cook Islands.

Did I establish an FAPT for our friend? Not a chance. The transaction would have been the world's most blatant fraudulent conveyance, obviously done solely to hinder, delay, and defeat a known creditor. The bank might not have been able to get anything from our friend, but they wouldn't have needed to. They would have been able to get everything from me, for having aided and abetted a fraudulent conveyance.

And so we repeat for one final time: The time to do your asset protection planning is *before* the creditors come calling, not after.

Appendix A: A Model Transmutation Agreement

TRANSMUTATION AGREEMENT

This conveyance establishes sole and separate property of a spouse, R&T 11911.

THIS AGREEMENT, made and entered into this 14th day of February, 1995.

RECITALS:

WHEREAS, John Brown (hereinafter ''husband'') and Lydia Brown (hereinafter ''wife,'') are husband and wife; and

WHEREAS, during the course of their marriage they have acquired numerous items of real and personal property with their combined funds, and

WHEREAS, the undersigned desire that all of their present or hereafter-acquired property be their separate property,

NOW, THEREFORE, the undersigned stipulate and agree as follows:

1. **Purpose.** The parties to this Agreement intend merely to define and clarify their respective property interests existing at the time of execution of this Agreement, and also to transmute the character of some of their present and after-acquired property from community property to their respective separate property.

This Agreement is not made in contemplation of a separation or dissolution.

2. **Transmutation of Community Property to Separate Property.**

(a) Wife hereby agrees to release, waive and quitclaim any and all of Wife's present or after-acquired interest in and to those assets described in Exhibit ''A'', attached hereto and incorporated herein by this reference, and to transmute the character of all of the assets described in Exhibit ''A'' from community property to the separate property of Husband. Wife understands that hereafter Wife shall have no interest of any kind in and to Husband's interest in the assets described in Exhibit ''A'' of any kind, which shall for all purposes be the sole and separate property of Husband.

Wife understands that some of the assets described in Exhibit ''A'' represent interests in various corporations. Wife understands that in waiving and releasing her rights in and to said interests, she is also waiving and releasing any and all voting rights and other rights conferred to a shareholder by statute.

Wife further understands that the aggregate of fair market value of all of the assets described in Exhibit ''A'' is greater than the aggregate of fair market value of assets described in Exhibit ''B''. Wife agrees that the allocation of assets is fair and reasonable, in that the assets allocated to Husband are (i) inherently illiquid, representing the stock or closely-held corporations, and (ii) are minority interests, subject to the management rights of others.

(b) Husband hereby agrees to release, waive and quitclaim any and all of Husband's present or after-acquired interest in and to those assets described in Exhibit ''B'', attached hereto and incorporated herein by this reference, and to transmute the character of all of the assets described in Exhibit ''B'' from community property to the separate property of Wife. Husband understands that hereafter Husband shall have no interest of any kind in and to Wife's interest in the assets described in Exhibit ''B'' of any kind, which shall for all purposes be the sole and separate property of Wife.

(c) Husband and Wife hereby agree that any and all dividends, interest, cash, stock or property distributions, properties received by way of exchange, gains, losses and other benefits accruing to either the Husband or Wife from any of the assets described in either Exhibit ''A'' or Exhibit ''B'' shall be the sole and separate property of the Husband or Wife, as the case may be.

3. **Transmutation of After-Acquired Property.** The parties hereto stipulate and agree that any and all property, assets, rights, debts, duties and obligations, whether real or personal, tangible or intangible, regardless of how designated, hereafter acquired, shall not become the community property of the parties hereto, but shall be the sole and separate property of the party who acquires said property or in whose name said property is titled. In the event that a property right of any kind is titled in the name of one of the parties hereto, then such title shall constitute an irrebuttable presumption that such property or property right is the sole and separate property of the party in whom such property right is titled. The foregoing statement is intended to serve as an express declaration by both of the parties hereto for the purposes of Section 5110.730 of the California Civil Code.

4. **Community Nature of Salaries.** All of the foregoing notwithstanding, the parties hereto stipulate
and agree that the wages, salaries, commissions, bo-
nuses and other emoluments directly attributable to
the employment of one of the parties hereto shall remain their community property.

5. **Release of Marital Rights to Separate Property.**

(a) The parties mutually agree to waive and release any and all equitable or legal claims and
rights, actual, inchoate, or contingent which he or
she might acquire in the separate property of the
other by reason of their marriage, including but not
limited to:

(1) The right to a family allowance;

(2) The right to a probate homestead;

(3) The right to claims of dower, curtesy or
any statutory substitutes provided by the laws of the
state in which the parties or either of them die domiciled or in which they own real property;

(4) The right to take against the will of the
other;

(5) The right to a distributive share in the
estate of the other should he or she die intestate;

(6) The right to declare a homestead in the
separate property of another;

(7) The right to act as administrator of the
other.

(b) Nothing in this Agreement shall be deemed to constitute a waiver by either party of any bequest or devise that the other party may choose to make to him or her by will or codicil. However, the parties acknowledge that neither of them have made promises of any kind to the other regarding any bequests or devises.

6. **Execution of Other Documents.** Each party agrees, upon the request of the other, to execute, deliver, and properly acknowledge whatever additional instruments may be required to carry out the intention of this Agreement and to execute, deliver and properly acknowledge any deeds or other documents in order that good and marketable title to any separate property can be conveyed by one party free from any claim of the other party acquired by him or her by reason of marriage.

7. **Representation by Separate Counsel.** The parties acknowledge that they have had the opportunity to be represented by separate counsel in the negotiations leading up to this Agreement, and in the execution of this Agreement.

8. **Governing Law.** This Agreement shall be governed by the laws of the State of California.

Dated:

_____   _____

John Brown   Lydia Brown

State of California   )
) ss.
County of Los Angeles)

On _____, 199__, before me, _____, a Notary

Public in and for said County and State, personally appeared John Brown and Lydia personally known to me or proved to me on the basis of satisfactory evidence to be the person(s) whose names are subscribed to the within instrument, and acknowledged to me that they executed the same in their authorized capacities, and that by their signatures on the instrument the persons or the entities upon behalf of which the persons acted, executed the instrument.

WITNESS my hand and official seal.

Signature: _____

Exhibit ''A''

1. All of Wife's interest in and to the stock of XYZ, Inc., a California corporation, being an interest in Twenty Percent (20%) of all of the issued and out-standing stock of XYZ, Inc., having an agreed-upon value of $3,000,000.

2. All of Wife's interest in and to ABC Investment Co., a California limited partnership, being a 12.5% interest in the capital of said partnership, having an agreed-upon value of $1,000,000.

Exhibit ''B''

1. All of Husband's interest in and to the following parcels of real property:

   a. Lot 44 of Tract No. 44481, in the City of Beverly Hills, County of Los Angeles, State of California, as per map recorded in Book 644 Pages 30 to 32 inclusive of maps, in the office of the County Recorder of said county.

    b. Lot 48 of Tract No. 21154, in the City of Los Angeles, County of Los Angeles, State of California, as per map recorded in Book 76, Pages 89 to 91 inclusive of maps, in the office of the County Recorder of said county.

2. All of Husband's interest in and to the stock of SOS, Inc., a California corporation, being Ten Percent (10%) of all of the issued and outstanding stock of SOS, Inc., having an agreed-upon value of $400,000.

3. All of Husband's interest in and to the stock of Front Property Investment, Inc., a California corporation, being Twenty Percent (20%) of all of the issued and outstanding stock of Front Property Investment, Inc., having an agreed-upon value of $300,000.

4. All of Husband's interest in the Merrill-Lynch account #24-667891.

Appendix B:
A Model Family
Limited Partnership

ARTICLES OF
THE BROWN FAMILY LIMITED PARTNERSHIP
AN ILLINOIS LIMITED PARTNERSHIP

THESE ARTICLES OF LIMITED PARTNERSHIP are entered into as of this _____ day of December, 1995, by and between Lydia Brown, the initial General Partner, and those persons listed in Schedule ''A'', attached hereto and incorporated herein by reference who are the initial Limited Partners of The Brown Family Limited Partnership, an Illinois limited partnership, [hereinafter referred to as the ''Partnership''].

In consideration of the mutual covenants and promises set forth in this agreement the Partners agree as follows:

ARTICLE I

GENERAL

1.1 <u>Formation</u>. The Partnership was created, or contemporaneously with the execution of this instrument will be created, pursuant to the laws of the State of Illinois. The Partnership was or will be formed upon the filing with the Illinois Secretary of State of the Partnership's duly executed Certificate of Limited Partnership. The Partners thereafter shall, from time to time, execute such further documents and take such further action as shall be deemed appropriate by the General Partner to comply with the requirements of law for the formation and operation of a limited partnership in all other counties, states, or other jurisdictions where the Partnership may elect to do business.

1.2 <u>Name</u>. The name of the Partnership shall be The Brown Family Limited Partnership.

1.3 <u>Location of the Principal Place of Business; Registered Agent and Office</u>. The principal place of business and registered office of the Partnership shall be at 20 N. Main Dr., Chicago, IL. 60601, or such other address within the State of Illinois as from time to time selected by the General Partner. The registered agent of the Partnership shall be Lydia Brown. If the General Partner changes the name of the registered agent and/or registered office, she shall notify the Partners.

1.4 <u>Records to be Kept at Registered Office</u>. The Partnership shall continuously maintain at its registered office all of the following:

(a) A current list of the full name and last known business or residence address of each Partner together with the contribution and the share in profits and losses of each Partner.

(b) The names and addresses of each person acting as a custodian, guardian or other fiduciary of the minor Limited Partner.

(c) A copy of the Certificate and Articles of Limited Partnership and all amendments thereto, together with any powers of attorney pursuant to which the articles of organization or any amendments thereto were executed.

(d) Copies of the Partnership's federal, state and local income tax or information returns and reports, if any, for the six most recent taxable years.

(e) Copies of the Partnership's financial statements for the six most recent fiscal years.

(f) The books and records of the Partnership as they relate to the internal affairs of the Partnership for at least the current and the four most recent fiscal years.

(g) In the event that the Partnership at any time owns an interest in real property, upon the request of an assessor, the Partnership shall make available, at the Partnership's registered office, a true copy of the business records relevant to the amount, cost, and value of all property that the Partnership owns, claims, possesses or controls within the county.

1.5 <u>Term</u>. The term of this Partnership shall commence on the date of filing of the Certificate of Limited Partnership with the Illinois Secretary of State, and shall continue until any of the following:

(a) December 31, 2029;

(b) Upon the death, withdrawal, resignation, expulsion, bankruptcy, or dissolution of a Partner, unless the business of the Partnership is continued by a vote of all of the remaining Partners within 90 days of the happening of that event;

(c) the entry of a decree of dissolution of the Partnership.

ARTICLE II

PARTNERS

2.1 <u>Nature of Interest</u>. A Partnership interest in the Partnership shall constitute the personal property of the Partner or assignee. A Partner or assignee has no interest in the specific Partnership property.

2.2 <u>Admission of Partners to Partnership</u>. Any person or entity other than the persons or entities listed in Schedule A shall become a Partner upon the affirmative vote of all of the Partners. In the event such person or entity is admitted as a Partner in the Partnership, such Partner shall become a party to these Articles of Limited Partnership, and shall have the same rights, duties, obligations and benefits of existing Partners.

2.3 <u>Assignment of a Partner's Interest</u>. Except as provided in Section 2.4, hereinbelow, a Partner may assign his interest in the Partnership, <u>provided that</u> the Partner shall first have received the written consent of all of the other Partners to the assignment. An assignee who has become a Partner has, to the extent assigned, the rights and powers, and is subject to the restrictions and liabilities, of a Partner under this Agreement and under the Act. However, an assignee is not obligated for liabilities unknown to the assignee at the time the assignee became a Partner and that could not be ascertained from the Articles of Limited Partnership.

2.4 <u>No Involuntary Assignments</u>. No person shall accede to the rights of any Partner hereto except upon the voluntary assignment of a Partner's rights, and the unanimous written consent of said assignment, pursuant to the provisions of Section 2.3, hereinabove. In the event any person or entity (herein referred to as the ''Involuntary Assignee'') accedes to the interest of a Partner as a result of the execution of a judgment, levy, seizure or other involuntary means, the Involuntary Assignee shall obtain only the distributive rights of such Partner. A court may charge the Partnership interest of the Partner with payment of the unsatisfied debt. However, upon receipt of any such charging order, the General Partner or Partner receiving such charging order shall notify the other Partners, in which event:

(a) No distribution otherwise required to be made to the Partner shall be made to the Partner or to the Involuntary Assignee; and

(b) The Involuntary Assignee shall offer the interest of the Partner to the Partnership, and the Partnership may, but shall not be required to, acquire the interest held by the Involuntary Assignee. The consideration that the Partnership shall pay to the Involuntary Assignee for the Partner's interest shall be the lesser of (i) the fair market value of the Partner's interest, determined by a qualified appraiser selected by the Partnership and the Involuntary Assignee, or (ii) the book value of the Partner's pro rata interest in the assets of the Partnership.

2.5 Death or Incompetency of a Partner. If a Partner who is an individual dies or is adjudged by a court of competent jurisdiction to be incompetent to manage the Partner's person or property, the Partner's executor, administrator, guardian, conservator or other legal representative may exercise all of the Partner's right for the purpose of settling the Partner's estate or administering the Partner's property, including any power the Partner had under this Agreement to give an assignee the right to become a Partner.

ARTICLE III

CAPITAL ACCOUNTS; CAPITAL CONTRIBUTIONS

3.1 Initial Capital Contributions. Each of the initial Partners shall make, or have already made, those initial capital contributions to the Partnership listed beside their names in Schedule A, attached hereto. After a Partner has made a contribution to the capital of the Partnership and has become a Partner, said Partner shall have no right to withdraw his capital contribution.

3.2 <u>Additional Capital Contributions</u>. No Partner shall be required to contribute additional capital to the Partnership at any time during the term of the Partnership, and no Partner shall suffer any penalty for failure to make voluntary contributions to the capital of the Partnership. The foregoing notwithstanding, in the event that any Partner makes additional voluntary contributions to the Partnership, which contributions shall be only for a valid purpose related to the Partnership's business, then upon the sale of any Partnership assets, any Net Capital Gain from the sale of Partnership assets shall be first allocated and distributed to those Partners who made voluntary capital contributions to the extent of those voluntary contributions, before Net Capital Gains are allocated to other Partners in accordance with their Partnership interests. A voluntary contribution of capital to the Partnership shall not otherwise result in an increase in the interest of a Partner in the Partnership owned by the Partner having made such voluntary contribution, or in an increase in such Partner's right to allocations and distributions of Partnership Cash Flow, or annual income.

3.3 <u>Establishment of Capital Accounts</u>. A capital account shall be established for each Partner. The account shall be credited with the amount of each Partner's capital contributions, including voluntary capital contributions, a) increased by: (i) his share of Partnership taxable Net Income and Net Gain and (ii) his share of Partnership income and gain not included in (i), and (b) decreased by Partnership distributions to him, (ii) his share of Partnership tax deductions and tax losses, and (iii) his share of expenses not included in (ii).

3.3.1 Special Allocations.

(a) Except as provided in Section 3.3.1(b) hereof, in the event any Partner unexpectedly receives any adjustments, allocations or distributions described in paragraphs (4), (5) and (6) of Treasury Regulations Section 1.704-1(b)(2)(ii)(d), items of Partnership income and gain shall be specially allocated to such Partner in an amount and manner sufficient to eliminate, to the extent required in the Regulations, the Adjusted Capital Account deficit of such Partner as quickly as possible. This Section 3.1.1(a) is intended to constitute a ''qualified income offset'' provision described in Treasury Regulations Section 1.704-1(b)(2)(ii)(d) and shall be interpreted consistently therewith.

(b) Notwithstanding any other provision of this Article III, if there is a net decrease in the Partnership's Minimum Gain during any Partnership fiscal year, each Partner who would otherwise have an Adjusted Capital Account Deficit at the end of such year shall be specially allocated items of Partnership income and gain for such year (and, if necessary, subsequent years) in an amount and manner sufficient to eliminate such adjusted Capital Account Deficit as quickly as possible. The items to be so allocated shall be determined in accordance with Treasury Regulations Section 1.704-1(b)(4)(iv)(e). This Section 3.1.1(b) is intended to constitute a ''minimum gain chargeback'' provision within the meaning of such Section of the Treasury Regulations and shall be interpreted consistently therewith.

3.3.3 The provisions of subsections 3.3.1 and 3.3.2 notwithstanding, the General Partner or the Partners, acting unanimously upon the written advice of counsel, may refuse to allocate in accordance with a Minimum Gain Chargeback and/or Qualified Income Offset if in their discretion an alternative allocation would have ''substantial economic effect'' for federal income tax purposes.

3.3.4 Upon dissolution of the Partnership:

(a) the Partnership will be dissolved and its assets shall be distributed as follows:

(1) all of the Partnership's debts and liabilities to persons other than the Partners shall be paid and discharged;

(2) all of the Partnership's debts and liabilities to the Partners shall be paid and discharged;

(3) the net assets of the Partnership shall be distributed to those Partners who have positive capital account balances, in accordance with the ratio of Partners' total capital account balances;

(b) In no event shall any Partner be required to restore any deficit capital account upon the dissolution of the Partnership.

ARTICLE IV

PARTNERSHIP ALLOCATIONS

4.1 Allocations According to Partners' Capital Contributions. Subject to the provisions of Section 3.2 relating to voluntary capital contributions, Partners will be allocated Net Income or Loss from Partnership operations and Net Gain and Loss from the sale or exchange of Partnership assets in accordance with each Partner's percentage of total Partners' capital contributions.

    4.2 <u>Determination of Share in Event of Transfer</u>. All items of income, gain, loss, deduction or credit (other than those attributable to the sale, exchange, refinancing or other disposition of any or all of the Property) for a calendar year allocable to any Partner which may have been transferred during the year shall be allocated between the transferor and transferee based upon the period of days that each was a Partner, without regard to the actual results of Partnership operations during any particular period and without regard to whether cash distributions were made to the transferor or transferee during any particular period.

ARTICLE V

MANAGEMENT

    5.1 <u>Management Rights Vested in General Partner</u>. The right to operate the Partnership shall be vested in the General Partner. The Initial General Partner shall be Lydia Brown. The General Partner shall have the power and authority to perform the following duties:

        (a) obtain and pay for out of Partnership funds the preparation of required Partnership tax returns;

        (b) maintain accounts in banking institutions or savings and loan associations whose deposits are insured by an agency of the United States Government or the State of Illinois or purchase certificates of deposit, money market fund securities or similar securities;

     (c) pay the obligations of the Partnership and collect obligations owed to the Partnership;

     (d) perform normal administrative and ministerial acts;

     (e) furnish financial statements to the Partners at such time and in such form as the General Partner shall deem appropriate;

     (f) maintain reserves for the purpose of paying property taxes, insurance costs, mortgage installments, and any and all other types of costs or expenses as required or desired by the General Partner;

     (g) employ accountants, legal counsel, managing agents, or other experts to perform services for the Partnership and compensate them from Partnership funds;

     (h) borrow money and incur secured and unsecured indebtedness on behalf of the Partnership and execute on behalf of the Partnership (without obligation on third party's part for inquiry as to actual authority or as to disposition of funds) all contracts, leases, notes, mortgages, deeds, evidences of indebtedness or security agreements;

     (i) purchase, trade, lease, liquidate and sell the Property of the Partnership upon such terms, conditions and prices as the General Partner deems acceptable;

     (j) enter into any and all other agreements on behalf of the Partnership;

(k) make those accounting decisions the General Partner deems in the best interest of the Partnership.

5.2 <u>Form of Execution of Documents</u>. Any document or instrument, of any and every nature, including without limitation, any agreement, contract, deed, promissory note, mortgage or deed of trust, security agreement, financing statement, pledge, assignment, bill of sale and certificate, which is intended to bind the Partnership or convey or encumber title to its real or personal property shall be valid and binding for all purposes if executed by the General Partner.

5.2.1 The General Partner shall be entitled to reasonable compensation for acting as General Partner. A General Partner shall be entitled to reimbursement for his or her actual expenses incurred in carrying out his or her duties as General Partner.

5.3 <u>Indemnification</u>. The Partnership shall indemnify and defend any Partner against any and all judgments, claims, suits, liabilities, expenses, costs and damages arising out of or incident to a person's status or actions as a Partner, other than those arising out of the intentional conduct or fraud of said Partner. The foregoing indemnification shall not extend to any suit brought by the Partnership against any Partner.

5.4 <u>Limitations on General Partner's Authority</u>. The General Partners shall not have authority to:

(a) do any act which would make it impossible to carry on the ordinary business of the Partnership;

(b) confess a judgment against the Partnership;

(c) sell, pledge, refinance or exchange all or substantially all of the assets of the Partnership, without the affirmative vote of Limited Partners owning a majority in interest of the outstanding Units; and

(d) dissolve the Partnership without the prior affirmative vote of Limited Partners owning two thirds in interest of the outstanding Unit.

5.5 Limited Partners.

(a) No Limited Partner shall take part in the management of the Partnership business, transact any business for the Partnership, or have the power to bind the Partnership. No Limited Partner shall be personally liable for the debts of the Partnership nor for any of the losses thereof beyond the amount of required capital contributions and his share of the undistributed profits of the Partnership. The General Partner may from time to time seek suggestions and expressions of opinion from the Limited Partners on major policy decisions, but need not accept such suggestions or expressions, and at all times the control and management of the Partnership shall rest solely with the General Partner.

(b) A Limited Partner may loan money to or act as surety for the Partnership and shall have the same rights and obligations with respect thereto as a person who is not a Partner.

5.6 No Regular Meetings. There shall be no required periodic or annual meetings of the Partners, and no inference of any kind shall be drawn from the failure of the Partners of the Partnership to conduct a meeting. However, meetings of the Partners to vote upon any matters as to which the Limited Partners are authorized to take action under this Agreement may be called at any time by the General Partner or by one or more Limited Partners holding more than 10% of the outstanding Units by delivering written notice, either in person or by registered mail, of such call to a General Partner. Within 10 days following receipt of such request, the General Partner shall cause a written notice, either in person or by registered mail, to be given to the Limited Partners entitled to vote at such meeting that a meeting will be held at a time and place fixed by the General Partner, convenient to the Limited Partners, which is not less than 15 days nor more than 60 days after the giving of notice of the meeting. Included with the notice of a meeting shall be a detailed statement of the action proposed, including a verbatim statement of the wording of any resolution proposed for adoption by the Limited Partners and of any proposed amendment to this Agreement. There shall be deemed to be a quorum at any meeting of the Partnership at which Limited Partners attending such meeting own a majority of the outstanding Units. The General Partner shall be entitled to notice of and to attend all meetings of the Limited Partners, regardless of whether called by the General Partner.

5.6.1 Voting Rights of Limited Partners. No Limited Partner, as such, shall take part in the management of, or transact any business for, the Partnership, nor have the power to sign for or bind the Partnership to any agreement or document. Notwithstanding the foregoing, a majority in interest of the Limited Partners may, without the concurrence of a General Partner vote to:

(a) Amend this Agreement subject to the conditions that such amendment:

(1) may not in any manner allow the Limited Partners to take part in the control of the Partnership's business, and

(2) may not, without the consent of the General Partner, alter the rights, powers and duties of the General Partner, the interest of the General Partner in profits or losses or;

(b) dissolve the Partnership;

(c) remove a General Partner;

5.6.2 <u>Conditions To Action By Limited Partners</u>. The right of the Limited Partners to vote to amend this Agreement, to dissolve the Partnership, and to remove the General Partner, and elect a replacement therefor shall not come into existence or be effective in any manner unless and until:

(a) the Partnership has received an opinion of counsel, which counsel is satisfactory to a majority in interest of the Limited Partners as to the legality of such action; and

(b) either

(1) the Partnership has received an opinion of counsel, which counsel is satisfactory to a majority in interest of the Limited Partners, that such action may be effected without subjecting the Limited Partners to liability as general partners under the Uniform Limited Partnership Act of the State of Illinois or under the laws of such other jurisdiction in which the Partnership is formed or qualified; or

(2) an Illinois court having original jurisdiction in the premises has entered a judgment to the foregoing effect; and

(c) either

(1) the Partnership has received an opinion of counsel, which counsel is satisfactory to a majority in interest of the Limited Partners, that such action may be effected without changing the Partnership's status for tax purposes; or

(2) either a court having original jurisdiction has entered a judgment, or the Internal Revenue Service has issued a ruling, to the foregoing effect.

For purposes of this Article 8.3, counsel will be deemed satisfactory to the Limited Partners if proposed by the General Partner and affirmatively approved in writing within 45 days by a majority in interest of the Limited Partners; provided that the holders of a majority or more of the outstanding Partnership interests propose counsel for this purpose, such proposed counsel, and not such approval by the Limited Partners.

5.7 Reports to Partners. The General Partner shall prepare and shall make available to each Partner on or before March 15th of each year, the federal income tax information return of the Partnership for the preceding fiscal year, showing the distributive share of each item of income, gain or loss, deduction or credit which a Partner is required to take into account separately on his individual federal income tax return. The General Partner shall also furnish to any Partner, at the Partner's expense, such other reports on the Partnership's operations and conditions as he may reasonably request.

(a) In addition to the foregoing, the General Partner shall cause information reports to be mailed

to all the Partners at reasonable intervals during
each year.

ARTICLE VI

ARBITRATION OR LITIGATION

6.1 <u>Option to Arbitrate</u>. At his or its option,
any party may submit any controversy, claim or matter
of difference (''Controversy'') to arbitration (''Arbitration'') by filing a written demand pursuant to the
provisions of this Article VI or commence an action
(''Litigation'') in accordance with the applicable
rules of civil procedure in any court of law having
jurisdiction over the parties and the subject matter
of such Controversy. If a party submits a Controversy
to Arbitration through written demand, then during the
pendency of the Arbitration between the parties, any
Controversy which cannot be resolved by the parties
may be submitted to Arbitration, but may not be the
subject of Litigation. If a party shall commence Litigation prior to the effective date of any demand for
Arbitration, then during the pendency of the Litigation between the parties, any Controversy which cannot
be resolved by the parties may be the subject of Litigation but may not be submitted to Arbitration. If a
party has submitted the Controversy to Arbitration and
the responding party has a claim which would be considered a compulsory cross-complaint under Code of
Civil Procedure the responding party shall assert the
compulsory counterclaim in the Arbitration proceeding
or it shall be deemed waived.

6.2 <u>Scope</u>. Without limiting the generality of the
foregoing, the following shall be considered Controversies for this purpose:

(a) All questions relating to the breach of
any obligation or condition of this agreement;

(b) All questions relating to any representations, negotiations and other proceedings leading to the execution of this agreement;

(c) Failure of any party to deny or reject a claim or demand of any other party; and

(d) All questions as to whether a right to arbitrate exists.

6.3 <u>Place</u>. If a Controversy is submitted to Arbitration the proceedings shall be conducted in Chicago, Illinois, according to the rules and practices of the American Arbitration Association from time to time in force, except that: (i) if such rules and practices shall conflict with the Code of Civil Procedure or any other provisions of Illinois law then in force, such Illinois rules and laws shall govern; and (ii) all parties shall be entitled to discovery concerning the Controversy to the same extent as permitted by the California Rules of Civil Procedure then in effect.

6.4 <u>Time Limits</u>. Arbitration of any Controversy shall be initiated by delivery to the other party of a written demand that Arbitration commence. Such demand must be made within a reasonable period of time after the Controversy arises, but in no event shall the Controversy be submitted to Arbitration if the date of delivery of the demand for Arbitration is not within the time limit of the California or Federal Statute of Limitations which would be applicable if the Controversy were asserted in Litigation. Arbitration may proceed in the absence of any party if demand for the proceedings has been given to such party.

6.5 <u>Awards</u>. Any Arbitration award shall be final and binding on all parties to an extent and in the manner provided by the Code of Civil Procedure. All awards may be filed with the clerk of one or more courts, state or federal, having jurisdiction over the party against whom such an award is rendered or his property, as a basis of judgment and of the issuance of execution for its collection. No party shall be considered in default under this agreement during the pendency of Arbitration proceedings relating to such default.

6.6 <u>Attorney's Fees; Costs</u>. If Arbitration or Litigation is brought for the enforcement of this agreement, or because of an alleged dispute, breach, default or misrepresentation in connection with any of the provisions of this agreement, the successful or prevailing party shall be entitled to recover reasonable attorney's fees and other costs incurred in that action or proceeding, in addition to any other relief to which it may be entitled.

ARTICLE VII

NOTICES

7.1 <u>Method for Notices</u>. All notices provided for in this agreement shall be sent by certified or regular mail addressed as set forth below. Notice shall be effective when deposited in the U.S. Mails, postage prepaid.

7.2 <u>Computation of Time</u>. In computing any period of time under this agreement, the day of the act, event or default from which the designated period of time begins to run shall not be included. The last day of the period so computed shall be included unless it is a Saturday, Sunday or legal holiday, in which event the period shall run until the end of the next day which is not a Saturday, Sunday or legal holiday.

ARTICLE VIII

AMENDMENTS

These Articles of Limited Partnership may be amended only upon the prior written consent of all of the Partners.

ARTICLE IX

MISCELLANEOUS PROVISIONS

9.1 <u>Integration</u>. This agreement embodies the entire agreement and understanding among the Partners and supersedes all prior agreements and understandings, if any, among them.

9.2 <u>Applicable Law</u>. This agreement and the rights of the Partners shall be construed and enforced in accordance with the laws of the State of Illinois.

9.3 <u>Counterparts</u>. This agreement may be executed in counterparts and all counterparts so executed shall constitute one agreement binding on all the parties hereto, notwithstanding that all the parties are not signatory to the original or the same counterpart, except that no counterpart shall be authentic unless signed by a Partner.

9.4 <u>Separability</u>. In case any one or more the provisions contained in this agreement or any application thereof shall be held to be invalid, illegal or unenforceable in any respect, the validity, legality and enforceability of the remaining provisions any other application thereof shall not in any way be affected or impaired.

9.5 <u>Binding Effect</u>. Except as herein otherwise provided to the contrary, this agreement shall be binding upon and inure to the benefit of the Partners and their respective heirs, representatives, successors and assigns.

9.6 <u>Headnotes</u>. Headnotes are used merely for reference purposes and do not affect the content of any Article or section.

9.7 <u>Gender</u>. Whenever the context of this instrument so requires words used in the masculine gender include the feminine and neuter; the singular includes the plural and the plural and singular.

IN WITNESS WHEREOF, the undersigned, being all of the Partners of The Brown Family Limited Partnership, an Illinois Limited Partnership, have executed and acknowledged this Agreement as of the day and year first above written.

By:

_____

Lydia Brown
General Partner

Limited Partners:

_____

The Brown Family Trust
By Lydia Brown, Trustee

_____

Ed Brown, Limited Partner

_____

Jane Brown, Limited Partner

SCHEDULE A

Limited Partners

Limited Partner	Interest	Capital Contribution
The Brown Family Trust	97%	See attached
Ed Brown	1%	$100.00
Jane Brown	1%	$100.00

SCHEDULE B

General Partner

	Interest
Lydia Brown	1%

Appendix C: IRS
Form 3520

Form **3520**	U.S. Information Return	
(Rev. June 1995)	**Creation of or Transfers to Certain Foreign Trusts**	OMB No. 1545-0159
Department of the Treasury Internal Revenue Service	(Under section 6048 of the Internal Revenue Code) *Attach additional sheets if more space is needed.*	

All information must be written in the English language. Show amounts in U.S. dollars.

Name of U.S. person(s) filing return	Identifying number(s)

Number, street, and room or suite no. (If a P.O. box, see instructions.)

City or town, state, and ZIP code

1 Title of person filing return (check applicable box)

☐ Grantor   ☐ Transferor   ☐ Fiduciary of an estate in the case of testamentary trust

2 If fiduciary of an estate, give name and social security number of the decedent.

3 Name of the trust

4 Foreign country under whose laws the trust was created	**5** Date trust was created
6 Name and business address of foreign trustee(s)	**7** Date of transaction
	8 Amount of money and value of property transferred $

9	Name of beneficiary	Address of beneficiary	Date of birth	Identifying number (if any)
a				
b				
c				
d				
e				
f				
g				

10 Name and address of the person(s) creating the trust

11 Termination date. If no termination date, attach a statement describing the conditions that will cause the trust to terminate.

12 Is trustee required to distribute all trust income currently? .... ☐ Yes ☐ No

If "No," attach a statement showing each beneficiary's **(a)** right to receive income or corpus, or both; **(b)** proportionate interest in the income or corpus, or both; and **(c)** any condition governing the time a distribution to the beneficiary may be made, such as specific date or age. You may attach a copy of the trust instrument instead of the statement.

13 Attach a statement listing the property transferred to the foreign trust in the transaction for which this return is being filed. Include in the statement a detailed description of each item transferred, its adjusted basis and fair market value on the date transferred, and the consideration, if any, paid by the foreign trust for the property.

For Paperwork Reduction Act Notice, see instructions on page 2.   Cat No. 19594V   Form **3520** (Rev. 6-95)

Y50005
10-23-95

14 Name and address (Number and street, city, state or province, ZIP or postal code, and country) of person(s) having custody of the books of account and records of the foreign trust

15 Location of the books of account and records if different from above

Signature - Under penalties of perjury, I declare that I have examined this return, including any accompanying reports, schedules, or statements, and to the best of my knowledge and belief, it is true, correct, and complete.

Signature ▶   Title (if any) ▶   Date ▶

Appendix D: IRS Form 3520-A

Form **Form 3520-A**	**Annual Return of**	
(Rev. August 1995) Department of the Treasury Internal Revenue Service	**Foreign Trust With U.S. Beneficiaries** (Attach additional sheets if more space is needed.)	OMB No. 1545-0160

All information must be written in English.

For calendar year 19	, or fiscal year beginning	, 19	, and ending	, 19
			Identifying number	
			Service center where person filing this return files income tax returns	

1 Title of person filing return (check applicable box):
☐ Grantor ☐ Transferor

2 Are you the sole U.S. grantor or transferor? .... ☐ Yes ☐ No
If "No," attach list of all other U.S. grantors or transferors showing name, address, and identifying number.

3 Name and address of the foreign trust

4 Country under whose laws the trust was created	**5** Date the trust was created
6 Name and business address of foreign trustee	**7 Termination date** (If no termination date, attach a statement describing the conditions that will cause the trust to terminate.)

			Identifying number, if any	U.S. citizen	
8 Name of U.S. beneficiary		Address of U.S. beneficiary		Yes	No
(a)					
(b)					
(c)					
(d)					
(e)					
(f)					

9 Amendments to trust during this year. Explain (attach statement if necessary):

10 Is trustee required to distribute all trust income currently? ....

11 Has the location of the trust changed since its creation? ....
If "Yes," attach explanation.

12 Was Form 3520 filed for this trust? ....
If "Yes," enter date filed ▶

13 Enter date of last transfer of property to trust by grantor or transferor filing this return ▶

14 Has grantor or transferor filed form TD 90-22.1 for this trust? ....

15 Did the trust acquire a U.S. beneficiary during the current year? ....
If "Yes," enter amount of deemed accumulation distribution to grantor (see section 679(b) and attach computation) ▶

16 Attach a statement showing each U.S. beneficiary's **(a)** right to receive income or corpus, or both; **(b)** proportionate interest in the income or corpus, or both;
and **(c)** any condition governing the time a distribution may be made to a U.S. beneficiary, such as a specific date or age. You may attach a copy of the trust
instrument instead of the statement. If either the statement or trust instrument was submitted in a prior year, you do not have to resubmit the information
unless it has changed. If you previously sent the information and it remains unchanged, enter the year the original information was submitted.

Under penalties of perjury, I declare that I have examined this return, including any accompanying reports, schedules, or statements, and to the best of my knowledge and belief, it is true, correct, and
complete.

Signature ▶	Title ▶	Date ▶
Y50007 10-23-95	D193 For Paperwork Reduction Act Notice, see instr.	Form **3520-A** (Rev. 8-95)

Form 3520-A (Rev. 8-95)   Page **2**

Part I	**Foreign Trust Income Statement** Show all amounts in U.S. dollars	**(a)** Totals from books and records of this foreign trust	**(b)** Portion to be reported by grantor or transferor

Income

1	Dividends		
2	Interest		
3	Income from partnerships and other fiduciaries		
4	Gross rents and royalties		
5	Gross profit (loss) from trade or business		
6	Net gain (loss) from capital assets		
7	Ordinary gains and (losses)		
8	Other income (state nature of income) ▶ _____		
9	Total income (add lines 1 through 8)		

Expenses

10	Interest		
11	Taxes (attach schedule)		
12	Fiduciary's portion of depreciation and depletion (explain depletion) ▶ _____		
13	Charitable contributions		
14	Other expenses ▶ _____		
15	Total expenses (add lines 10 through 14)		
16	Net income (subtract line 15 from line 9)		

Amount from line 16, column (b), should be entered in Schedule E (Form 1040), Form 1065, Form 1041, or Forms 1120 and 1120S (if less than 100% of column (a), attach computations).

Part II	**Balance Sheets** Show all amounts in U.S. dollars	**Beginning of Tax Year**		**End of Tax Year**	
	Assets	**(a)** Amount	**(b)** Total	**(c)** Amount	**(d)** Total
1	Cash:				
a	Savings and interest-bearing accounts				
b	Other				
2	Net accounts receivable				
3	Notes receivable (attach schedule)				
4	Inventories				
5	Government obligations:				
a	U.S. and instrumentalities				
b	State, subdivisions thereof				
6	Investments in non-Govt. bonds, etc. (attach schedule)				
7	Investments in corporate stocks (attach schedule)				
8	Mortgage loans (number of loans ▶ _____)				
9	Other investments (attach schedule)				
10	Depreciable (depletable) assets (attach schedule)				
	Less accumulated depreciation				
11	Land				
12	Other assets (attach schedule)				
13	Total assets				
	Liabilities				
14	Accounts payable				
15	Contributions, gifts, grants, etc., payable				
16	Mortgages and notes payable (attach schedule)				
17	Other liabilities (attach schedule)				
18	Total liabilities				
	Net Worth				
19	Accumulated trust income				
20	Other (attach schedule)				
21	Total net worth				
22	Total liabilities and net worth (line 18 plus line 21)				

Y50008
10-23-95

Appendix E: IRS Form 926

Form **926** (Rev. November 1992) Department of the Treasury Internal Revenue Service	Return by a U.S Transferor of Property to a Foreign Corporation, Foreign Estate or Trust, or Foreign Partnership	OMB No. 1545-0026 Expires 8-31-95

Name of transferor	Identifying number
Number, street, and room or suite no. (If a P.O. box, see instructions.)	Date of transfer (month, day, year)
City or town, state, and ZIP code	Place of organization or creation if a corporation, partnership, estate, or trust

Part I   **Foreign Transferee Information**

1 Name of transferee	2 Identifying number, if any

3 Address (including country)

4 a Check type of foreign transferee: ☐ Corporation ☐ Estate ☐ Trust ☐ Partnership

   b Place of organization or creation

   c If an estate or trust, enter name and address of fiduciary

   d If stock or securities are transferred to a corporation or partnership, enter percentage of transferor's interest in the stock of the
transferee corporation or the partnership after the transfer .... ►   %

5   Name and address of each: (**a**) partner if a partnership or (**b**) beneficiary if an estate or trust (attach additional sheets, if needed)

Name	Address

Part II   **Transfers Exempt from Excise Tax**

6 a Is the transfer to an exempt transferee? .... ☐ Yes ☐ No

   b Check this box if you are making an election under section 1057 .... ☐

   c Is the transfer a transfer described in section 367? .... ☐ Yes ☐ No

   d If "No" have you made an election to apply principles similar to the principles of section 367? .... ☐ Yes ☐ No

   e If the answer to 6c or 6d is "Yes," attach the information required under section 6038B. If the answer to 6d is "Yes," also
attach a statement explaining the application of principles similar to the principles of section 367 to the transfer.

   f If stock or securities are being transferred to a foreign corporation, have you attached an agreement to recognize
gain upon a later disposition by the transferee? .... ☐ Yes ☐ No

7   Attach a statement summarizing all facts relating to the transfer and a copy of the plan under which the transfer was made.

Part III   **Figuring the Excise Tax (Complete this part only for transfers subject to the excise tax)**

(a) Description of property transferred	(b) Number of items transferred	(c) Fair market value on the date of transfer	(d) Cost or other basis (See section 1011)	(e) Amount of gain recognized at the time of transfer	(f) Excess (Column (c) less sum of columns (d) and (e)-enter zero if no excess)

8 Total ....

9 Excise tax (multiply line 8 by 35%) ....

Please Sign Here	Under penalties of perjury, I declare that I have examined this return, including accompanying schedules and statements, and to the best of my knowledge and belief, it is true, correct, and complete. Declaration of preparer (other than taxpayer) is based on all information of which preparer has any knowledge.

► Signature   Date   ► Title

Paid Preparer's Use Only	Preparer's signature ►		Date	Check if self-employed ► ☐	Preparer's social security no.
	Firm's name (or yours if self-employed), and address ►			E.I. No. ►	
				ZIP code ►	

C40088   09-10-95   For Paperwork Reduction Act Notice, see instr.

Appendix F: IRS Form 90-22.1

Department of the Treasury	**REPORT OF FOREIGN BANK AND FINANCIAL ACCOUNTS**	Form Approved: OMB No. 1505-0063
TD F 90-22.1 10/92	For the calendar year 19 _____	Expiration Date: 9/95
SUPERSEDES ALL PREVIOUS EDITIONS	**Do not file this form with your Federal Tax Return**	

This form should be used to report financial interest in or signature authority or other authority over one or more bank accounts, securities accounts, or other financial accounts in foreign countries as required by Department of the Treasury Regulations (31 CFR 103). You are not required to file a report if the aggregate value of the accounts did not exceed $10,000. Check all appropriate boxes. SEE INSTRUCTIONS FOR DEFINITIONS. File this form with Dept. of the Treasury, P.O. Box 32621, Detroit, MI 48232.

1. Name (Last, First, Middle)

2. Social security number or employer identification number if other than individual

3. Name in item 1 refers to
   ☐ Individual
   ☐ Partnership
   ☐ Corporation
   ☐ Fiduciary

4. Address (Street, City, State, Country, ZIP)

5. ☐ I had signature authority over one or more foreign accounts, but had no "financial interest" in such accounts. Indicate for these accounts:

(a)   Name and social security number or taxpayer identification number of each owner _____

(b)   Address of each owner _____

(Do not complete item 9 for these accounts)

6. ☐ I had a "financial interest" in one or more foreign accounts owned by a domestic corporation, partnership or trust which is required to file TD F 90-22.1. Indicate for these accounts:

(a) Name and taxpayer identification number of each such corporation, partnership or trust _____

(b) Address of each such corporation, partnership or trust _____

(Do not complete item 9 for these accounts)

7. ☐ I had a "financial interest" in one or more foreign accounts, but the total maximum value of these accounts did not exceed $10,000 at any time during the year. (If you checked this box, do not complete item 9).

8. ☐ I had a "financial interest" in 25 or more foreign accounts. (If you checked this box, do not complete item 9.)

9. If you had a "financial interest" in one or more but fewer than 25 foreign accounts which are required to be reported, and the total maximum value of the accounts exceeded $10,000 during the year, write the total number of those accounts in the box below: Complete items (a) through (f) below for one of the accounts and attach a separate TD F 90-22.1 for each of the others. Items 1, 2, 3, 9, and 10 must be completed for each account.
Check here if this is an attachment. ☐

(a) Name in which account is maintained

(b) Name of bank or other person with whom account is maintained

(c) Number and other account designation, if any

(d) Address of office or branch where account is maintained

(e) Type of account. (If not certain of English name for the type of account, give the foreign language name and describe the nature of the account. Attach additional sheets if necessary.)
     ☐ Bank Account   ☐ Securities Account   ☐ Other (specify)

(f) Maximum value of account
     ☐ Under $10,000   ☐ $10,000 to $50,000   ☐ $50,000 to $100,000   ☐ Over $100,000

10. Signature

11. Title (Not necessary if reporting a personal account)

12. Date

PRIVACY ACT NOTIFICATION

Pursuant to the requirements of Public Law 93-579, (Privacy Act of 1974), notice is hereby given that the authority to collect information on TD F 90-22.1 in accordance with 5 U.S.C. 552(e)(3) is Public Law 91-508; 31 U.S.C. 1121; 5 U.S. C. 301, 31 CFR Part 103.

The principal purpose for collecting the information is to assure maintenance of reports or records where such reports or records have a high degree of usefulness in criminal, tax, or regulatory investigations or proceedings. The information collected may be provided to those officers and employees of any constituent unit of the Department of the Treasury who have a need for the records in the performance of their duties. The records may be referred to any other department or agency of the Federal Government upon the request of the head of such department or agency for use in a criminal, tax, or regulatory investigation or proceeding.

Disclosure of this information is mandatory. Civil and criminal penalties, including under certain circumstances a fine of not more than $500,000 and imprisonment of not more than five years, are provided for failure to file a report, supply information, and for filing a false or fraudulent report.

Disclosure of the social security number is mandatory. The authority to collect this number is 31 CFR 103. The social security number will be used as a means to identify the individual who files the report.

419951
12-02-94

Appendix G: IRS Forms 433-A, 433-B, 433-D, and 656

Form **433-A** (Rev. September 1995)	Department of the Treasury - Internal Revenue Service **Collection Information Statement for Individuals**

NOTE: Complete all blocks, except shaded areas. Write "N/A" (not applicable) in those blocks that do not apply. Instructions for certain line items are in Publication 1854.

1. Taxpayer(s) name(s) and address	2. Home phone number	3. Marital status
County _____	4.a. Taxpayer's social security number	b. Spouse's social security number

Section I.   Employment Information

5. Taxpayer's employer or business (name and address)	a. How long employed	b. Business phone number	c. Occupation
	d. No. of exemptions claimed on Form W-4	e. Pay period: ☐ Weekly ☐ Bi-weekly ☐ Monthly ☐ _____ Payday: _____ (Mon-Sun)	f. (Check appropriate box) ☐ Wage earner ☐ Sole proprietor ☐ Partner

6. Spouse's employer or business (name and address)	a. How long employed	b. Business phone number	c. Occupation
	d. No. of exemptions claimed on Form W-4	e. Pay period: ☐ Weekly ☐ Bi-weekly ☐ Monthly ☐ _____ Payday: _____ (Mon-Sun)	f. (Check appropriate box) ☐ Wage earner ☐ Sole proprietor ☐ Partner

Section II.   Personal Information

7. Name, address and telephone number of next of kin or other reference	8. Other names or aliases	9. Previous address(es)

10. Age and relationship of dependents living in your household (exclude yourself and spouse)

11. Date of birth ▶	a. Taxpayer	b. Spouse	12. Latest filed income tax return (tax year)	a. Number of exemptions claimed	b. Adjusted Gross Income

Section III.   General Financial Information

13. Bank accounts (include savings & loans, credit unions, IRA and retirement plans, certificates of deposit, etc.) Enter bank <u>loans</u> in item 28.

Name of Institution	Address	Type of Account	Account No.	Balance
			Total (Enter in Item 21)	

M50387 LHA
10-24-95

Form **433-A** (Rev. 9-95)

Section III - continued　　　　　**General Financial Information**

14. Charge cards and lines of credit from banks, credit unions, and savings and loans. List all other charge accounts in item 28.

Type of Account or Card	Name and Address of Financial Institution	Monthly Payment	Credit Limit	Amount Owed	Credit Available
	Totals (Enter in Item 27) ▶				

15. Safe deposit boxes rented or accessed (List all locations, box numbers, and contents)

16. Real Property (Brief description and type of ownership)	Physical Address
a.	
	County _____
b.	
	County _____
c.	
	County _____

17. Life Insurance (Name of Company)	Policy Number	Type	Face Amount	Available Loan Value
		Whole / Term		
		Whole / Term		
		Whole / Term		
		Total (Enter in Item 23) ▶		

18. Securities (stocks, bonds, mutual funds, money market funds, government securities, etc.):

Kind	Quantity of Denomination	Current Value	Where Located	Owner of Record

19. Other information relating to your financial condition. If you check the yes box, please give dates and explain on page 4, Additional Information or Comments:

	Yes	No		Yes	No
a. Court proceedings	☐	☐	b. Bankruptcies	☐	☐
c. Repossessions	☐	☐	d. Recent transfer of assets for less than full value	☐	☐
e. Anticipated increase in income	☐	☐	f. Participant or beneficiary to trust, estate, profit sharing, etc.	☐	☐

Form **433-A** **page 2** (Rev. 9-95)
M50388
10-24-95

Section IV.   **Assets and Liabilities**

Description		Current Market Value	Current Amount Owed	Equity in Asset	Amount of Monthly Payment	Name and Address of Lien/Note Holder/Lender	Date Pledged	Date of Final Payment
20. Cash								
21. Bank accounts (from item 13)								
22. Securities (from item 18)								
23. Cash or loan value of insurance								
24. Vehicles (model, year, license, tag#)								
	a.							
	b.							
	c.							
25. Real property (From Section III, item 16)	a.							
	b.							
	c.							
26. Other assets								
	a.							
	b.							
	c.							
	d.							
	e.							
27. Bank revolving credit (from item 14)								
28. Other Liabilities (including bank loans, judgments, notes, and charge accounts not entered in Item 13.)	a.							
	b.							
	c.							
	d.							
	e.							
	f.							
	g.							
29. Federal taxes owed (prior years)								
30. Totals				$	$			

Internal Revenue Service Use Only Below This Line

Financial Verification/Analysis

Item	Date Information or Encumbrance Verified	Date Property Inspected	Estimated Forced Sale Equity
Personal Residence			
Other Real Property			
Vehicles			
Other Personal Property			
State Employment (Husband and Wife)			
Income Tax Return			
Wage Statements (Husband and Wife)			
Sources of Income/Credit (D&B Report)			
Expenses			
Other Assets/Liabilities			

Section V. **Monthly Income and Expense Analysis**

Total Income			Necessary Living Expenses		
Source	**Gross**			**Claimed**	**(IRS use only) Allowed**
31. Wages/Salaries (Taxpayer)	$		42. National Standard Expenses[1]	$	$
32. Wages/Salaries (Spouse)			43. Housing and utilities[2]		
33. Interest - Dividends			44. Transportation[3]		
34. Net business income (from Form 433-B)			45. Health care		
35. Rental income			46. Taxes (income and FICA)		
36. Pension (Taxpayer)			47. Court ordered payments		
37. Pension (Spouse)			48. Child/dependent care		
38. Child Support			49. Life insurance		
39. Alimony			50. Secured or legally-perfected debts (specify)		
40. Other			51. Other expenses (specify)		
41. **Total Income**	$		52. **Total Expenses**	$	$
			53. (IRS use only) Net difference (income less necessary living expenses)		

Certification	Under penalties of perjury, I declare that to the best of my knowledge and belief this statement of assets, liabilities, and other information is true, correct, and complete.	
54. Your Signature	55. Spouse's signature (if joint return was filed)	56. Date

Notes

1. Clothing and clothing services, food, housekeeping supplies, personal care products and services, and miscellaneous.

2. Rent or mortgage payment for the taxpayer's principal residence. Add the average monthly payment for the following expenses if they are not included in the rent or mortgage payment: property taxes, homeowner's or renter's insurance, parking, necessary maintenance and repair, homeowner dues, condominium fees and utilities. Utilities includes gas, electricity, water, fuel oil, coal, bottled gas, trash and garbage collection, wood and other fuels, septic cleaning and telephone.

3. Lease or purchase payments, insurance, registration fees, normal maintenance, fuel, public transportation, parking and tolls.

Additional information or comments:

Internal Revenue Service Use Only Below This Line

Explain any difference between Item 53 and the installment agreement payment amount:

Name of originator and IDRS assignment number:	Date

345 10/91   1059-3

Department of the Treasury - Internal Revenue Service

Form **433-B**   **Collection Information Statement for Businesses**

(Rev. June 1991)   (If you need additional space, please attach a separate sheet)

NOTE: Complete all blocks, except shaded areas. Write "N/A" (not applicable) in those blocks that do not apply.

1. Name and address of business	2. Business phone number	
	3. (Check appropriate box)	
	☐ Sole proprietor ☐ Other (specify)	
	☐ Partnership	
County	☐ Corporation	
4. Name and title of person being interviewed	5. Employer Identification Number	6. Type of business

7. Information about owner, partners, officers, major shareholder, etc.

Name and Title	Effective Date	Home Address	Phone Number	Social Security Number	Total Shares or Interest

Section I.   **General Financial Information**

	Form	Tax Year ended	Net income before taxes
8. Latest filed income tax return ▶			

9. Bank accounts (List all types of accounts including payroll and general, savings, certificates of deposit, etc.)

Name of institution	Address	Type of Account	Account Number	Balance
		Total (Enter in Item 17) ▶		

10. Bank credit available (Lines of credit, etc.)

Name of Institution	Address	Credit Limit	Amount Owed	Credit Available	Monthly Payments
Totals (Enter in Items 24 or 25 as appropriate)		▶			

11. Location, box number, and contents of all safe deposit boxes rented or accessed

Section I - continued　　　　　　**General Financial Information**

12.　Real property

Brief Description and Type of Ownership	Physical Address
a.	County
b.	County
c.	County
d.	County

13.　Life insurance policies owned with business as beneficiary

Name Insured	Company	Policy Number	Type	Face Amount	Available Loan Value
	Total (Enter in item 19)			▶	

14.　Additional information regarding financial condition　(Court proceedings, bankruptcies filed or anticipated, transfers of assets for less than full value, changes in market conditions, etc.; include information regarding company participation in trusts, estates, profit-sharing plans, etc.)

b.　If you know of any person or organization that borrowed or otherwise provided funds to pay net payrolls:	a.　Who borrowed funds?
	b.　Who supplied funds?

15.　Accounts/Notes receivable　(Include current contract jobs, loans to stockholders, officers, partners, etc.)

Name	Address	Amount Due	Due Date	Status
		$		
	Total (Enter in Item 18)　▶	$		

Section II.								
Asset and Liability Analysis								
Description (a)	Cur. Mkt. Value (b)	Liabilities Bal. Due (c)	Equity in Asset (d)	Amt. of Mo. Pymt. (e)	Name and Address of Lien/Note Holder/Obligee (f)	Date Pledged (g)	Date of Final Pymt. (h)
16. Cash on hand							
17. Bank accounts							
18. Accounts/Notes receivable							
19. Life insurance loan value							
20. Real property (from Item 12) a.							
b.							
c.							
d.							
21. Vehicles (Model, year, and license) a.							
b.							
c.							
22. Machinery and equipment (Specify) a.							
b.							
c.							
23. Merchandise inventory (Specify) a.							
b.							
24. Other assets (Specify) a.							
b.							
25. Other liabilities (Including notes and judgments) a.							
b.							
c.							
d.							
e.							
f.							
g.							
h.							
26. Federal taxes owed							
27. Total							

M40393
08-17-95

Page 3

Form 433-B (Rev. 6-91)

Section III.   **Income and Expense Analysis**

The following information applies to income and expenses during the period _____ to _____	Accounting method used

Income		Expenses	
28. Gross receipts from sales, services, etc.	$	34. Materials purchased	$
29. Gross rental income		35. Net wages and salaries / Number of Employees	
30. Interest		36. Rent	
31. Dividends		37. Allowable installment payments (IRS use only)	
32. Other income (Specify)		38. Supplies	
		39. Utilities/Telephone	
		40. Gasoline/Oil	
		41. Repairs and maintenance	
		42. Insurance	
		43. Current taxes	
		44. Other (Specify)	
33. Total Income ▶	$	45. Total Expenses (IRS use only) ▶	$
		46. Net difference (IRS use only) ▶	$

Certification   Under penalties of perjury, I declare that to the best of my knowledge and belief this statement of assets, liabilities, and other information is true, correct, and complete.

47. Signature	48. Date

Internal Revenue Service Use Only Below This Line

Financial Verification/Analysis

Item	Date Information or Encumbrance Verified	Date Property Inspected	Estimated Forced Sale Equity
Sources of Income/Credit (D&B Report)			
Expenses			
Real Property			
Vehicles			
Machinery and Equipment			
Merchandise			
Accounts/Notes Receivable			
Corporate Information, if Applicable			
U.C.C.: Senior/Junior Lienholder			
Other Assets/Liabilities:			

Explain any difference between Item 46 (or P&L) and the installment agreement payment amount:

Name of Originator and IDRS assignment number	Date

Form **433-D**
(Rev. April 1994)

Installment Agreement

check box if pre-assessed modules included ☐

Name and address of taxpayer(s)	Social security or employer identification number
	(primary) (secondary)
┌	Telephone number
	(home)
	(business)
	Kinds of taxes (form numbers) Tax periods
└	Amount owed as of _____ Earliest CSED
	$

Employer (name and address)	Financial institutions (names and addresses)	For assistance: Call 1-800-829-1040 or write:
		_____ Service Ctr.
		_____
		City, State and Zip Code

I/We agree that the federal taxes shown above, PLUS ALL PENALTIES AND INTEREST PROVIDED BY LAW, will be paid as follows:
$ _____ will be paid on _____ and $ _____ will be paid no later than the _____ of each month thereafter until the total liability is paid in full. I/we also agree that the above installment payment will be increased or decreased as follows:

Date of increase (or decrease)			AGREEMENT LOCATOR NUMBER: _____
Amount of increase (or decrease)	$		(circle)
New installment amount	$		**0** No future action is required

AGREEMENT LOCATOR NUMBER: _____
(circle)
0 No future action is required
5 Financial review date: ___ / ___ m m   y y
8 SCCB - Monitor ES compliance: ____
Amount per quarter $ ____
(If amount(s)/quarters will vary, provide details.)

Conditions of this agreement:

- We must receive each payment by the date shown above; if you have a problem, contact us immediately.
- This agreement is based on your current financial condition. We may change or cancel it if our information shows that your ability to pay has changed significantly.
- We may cancel this agreement if you don't give us updated financial information when we ask for it.
- While this agreement is in effect, you must file all federal tax returns and pay any taxes you owe on time.
- We will apply your federal or state tax refunds (if any) to the amount you owe until it is fully paid. (This includes the Alaska Permanent Fund dividend for Alaska residents.)

- If you don't meet the conditions of this agreement, we will cancel it, and may collect the entire amount you owe by levy on your income, bank accounts or other assets, or by seizing your property.
- We may cancel this agreement at any time if we find that collection of the tax is in jeopardy.
- We will apply all payments on this agreement in the best interest of the United States.
- The IRS Collection Division must accept this agreement, and it may require managerial approval. If it is not accepted or approved, we will notify you.

Additional Conditions: (To be filled in by IRS)

- **A NOTICE OF FEDERAL TAX LIEN** (check one)
  - ☐ HAS ALREADY BEEN FILED
  - ☐ WILL BE FILED IMMEDIATELY
  - ☐ WILL BE FILED WHEN TAX IS ASSESSED
  - ☐ MAY BE FILED IF THIS AGREEMENT DEFAULTS

Your signature	Title (if corporate officer or partner)	Date	Originator's name, title and IDRS assignment number (or district):
Spouse's signature (if a joint liability)		Date	
Agreement examined or approved by (signature, title, function)		Date	Originator Code:

YOU MAY HAVE YOUR INSTALLMENT AGREEMENT PAYMENT DEDUCTED FROM YOUR CHECKING ACCOUNT EACH MONTH (DIRECT DEBIT); IF YOU CHOOSE THIS OPTION, FOLLOW THE DIRECTIONS ON PAGE 2 OF YOUR COPY OF THIS FORM.

If you agree to Direct Debit, initial here:

_____
and attach a blank voided check.

- I (we) authorize the IRS and the depository (bank) identified on the attached voided check to deduct payments (debit) from my (our) checking account or correct errors on the account. This authorization remains in effect until I (or either of us) notify IRS in writing to stop or until the liability covered by this agreement is satisfied.
- I (we) understand that if the depository is unable to honor IRS's request for payment due to insufficient funds in my (our) account on the payment due date I (we) will be charged a penalty of $15 or two percent of the payment request, whichever is greater. If the payment request is for less than $15, the penalty is the amount of the request.

Part 1 - IRS Copy

M40395
08-28-95

Form 433-D (Rev. 4-94)

Form **433-D** (Rev. April 1994)	**Installment Agreement**	check box if pre-assessed modules included ☐

Name and address of taxpayer(s)	Social security or employer identification number
	(primary) (secondary)
	Telephone number
	(home) (business)
	Kinds of taxes (form numbers)	Tax periods
	Amount owed as of _____	Earliest CSED
	$	

Employer (name and address)	Financial institutions (names and addresses)	For assistance: Call 1-800-829-1040 or write: _____ Service Ctr.
		_____
		City, State and Zip Code

I/We agree that the federal taxes shown above, <u>PLUS ALL PENALTIES AND INTEREST PROVIDED BY LAW</u>, will be paid as follows:

$ _____ will be paid on _____ and $_____ will be paid no later than

the _____ of each month thereafter until the total liability is paid in full. I/we also agree that the above installment payment will be increased

or decreased as follows:

Date of increase (or decrease)			AGREEMENT LOCATOR NUMBER: _____
Amount of increase (or decrease)	$		(circle) 0 No future action is required
			5 Financial review date: ___ / ___ m m y y
New installment amount	$		6 SCCB - Monitor ES compliance: Amount per quarter $ _____ (If amount(s)/quarters will vary, provide details.)

Conditions of this agreement:

- We must receive each payment by the date shown above; if you have a problem, contact us immediately.
- This agreement is based on your current financial condition. We may change or cancel it if our information shows that your ability to pay has changed significantly.
- We may cancel this agreement if you don't give us updated financial information when we ask for it.
- While this agreement is in effect, you must file all federal tax returns and pay any taxes you owe on time.
- We will apply your federal or state tax refunds (if any) to the amount you owe until it is fully paid. (This includes the Alaska Permanent Fund dividend for Alaska residents.)

- If you don't meet the conditions of this agreement, we will cancel it, and may collect the entire amount you owe by levy on your income, bank accounts or other assets, or by seizing your property.
- We may cancel this agreement at any time if we find that collection of the tax is in jeopardy.
- We will apply all payments on this agreement in the best interest of the United States.
- The IRS Collection Division must accept this agreement, and it may require managerial approval. If it is not accepted or approved, we will notify you.

Additional Conditions: (To be filled in by IRS)

- **A NOTICE OF FEDERAL TAX LIEN** (check one)
  - ☐ HAS ALREADY BEEN FILED
  - ☐ WILL BE FILED IMMEDIATELY
  - ☐ WILL BE FILED WHEN TAX IS ASSESSED
  - ☐ MAY BE FILED IF THIS AGREEMENT DEFAULTS

Your signature	Title (if corporate officer or partner)	Date	Originator's name, title and IDRS assignment number (or district):
Spouse's signature (if a joint liability)		Date	
Agreement examined or approved by (signature, title, function)		Date	Originator Code:

YOU MAY HAVE YOUR INSTALLMENT AGREEMENT PAYMENT DEDUCTED FROM YOUR CHECKING ACCOUNT EACH MONTH (DIRECT DEBIT); IF YOU CHOOSE THIS OPTION, FOLLOW THE DIRECTIONS ON PAGE 2 OF YOUR COPY OF THIS FORM.

If you agree to Direct Debit, initial here:
_____
and attach a blank voided check.

- I (we) authorize the IRS and the depository (bank) identified on the attached voided check to deduct payments (debit) from my (our) checking account or correct errors on the account. This authorization remains in effect until I (or either of us) notify IRS in writing to stop or until the liability covered by this agreement is satisfied.
- I (we) understand that if the depository is unable to honor IRS's request for payment due to insufficient funds in my (our) account on the payment due date I (we) will be charged a penalty of $15 or two percent of the payment request, whichever is greater. If the payment request is for less than $15, the penalty is the amount of the request.

Part 1 - Taxpayer's Copy

M40396
08-28-95

Form **433-D** (Rev. 4-94)

Form **433-D**
(Rev. April 1994)

Installment Agreement

check box if
pre-assessed
modules included ☐

| Name and address of taxpayer(s) | Social security or employer identification number |
| | (primary)   (secondary) |

┌   ┐   Telephone number
                                             (home)   (business)

                                             Kinds of taxes *(form numbers)* | Tax periods

└   ┘   Amount owed as of _____ | Earliest CSED
                                             $

Employer (name and address)	Financial institutions (names and addresses)	For assistance: Call 1-800-829-1040 or write:
		_____ Service Ctr.
		City, State and Zip Code

I/We agree that the federal taxes shown above, <u>PLUS ALL PENALTIES AND INTEREST PROVIDED BY LAW</u>, will be paid as follows:

$ _____ will be paid on _____ and $ _____ will be paid no later than

the _____ of each month thereafter until the total liability is paid in full. I/we also agree that the above installment payment will be increased

or decreased as follows:

Date of increase (or decrease)			AGREEMENT LOCATOR NUMBER: _____
Amount of increase (or decrease)	$		*(circle)*
New installment amount	$		

0 No future action is required
5 Financial review date: ____ / ____
          m m   y y
6 SCCB - Monitor ES compliance:
     Amount per quarter $
     (If amount(s)/quarters will vary, provide details.)

Conditions of this agreement:

- We must receive each payment by the date shown above; if you have a problem, contact us immediately.
- This agreement is based on your current financial condition. We may change or cancel it if our information shows that your ability to pay has changed significantly.
- We may cancel this agreement if you don't give us updated financial information when we ask for it.
- While this agreement is in effect, you must file all federal tax returns and pay any taxes you owe on time.
- We will apply your federal or state tax refunds (if any) to the amount you owe until it is fully paid. (This includes the Alaska Permanent Fund dividend for Alaska residents.)

Additional Conditions: (To be filled in by IRS)

- If you don't meet the conditions of this agreement, we will cancel it, and may collect the entire amount you owe by levy on your income, bank accounts or other assets, or by seizing your property.
- We may cancel this agreement at any time if we find that collection of the tax is in jeopardy.
- We will apply all payments on this agreement in the best interest of the United States.
- The IRS Collection Division must accept this agreement, and it may require managerial approval. If it is not accepted or approved, we will notify you.

- **A NOTICE OF FEDERAL TAX LIEN** (check one)
  - ☐ HAS ALREADY BEEN FILED
  - ☐ WILL BE FILED IMMEDIATELY
  - ☐ WILL BE FILED WHEN TAX IS ASSESSED
  - ☐ MAY BE FILED IF THIS AGREEMENT DEFAULTS

Your signature	Title *(if corporate officer or partner)*	Date	Originator's name, title and IDRS assignment number (or district):
Spouse's signature *(if a joint liability)*		Date	
Agreement examined or approved by *(signature, title, function)*		Date	Originator Code:

YOU MAY HAVE YOUR INSTALLMENT AGREEMENT PAYMENT DEDUCTED FROM YOUR CHECKING ACCOUNT EACH MONTH (DIRECT DEBIT); IF YOU CHOOSE THIS OPTION, FOLLOW THE DIRECTIONS ON PAGE 2 OF YOUR COPY OF THIS FORM.

If you agree to Direct Debit, initial here:

_____

and attach a blank voided check.

- I (we) authorize the IRS and the depository (bank) identified on the attached voided check to deduct payments (debit) from my (our) checking account or correct errors on the account. This authorization remains in effect until I (or either of us) notify IRS in writing to stop or until the liability covered by this agreement is satisfied.
- I (we) understand that if the depository is unable to honor IRS's request for payment due to insufficient funds in my (our) account on the payment due date I (we) will be charged a penalty of $15 or two percent of the payment request, whichever is greater. If the payment request is for less than $15, the penalty is the amount of the request.

Part 1 - Bank Copy (Direct Debit Only)

Form **656** (Rev. Sept. 1993)	Department of the Treasury - Internal Revenue Service **Offer in Compromise**		

(1) Name and Address of Taxpayers	**For Official Use Only**	
	Offer is (Check applicable box) ☐ Cash (Paid in full) ☐ Deferred payment	Serial Number (Cashier's stamp)
(2) Social Security Number (3) Employer Identification Number	Alpha CSED Ind.	
To: **Commissioner of Internal Revenue Service**	Amount Paid $	

(4) I/we (includes all types of taxpayers) **submit this offer to compromise the tax liabilities plus any interest, penalties, additions to tax, and additional amounts required by law (tax liability)** for the tax type and period checked below: (Please mark "X" for the correct description and fill in the correct tax period(s), adding additional periods if needed.)

☐   Income tax for the year(s) 19___ , 19 ___ , 19 ___ , and 19___

☐   Trust fund recovery penalty (formerly called the 100-percent penalty) as a responsible person of _____
_____ (enter business name) for failure to pay withholding
and Federal Insurance Contributions Act taxes (Social Security taxes) for the period(s) ended _____ , _____ ,
_____ , _____ (for example - 06/30/92)

☐   Withholding and Federal Insurance Contributions Act taxes (Social Security taxes) for the period(s) ended _____ , _____ ,
_____ , _____ (for example - 06/30/92)

☐   Federal Unemployment Tax Act taxes for the year(s) 19___ , 19 ___ , 19 ___ , and 19___

☐   Other (Be specific.) _____

(5) I/we offer to pay $ _____ .

If you aren't making full payment with your offer, describe below when you will make full payment (for example - within ten (10) days from the date the offer is accepted): See the instructions for Item 5.

_____
_____
_____

As required by section 6621 of the Internal Revenue Code, the Internal Revenue Service (IRS) will add interest to the offered amount from the date IRS accepts the offer until the date you completely pay the amount offered. IRS compounds interest daily, as required by section 6622 of the Internal Revenue Code.

(6) I/we submit this offer for the reason(s) checked below:

☐   Doubt as to collectibility ("I can't pay.") You must include a completed financial statement (Form 433-A and/or Form 433-B).

☐   Doubt as to liability ("I don't believe I owe this tax.") You must include a detailed explanation of the reason(s) why you believe you don't owe the tax.

IMPORTANT: SEE PAGE 2 FOR TERMS AND CONDITIONS

I accept waiver of the statutory period of limitations for the Internal Revenue Service	Under penalties of perjury, I declare that I have examined this offer, including accompanying schedules and statements, and to the best of my knowledge and belief, it is true, correct and complete.	
Signature of authorized Internal Revenue Service Official	**(8a)** Signature of Taxpayer-proponent	Date
Title Date	**(8b)** Signature of Taxpayer-proponent	Date

Dispose of prior issues.

M40402
08-17-95

Form **656** (Rev. 9-93)

(7) By submitting this offer, **I/we understand and agree to the following terms and conditions:**

(a) I/we voluntarily submit all payments made on this offer.

(b) IRS will apply payments made under the terms of this offer in the best interests of the government.

(c) If IRS rejects the offer or I/we withdraw the offer, IRS will return any amount paid with the offer. If I/we agree in writing, IRS will apply the amount paid with the offer to the amount owed. If I/we agree to apply the payment, the date the offer is rejected or withdrawn will be considered the date of payment. I/we understand that IRS will not pay interest on any amount I/we submit with the offer.

(d) I/we will comply with all the provisions of the Internal Revenue Code related to filing my/ our returns and paying my/our required taxes for five (5) years from the date IRS accepts the offer.

(e) I/we waive and agree to the suspension of any statutory periods of limitation (time limits provided for by law) for IRS assessment and collection of the tax liability for the tax periods checked in item (4).

(f) IRS will keep all payments and credits made, received, or applied to the amount being compromised before this offer was submitted. IRS will also keep any payments made under the terms of an installment agreement while this offer is pending.

(g) IRS will keep any refund, including interest, due to me/us because of overpayment of any tax or other liability, for tax periods extending through the calendar year that IRS accepts the offer. This condition doesn't apply if the offer is based only on doubt as to liability.

(h) I/we will return to IRS any refund identified in (g) received after submitting this offer. This condition doesn't apply if the offer is based only on doubt as to liability.

(i) The total amount IRS can collect under this offer can't be more than the full amount of the tax liability.

(j) I/we understand that I/we remain responsible for the full amount of the tax liability unless and until IRS accepts the offer in writing and I/we have met all the terms and conditions of the offer. IRS won't remove the original amount of the tax liability from its records until I/we have met all the terms and conditions of the offer.

(k) I/we understand that the tax I/we offer to compromise is and will remain a tax liability until I/we meet all the terms and conditions of this offer. If I/we file bankruptcy before the terms and conditions of this offer are completed, any claim the IRS files in the bankruptcy proceeding will be a tax claim.

(l) Once IRS accepts the offer in writing, I/we have no right to contest, in court or otherwise, the amount of the tax liability.

(m) The offer is pending starting with the date an authorized IRS official signs the form and accepts my/our waiver of the statutory periods of limitation. The offer remains pending until an authorized IRS official accepts, rejects, or withdraws the offer in writing. If I/we appeal the IRS decision on the offer, IRS will continue to treat the offer as pending until the Appeals Office accepts or rejects the offer in writing. If I/we don't file a protest within 30 days of the date IRS notifies me/us of the right to protest the decision, I/we waive the right to a hearing before the Appeals Office about this offer in compromise.

(n) The waiver and suspension of any statutory periods of limitation for assessment and collection of the amount of the tax liability described in item (4), continues to apply:

(i) while the offer is pending (see (m) above),

(ii) during the time I/we haven't paid all of the amount offered,

(iii) during the time I/we haven't completed all terms and conditions of the offer, and

(iv) for one additional year beyond the time periods identified in (i), (ii), and (iii) above.

(o) If I/we fail to meet any of the terms and conditions of the offer, the offer is in default, and IRS may:

(i) immediately file suit to collect the entire unpaid balance of the offer;

(ii) immediately file suit to collect an equal amount of the original amount of the tax liability as liquidated damages, minus any payments already received under the terms of this offer;

(iii) disregard the amount of the offer and apply all amounts already paid under the offer against the original amount of tax liability;

(iv) file suit or levy to collect the original amount of tax liability, without further notice of any kind.

IRS will continue to add interest, as required by section 6621 of the Internal Revenue Code, on the amount IRS determines is due after default. IRS will add interest from the date the offer is defaulted until I/we completely satisfy the amount owed. IRS compounds interest daily, as required by section 6622 of the Internal Revenue Code.

Index

Abstract of judgment, 92
Anti-alientation rule, 86–88
Anti-duress provision, 147–149
Assessments, tax, 179, 184,
        186–187, 191–196,
        202–203
    jeopardy and termination,
        193, n. 1
    statute of limitation on,
        187–189, 194
    extension of, 194
Attachments of assets, 29–30,
        34, 74
    anti-alientation rule, 86
    community property, 60–61
    exempt assets, 36
    general partners, 69
    Individual Retirement
        Accounts (IRAs), 88–89
    joint tenancy, 56
    Qualified Domestic Relations
        Orders, 86
    tenancy by entireties, 57

Bahamas, 157
Bankruptcy, 169–181
    alimony, 171, 176–177

automatic stay, 174, 176
Chapter 7, 173–175
Chapter 11, 172
Chapter 13, 175–178
child support, 171, 178
discharge, 26, 172
exempt assets, 170, 173
fraudulent conveyance, 173
petition in, 173
preferential transfers, 174
proof of claim, 174
qualified plans, 176–177
reorganization plans, 172
taxes, dischargeability of, 97,
        178–179
Belize, 157

Cayman Islands, 9, 156–157,
        213
Charging order, 74–78, 83–84,
        159
Close corporations, 93–94
Collateral Agreements, 207
Collection Information
        Statement, 198–200,
        204–205
Comity, 28, 133

Community property, 47, 51,
    58–64, 210, 213
  attachment of assets, 50–61
  divorce, 59
Comprehensive Environmental
    Response, Compensation
    and Liability Act
    (CERCLA), 15
Cook Islands, 9, 132–134,
    147–148, 155–157, 211
Corporations, 90–108
  articles of incorporation, 91,
    104–105
  close corporations, 93–94
  directors, 94–96, 98
  dividends, 94
  employee claims, 96
  fraudulent conveyances, 211
  generally, 91–92
  limited liability, 90–108
  officers, 95–96, 98
  professional corporations,
    106
  "S" corporations, 80–81
  shareholders, 92–94, 96
  taxes, 80, 96–98
Cyprus, 157

Debtor examinations, 30–32, 75
Deeds of trust. See Mortgages

Environmental Protection
    Agency (EPA), 15–16
ERISA, 85, 87–89

Estate taxes, 122
  foreign asset protection
    trusts, 142

Flight provision, 149–150
Foreign asset protection trusts,
    132–168, 211
  anti-duress provision, 147–149
  beneficiaries, 151
  discretionary nature of, 142
  flight provision, 149–150
  fraudulent convenyances,
    132, 135, 151
  as grantor trusts, 142, 153
  irrevocability, 137, 153
  protector, 153, 155
  reports, 144–145
  settlor, 151
  trustee, 152–154
Fraudulent conveyances,
    35–49, 210–211
  badges of fraud, 41–46
  bankruptcy, 173
  corporations, 211
  defined, 39
  foreign asset protection
    trusts, 132, 135, 151
  homestead exemption, 66
  limited liability companies,
    43, 212
  limited partnerships, 43, 79
  qualified plans, 89
  revocable trusts, 118
  between spouses, 54
  Statute of Elizabeth, 39

transmutation agreement, 63
Uniform Fraudulent
    Conveyances Act, 39, 42
Fuentes v. Shavin, 29
Full Faith and Credit Clause,
    28, 133, 154

Garnishment, 35–36
General partners, 159
    agents for partnerships,
        68–72
    apparent authority, 69, 72
    of limited partnerships, 72
    unlimited liability, 69–72, 80
Gift taxes, 121–141
    annual exemption from, 122,
        128, 139
    Crummey powers, 129
    grantor trust rules, 139–141
    irrevocable trusts, 121–123,
        127–129, 138–140
    present gifts, 128
Guarantees, personal, 103

Homestead exemption, 36,
    65–66, 162, 171, 180,
    212, 214

Individual Retirement
    Accounts (IRAs), 88–89
Installment Payment
    Agreement, 183,
    197–202, 204
Collection Information
    Statement, 198–200

Form 433-D, 197
    interest on, 198
Internal Revenue Service (IRS),
    182–208
    appeal, 193–195
    assessment, 179, 184,
        186–187, 191–196
    collateral agreement, 207
    collection, statute of
        limitations on, 197
    Collection Information
        Statement, 198–200
    Collections Division,
        186–188, 190, 197,
        205–207
    Criminal Investigations
        Division, 191
    Examinations Division, 186,
        192–193, 205
    installment payment
        agreement, 183, 197–202
    90-day letter, 194, 203
    Notice of Deficiency, 194
    offers in compromise, 183,
        203–207
    ombudsman, 207–208
    refund claims, 196, 203
    Revenue Officer (RO),
        197–208
    Taxpayer Assistance Order
        (TAO), 208
    Taxpayer Bill of Rights, 183,
        192
    30-day letter, 193–195
Isle of Man, 157, 213

Joint tenancy, 55–56, 113
  attachment of assets, 56
  probate avoidance, 55–56
Judgment liens, 32–34, 210
Judgments, 23–28, 209
  appeals bond, 25
  consent judgments, 27
  default judgments, 26–27
  foreign judgments, 27
  stay of execution, 25

Lender liability, 16
Levy, 34
Life insurance, 124–125
  creditors of, 125
  estate taxes, 126
  life insurance trusts, 126–129
Limited liability
  corporations, 90–108
  limitations of, 101–107
  limited liability companies, 83
  limited partners, 72–74
  personal guarantees, 103
  piercing the corporate veil,
    104–105
  secured debts, 103
  sole proprietorships, 99–101
  ultra vires doctrine, 105–106
Limited liability company
    (LLC), 70–71, 79–84
  charging orders, 83–84
  fraudulent conveyances, 43,
    212
  limited liability, 83
  managers of, 83

  members of, 81
  taxation, 83
Limited partners, 72–74
  limited liability, 72–74
  management rights, 72–73
Limited partnerships, 71–79,
    159–168
  charging orders, 74–78, 159
  dissolution of, 159
  formation, 71–72, 74
  fraudulent conveyances,
    43, 79
  general partner, 72, 73, 80,
    159
  generally, 72–74, 159–168

Marital property, 53–55, 59
Mortgages, 47, 161–162

Nauru, 154–155
Negligent entrustment, 12, 16
Notice of Deficiency, 194–196

Offer in Compromise, 183,
    202–207
  Form 656, 202
Ombudsman, 207–208

Panama, 154
Partners
  as agents for partnership,
    68–71
  general partners, 68
  taxation, 78–80
Partnerships
  general partnerships, 67–71, 79

limited partnerships, 71–79
partnership agreement,
   69, 74
taxation of, 78
Patterson v. Shumate, 87
Piercing the corporate veil,
   104–105
Probate, 112–117
  creditors, 115–117
    statute of limitations on,
    116
    joint tenancy property,
    55–56, 113
    living trusts, 115
    probate estate, 113
Product line doctrine, 15
Professional corporations, 106

Qualified Domestic Relations
   Orders, 86

Retirement plans, 85–88, 212
  anti-alienation rule, 86
  employee deductions, 86
Revenue Officer (RO), 197–208
Revised Uniform Limited
   Partnership Act (RULPA)
   71, 76–77, 81, 84
Right of survivorship, 113
Rule against perpetuities, 138,
   n. 1

"S" corporations, 80–81, 83
Separate property, 51–55, 59,
   61, 213
  marital property, 53–55

*Snaidach v. Family Finance
   Corp.*, 29
Sole proprietorship, 79, 99–101
  retirement plans, 87
Strict liability, 14
Switzerland, 157, 193, n. 1

Tax Court, United States, 193,
   195, 203
Taxpayer Assistance Orders
   (TAO), 208
Taxpayer Bill of Rights, 183,
   192, 207
Tenancy by entireties, 56–58,
   64, 213
Transmutation agreements,
   62–64, 210, 213
   fraudulent conveyances, 63
Trust Fund Recovery Penalty,
   97, 203
Trusts
  beneficiaries, 110, 151–152
  Crummey trusts, 129
  declaration of, 110
  discretionary trusts, 119–120,
   142
  foreign asset protection
   trusts, 132–168
  gift taxes, 121, 128–129
  grantor trusts, 123, 138–142,
   153
  income taxes, 123
  irrevocable, 118, 137–138
  life insurance trusts, 126–129
  living trusts, 56, 111,
   114–115

Trusts *(Continued)*
    parties to, 109–111
    principal, 110
    probate avoidance, 112, 199
    revocable trusts, 117–119,
        140
    settlor, 109–110, 118, 123,
        151
    spendthrift trusts, 120–121,
        151

testamentary trusts, 111
three-year rule, 129
trustee, 110, 152–154
Tulsa Professional Collection
    Services v. Pope, 116–117
Turks and Caicos Islands, 157

Ultra vires doctrine, 105–106
Uniform Partnership Act, 77